Foundations

A Reader for New College Students

FIFTH EDITION

VIRGINIA N. GORDON
THE OHIO STATE UNIVERSITY

THOMAS L. MINNICK
THE OHIO STATE UNIVERSITY

Australia • Brazil • Japan • Korea • Mexico • Singapore • Spain • United Kingdom • United States

WADSWORTH
CENGAGE Learning™

Foundations: A Reader for New College Students, Fifth Edition
Virginia N. Gordon
Thomas L. Minnick

Senior Publisher: Lyn Uhl

Director of College Success: Annie Todd

Senior Sponsoring Editor: Shani Fisher

Assistant Editor: Daisuke Yasutake

Editorial Assistant: Cat Salerno

Senior Marketing Manager: Kirsten Stoller

Marketing Coordinator: Ryan Ahern

Marketing Communications Manager: Martha Pfeiffer

Print Buyer: Julio Esperas

Senior Rights Acquisition Account Manager, Text: Katie Huha

Production Service: Pre-PressPMG

Senior Art Director: Linda Jurras

Cover Image: Permian/Big Stock Photo

Cover Designer: Hannah Wellman

Compositor: Pre-PressPMG

Library of Congress Control Number: 2009939344

ISBN-13: 978-1-4390-8605-6

ISBN-10: 1-4390-8605-2

Wadsworth
20 Channel Center Street
Boston, MA 02210
USA

Cengage Learning is a leading provider of customized learning solutions with office locations around the globe, including Singapore, the United Kingdom, Australia, Mexico, Brazil, and Japan. Locate your local office at: **international.cengage.com/region.**

Cengage Learning products are represented in Canada by Nelson Education, Ltd.

For your course and learning solutions, visit **www.cengage.com.**

Purchase any of our products at your local college store or at our preferred online store **www.CengageBrain.com.**

Printed in the United States of America
1 2 3 4 5 6 7 14 13 12 11 10

This edition of *Foundations* is dedicated
to the memory of
Marilyn E. Hagans
and in honor of
Albert J. Kuhn,
two extraordinary teachers of English.

Brief Contents

Contents

Unit 4
How Should I Expect to Learn?   81

Unit 5
What About Technology?   109

Unit 6
What Are My Rights and Responsibilities as a Student?   125

Unit 7
What Is Diversity and Why Is It Important?   157

Unit 8
What Should I Know About Careers?   199

Unit 9
Setting Future Goals: Now Is the Time To Start   223

Preface

Students entering college today will confront many universal experiences that decades of college students have dealt with before them. This anthology focuses on many of these issues through the writings of a wide variety of authors—from senior college students who share their first-year experiences, to other thoughtful writers who are experts in their field or well-known for other reasons. All offer ideas and insights that speak to the variety of issues that most first-year college students, regardless of age, will experience.

What's New In The Fifth Edition?

- A Foundations Companion Web site www.cengage.com/success/Gordon/Foundations5e now provides students with the ability to complete journal entry exercises online, save their responses to their desktop or e-mail them to their professor. The web site will also include vocabulary flashcards that correlate to each of the textbook Unit's readings.
- New essays written by graduating seniors share reflections of their first-year college experiences to provide peer insight.
- The Fifth Edition contains a total of 49 readings. 22 new readings include topics such as internships, money management, problem solving, and plagiarism. The textbook now closes with a commencement speech by First Lady Michelle Obama.
- Here is a complete list of new readings:

  William J. Cory and John Henry Newman, *Why Go To College? Two Classic Answers*
  GetRichSlowly.org, *The Value of a College Education*
  Ben Bernstein, *The Stakes are Low*
  Jennifer Rosella, *Four Pieces of Advice*
  Andrew Gordon-Seifert, *Things I Wish I Knew as a Freshman*
  Dave Ellis, *Three Paths to Financial Freedom*
  Cal Newport, *How to Win at College*
  Walter Pauk and Ross J. Q. Owens, *Using Time and Space Effectively*
  Howard Gardner, *Minds Viewed Globally*
  Karl Albrecht, *How to Become an Excellent Problem-Solver*
  Don Tapscott, *A Generation Bathed in Bits*
  Leonard Pitts, Jr., *Losing Stuff Has Never Been So Sad*
  Emailreplies.com, *Email Etiquette*

W. P. Carey, *College of Business College Cheating Is Bad for Business*
Rosemarie Menager and Lyn Paulos, *Avoiding Plagiarism*
Thomas Brown, *From Diversity to Inclusivity*
Skylar Covich, *A College Senior Speaks about Diversity: The Disability Perspective*
Donald Asher, *The Relationship between College and Work*
David Horne, *An Internship—Your First Big Career Break*
Arthur D. Rosenberg, *Adjust to Change*
Lev Grossman, *Grow Up? Not So Fast*
Michelle Obama, *The First Lady's Challenge to the Graduates*

The Unit headings focus on nine broad topics that are relevant to the first-year college experience. For example, some students may ask: "Why am I in college?" or "How can I succeed academically?" or "What should I know about careers?" The writers in each unit offer a variety of perspectives on these and many other questions that students might ponder. It is hoped that the ideas and insights expressed by such a broad spectrum of writers will help students recognize and perhaps be comforted by the universal character of the issues they face and better prepared to address and resolve them.

The reader format encourages dialogue among different points of view. Because such dialogue is essential to a learning community, students are encouraged to participate in the exploration of ideas, which is how their journey toward knowledge and self-awareness can best proceed. Instructors are also encouraged to participate in the dialogue, because students will benefit from their example. Journaling activities encourage students to reflect on what they read and how the topics may be relevant to their own college experience.

This Fifth Edition contains 22 new essays that convey perspectives that range from practical to thought-provoking. In Unit 1, for example, two historical answers to the question, "Why am I in college?" offer reasons that are relevant today. Other essays in this unit examine the value of a college education and answer the question, "What is a truly educated person?" So that beginning students appreciate the academic community of which they are members, included is a brief history of higher education and the contemporary American university as they have evolved through the last century.

Unit 2 focuses on what you can reasonably expect of college work and how you are likely to change during your college years. In this new edition, seniors who are about to graduate share their experiences as freshmen and offer insights into student life that many readers may find familiar. Money concerns are common to all students, so a new essay provides suggestions for money management. Other writers suggest how you will change intellectually and personally through the college years and how you can become more personally effective in college, work, and life.

In Unit 3, new essays have been added or updated to provide practical advice on how to succeed academically. Topics include suggestions for writing papers, how to develop good study and time management skills, and the importance of attending classes and turning assignments in on time. Because learning is such an integral part of the academic experience, the writings in Unit 4 offer a variety of perspectives on this important process. Included are practical matters such as the power of memory and how to understand your own learning styles. New essays examine the kind of minds that will be needed if we are to survive in the future and another offers advice on how to become a more effective problem solver.

New essays in Unit 5 offer different perspectives on technology, such as how the Internet has changed our lives, including its emerging social aspects and its hazards. Another essayist mourns the demise of part of the physical world brought about by our dependence on the digital world. Some practical advice on writing effective e-mails provides a more useful aspect of the topic. Some foreseeable challenges of new educational technology are predicted.

Unit 6 introduces the idea of college as a special kind of community, one defined by the common mission of its members: the search for knowledge and truth. Academic freedom (the freedom to express any point of view so that it can be studied and evaluated) is the essential condition of the college community. Because the search for truth is at the heart of the academic experience, certain kinds of behavior are intolerable within it, including, for example, cheating or plagiarism. A new essay discusses the increase of college cheating and how it threatens to demean the integrity of universities as a whole.

The essays in Unit 7 discuss the value of diversity and connectedness in a college setting. A college senior speaks about his perspective as a disabled student. Another new essayist discusses why college is one of the few places where "people from so many different experiences, backgrounds and beliefs come together for a common purpose." Dialogue essential to discovering truth places a high value on diversity because, through their diverse opinions and experiences, the varied members of an academic community enrich that dialogue and make it likelier to uncover many truths.

The essays in Unit 8 will help you better understand how your professional life is likely to develop and, therefore, how best to prepare for a career in the 21st century. Several new essays in Unit 8 provide a more practical approach to career planning, such as the importance of internships and preparing for the job search process early. Other essays examine the relationship between college and explore how to prepare for change in the workplace.

In Unit 9 new essays discuss the importance of goal setting and how planning for the future should be a natural part of academic decision-making. The advice offered in this unit emphasizes why academic, career, and life planning should start early. For example, understanding how to get along with the different generations that teach, administer, and inhabit today's college classrooms is useful in adapting to college life. First Lady Michelle Obama challenges the graduates in this commencement address to use their education as a "building block to a brighter future."

In compiling this anthology we have been helped by many students, colleagues, and friends, and we thank them. Mary Ellen Jenkins, assistant dean of the Colleges of the Arts and Sciences, undertook the essential task of securing permissions for reprinting material under copyright. Ellen Banks helped with aspects of the manuscript's preparation. The following reviews provided input on improvements for this fifth edition: Maureen Barry, Rochester Institute of Technology; Sharon Buzzard, Western Kentucky University; Juan J. Flores, Folsom Lake College; Douglas Posey, Lock Haven University of Pennsylvania; Karla Sanders, Eastern Illinois University; and Paul Tidman of Mount Union College.

Finally we want to acknowledge the lessons we have learned from generations of colleagues and students at The Ohio State University who enrolled in and taught University Survey, a course we were associated with for more than 25 years. In that time, more than 250,000 first-year students were introduced to the values and challenges of living and learning in an academic community.

How to Keep a Journal

After most of the readings in this textbook, you will find "Suggestions for Your Journal." We strongly encourage you to get into the habit of keeping a written journal of your reactions to and reflections on your assigned readings. Such journaling will result in a record of your development as you think through both the essays and your experiences as a new student at your college or university. Because many new college students may not know what a journal at its best can be, or how to keep one, we offer the definition and suggestions that follow.

Why keep a journal? The type of journal we are suggesting that you write is a "response" journal in which you will record your ideas and feelings in response to the readings that you are assigned in each unit. Writing a journal can reveal how your thought processes work and how they develop or change, serve as a memory aid, and provide an informal way of keeping track of your ideas that may be less threatening than more formal writing assignments like essays and research papers. Writing in your journal means working to find the right words to express yourself, and so keeping a journal can help you make your ideas more specific, more concrete.

The purpose of a journal is usually to provide a record, often day by day, of the writer's own internal or spiritual growth. In this regard, both journals and the closely related form, diaries, are similar to a document once needed on every sailing ship, the captain's log. The log was a book in which the chief officer of the ship kept a daily record of the ship's travels. Entries were usually brief, providing the ship's location in longitude and latitude and perhaps a sentence or two about important events of the voyage: "Sighted a large group of whales to the west," for example, or "Finished the last fresh provisions today." The ship's log therefore became the skeleton of a history. For some writers, a diary can be very similar to a log. Depending on how much detail an author chooses to include, a diary can be as lean as a ship's log or substantially more informative. An important difference is that the ship's log was intended to be available to others, such as the ship's owners. A diary is almost always intended to be a private document. A journal, in the sense that we hope you will use the word, is similar to a log or diary in that the entries can be made daily and should be dated. Unlike a personal diary, the best journals are written with the expectation that sometime someone besides the writer will probably read them. Yet they retain a sense of ease and intimacy as though the prospective readers were the author's good friends.

Keeping a journal can encourage you to think more critically by helping you to make connections between what an author has written and your agreements or disagreements with that author's point of view. For example, a typical journal entry may note:

> Date: February 1, 2010 (Most journal entries should be dated!)
> Essay: "Using Time and Space Effectively" by Walter Pauk and Ross J.Q. Owens
>
> As I read this essay I realized there are a lot of ways that I can improve how I use my time. When I go to the library to study I often run into friends and waste time. The authors suggested going to the library when almost nobody is there and I'm going to try this. I think their ideas about listening to your body were interesting. I never thought of how studying and body rhythms might be related. Reading in the morning and reviewing in the afternoon makes sense. I also like the idea of carrying pocket work and since I carry around my study notes on index cards, I might use them to refresh my memory when I'm on the bus or waiting for class. All in all there were some good ideas in this essay that I hadn't thought of before.

This entry starts with an idea from an assigned essay and develops it with the student's personal point of view, including her examples, generalizations, and relevant personal experiences. A journal entry is usually this length or longer: One perfect sentence might be adequate and expressive, but usually a reflective response will require some development. A paragraph is a common length for an entry, but some may be as long as several paragraphs—even amounting to an essay.

We recommend that you read every essay with an eye for what you personally can learn or take from that essay. Can you apply some comment or suggestion from that reading to your experience? How? Or why not? Our suggested topics are not meant to limit you but merely to serve as possible starting places. In addition, here are some practical tips for keeping a journal that many writers find helpful:

- In journal writing it is permissible to write as you would talk to a friend or trusted adviser. The content is more important than perfection of style, and you will often find the entries are more informative if you think about what you want to express without worrying too much about the style or form of expression you use.
- Write about the insights, feelings and emotions, or problems that you think about when reading the assigned essay. Don't worry if you may seem more negative than positive: It is entirely all right to disagree with an author.
- Sometimes as you are reading an assignment, it is handy to jot down notes with your reactions in a very brief form (just so you can understand them later!). Your journal entry can then be developed from these notes, as you think about them and put them into your own organization.
- Interact with and expand upon what the author is saying but do so in your own words, adding your own ideas.
- Use any creative format that you think best expresses your responses. You may want to write in the form of a dialogue between you and the author or of a letter to a friend or to your parents.

Your course instructor will tell you how your journal entries will be used in class—that is, how they will fit into the course structure and count in your final grade. Some students find that they enjoy keeping a journal and continue the practice even after they are required to do so by a class. Many successful authors keep journals for decades and take from them their ideas for longer essays or books. And some journals have become important historical documents because, like the captain's log of an important voyage, they help others to navigate along one of the paths that eventually we all must find and follow.

Unit 1

The Value of a College Education: Why Am I in College?

Enter to grow in wisdom. Depart to serve better thy

country and mankind.

—INSCRIPTION ON THE 1890 GATE TO HARVARD YARD

Students attend college for many reasons. In a national survey by Alexander Astin of UCLA, who has studied each class of first-year students for many years, the largest number of entering students (73 percent) indicated they were coming to college to prepare for a better job. Other common reasons that students gave were to make more money, find a philosophy of life, become a more cultured person, or satisfy their parents' wishes.

Examining your reasons for enrolling in higher education can help you determine what you can realistically hope to accomplish as a student. Because new students may find it difficult to set tentative educational and occupational goals, they usually find it helpful to understand what the college experience is intended to, and can, provide. Such an understanding establishes a foundation on which to shape your personal expectations.

College will open for you an unbelievable range of opportunities to explore diverse fields of knowledge, along with a variety of activities that will help you grow personally and socially. Although you could educate yourself outside the college environment, it is much more expedient and satisfying to learn with other students and from teachers who are committed to creating an environment that supports learning.

1

In college you will have the time and freedom to delve into many areas of interest that you may not have explored. You will also be exposed to areas of the human experience that you did not know existed. Imagine! In a four-year (now often longer) span of time, you can acquaint yourself with a wide range of human knowledge and experience. Even in a two-year institution, these same opportunities exist, although they will be more focused.

At no other time in your life will you have such a concentrated opportunity for learning. In high school, most of the courses you took were prescribed for you by others. In college, although some majors are more rigidly structured than others, you have more freedom to pursue your personal interests. You are in control of your own learning.

On the other hand, if one of your reasons for being in college is to obtain a job, consider what college can offer you in preparing for your future career. A U.S. Department of Labor study, done with the American Society for Training and Development, identified the following seven basic skills that workers in the future must possess if they are to be successful: learning to learn, competence, communication, personal management, adaptability, group effectiveness, and influence. Many people feel that you will be able to acquire and perfect these basic skills through your college experience. Consciously working to acquire these skills in the classroom, in campus activities, and in social and other contacts will enhance your effectiveness with them by the time you graduate.

The readings in this unit are intended to stimulate your thinking about why you are in college and what you expect from it. The essays present a broad perspective on higher education and its value to the individual, not only intellectually but also as the beginning of a lifelong pursuit of learning. The brief statements by William Cory and John Henry Newman provide a traditional perspective on the enduring objectives of "higher" education. The essay by Bennett offers the author's personal experience of growing toward those objectives. An article from the blog Get Rich Slowly attempts to quantify the financial advantage of a college education, and Bok briefly summarizes the history of American higher education in an essay included here because, when you want to know where you are, it can be helpful to know where you have been. These readings can help you compare your reasons for enrolling in college with some of the goals and objectives of higher education in general. You might also want to discuss with faculty, administrators, and other students your institution's mission and goals for preparing its students for the future.

Why Go to College?
Two Classic Answers

William Johnson Cory and John Henry Newman

The college or university that you attend is located not only in a physical place and time but also, we could say spiritually, in a tradition—a long tradition which has its precedents primarily in Europe. Among the most influential models in this tradition are English schools, notably Oxford and Cambridge Universities, which date from about 1167 and 1209, respectively. Embodied in that long tradition are values that generations of students have learned and adopted, and that are well defined by the characteristics of an educated person in the two following brief statements.

"You go to a great school"

WILLIAM JOHNSON CORY

William Cory (1823–1892) was a talented educator and poet and a brilliant writer of Latin verse. Considered an exemplary school teacher, called "the most brilliant Eton tutor of his day," he strove to educate boys who might become future leaders, and numbered among his former students members of Parliament, cabinet ministers, and several prime ministers.

At school you are engaged not so much in acquiring knowledge as in making mental efforts under criticism. A certain amount of knowledge you can indeed with average faculties acquire so as to retain; nor need you regret the hours you spent on much that is forgotten, for the shadow of lost knowledge at least protects you from many illusions. But you go to a great school not so much for knowledge as for arts and habits; for the habit of attention, for the art of expression, for the art of assuming at a moment's notice a new intellectual position, for the art of entering quickly into another person's thoughts, for the habit of submitting to censure and refutation, for the art of indicating assent or dissent in graduated terms, for the habit of regarding minute points of accuracy, for the art of working out what is possible in a given time, for taste, for discrimination, for mental courage, and for mental soberness. Above all, you go to a great school for self-knowledge.

"A Great but Ordinary End"

JOHN HENRY NEWMAN

John Henry Newman (1801–1890) was a priest and later cardinal in the Roman Catholic Church. He converted from Anglicanism in 1845. Both before and after becoming a Roman Catholic, he wrote a number of influential books, including *The Idea of a University* (1852) from which this excerpt is taken.

A University training is the great ordinary means to a great but ordinary end; it aims at raising the intellectual tone of society, at cultivating the public mind, at purifying the national taste, at supplying true principles to popular enthusiasm and fixed aims to popular aspiration, at giving enlargement and sobriety to the ideas of the age, at facilitating the exercise of political power, and refining the intercourse of private life.

It is the education which gives a man a clear conscious view of his own opinions and judgments, a truth in developing them, an eloquence in expressing them, and a force in urging them.

It teaches him to see things as they are, to go right to the point, to disentangle a *skein** of thought, to detect what is *sophistical*, and to discard what is irrelevant.

It prepares him to fill any *post* with credit, and to master any subject with facility.

It shows him how to accommodate himself to others, how to throw himself into their state of mind, how to bring before them his own, how to influence them, how to come to an understanding with them, how to bear with them.

He is at home in any society, he has common ground with every class; he knows when to speak and when to be silent; he is able to converse, he is able to listen; he can ask a question pertinently, and gain a lesson seasonably, yet never in the way; he is a pleasant companion, and a comrade you can depend upon; he knows when to be serious and when to *trifle*, and he has a sure tact which enables him to trifle with gracefulness and to be serious with effect.

He has the repose of mind which lives in itself, while it lives in the world, and which has resources for its happiness at home when it cannot go abroad. He has a gift which serves him in public, and supports him retirement, without which good fortune is but vulgar, and with which failure and disappointment have a charm. The art which tends to make a man all this, is in the object which it pursues as useful as the art of wealth or the art of health, though it is less susceptible of method, and less tangible, less certain, less complete in its result. (From Discourse VII of *The Idea of a University*, 1852)

 ## Vocabulary

As you think about these two selections, these definitions may be useful to you:
1. **skein**   literally, a bundle of yarn or thread wound loosely and coiled together; but metaphorically, a tangle: a tangled or complex mass of material

*Vocabulary words are italicized in each essay—ED.

2. **sophistical**   seemingly clever and plausible, but actually unsound and tending to mislead
3. **post**   job or position
4. **trifle**   as a noun, this word means an article or thing of very little value. Used as a verb, as in this example, we might say "to joke" or "to have fun with."

 ## Discussion Questions

1. In your experience, is William Cory correct in describing schoolwork as "not so much . . . acquiring knowledge as . . . making mental efforts under criticism"?
2. Cory stresses the personal impact of education throughout his comments, but Newman opens with a broader view of the social impact of education. Are these contradictory?
3. These selections both exemplify a traditional notion of the impact of college. However, much modern education aims at more practical objectives. James Tunstead Burtchaell, a priest who was Provost (i.e., chief academic officer) at Indiana's University of Notre Dame, makes this distinction:

> An institution that offers you training is trying to provide you with the information and skills you need for a specific career. A law school must acquaint you with how to interview clients, how to plead before a court, and how to draw up proper legal documents. A welding academy will teach you the materials and methods of the trade. Advanced training in computing will prepare you not simply to keypunch or to program, but to create software, to understand the mysteries of central processing, and then to grasp the theoretical underpinnings or applied mathematics. . . . All of that is training: Specific knowledge needed for specific professional or skilled work. It is not education.

Given this distinction, are you currently engaged in "education" or "training" or some combination of both?

 ## Suggestions for Your Journal

What elements of your education so far have provided you with self-knowledge? Which of the arts and habits that Cory says are the goal of education at a great school are important to you? Which would you most like to master? Do you care about "raising the intellectual tone of society, at cultivating the public mind, at purifying the national taste," as Newman implies you should? Why or why not?

The Lure of Learning

William J. Bennett

William J. Bennett is an accomplished scholar, teacher, and academic administrator. He was chair of the National Endowment for the Humanities in the early 1980s, Secretary of Education in the Reagan administration, and the nation's "Drug Czar" in the George H. W. Bush administration. Since leaving government service, Bennett has remained an active commentator on cultural issues, publishing more than a dozen books. He has stated that students should be taught "patriotism, self-discipline, thrift, honesty, and respect for elders." He received a Ph.D. in philosophy from the University of Texas and a law degree from Harvard.

This essay reflects Bennett's strong belief in the value of college teaching and its effect on students' learning. His career as an outstanding professor was obviously influenced by those who taught him and brought life to the subjects.

When I arrived at college as a freshman some time ago, I had definite ideas about how I wanted to use my four years of higher education. I wanted to major in English because I wanted to become *sophisticated*. I wanted to become sophisticated because I wanted to land a good job and make big money.

But because of my college's course requirements, I found myself in an introductory philosophy class, confronted by Plato's *Republic* and a remarkable professor who knew how to make the text come alive. It seemed to me and many of my fellow classmates as if we had come face to face with a reincarnation of Socrates himself. Before we knew it, we were ensnared by the power of a 2,000-year-old dialogue.

In our posture of youthful cynicism and arrogance, we at first resisted the idea that the question of justice should really occupy our time. But something happened to us that semester as we fought our way through the *Republic,* arguing about notions of right and wrong. Along the way, our insides were shaken up a little bit. Without quite knowing it, we had committed ourselves to the serious enterprise of raising and wrestling with questions. And once caught up in that enterprise, there was no turning back. We had met up with a great text and a great teacher; they had taken us, and we were theirs.

Every student is entitled to that kind of experience at college. And if I could make one request of future undergraduates, it would be that they open the door to that possibility. College should shake you up a little, get you breathing, quicken your senses and animate a conscious examination of life's enduring questions. Know thyself, Socrates said. Higher education worthy of the name aspires to nothing less than the wisdom of that *dictum*.

These are lofty ambitions. What do they mean in the context of four years of campus life?

A college is many things. It is a collection of dormitories, libraries, social clubs, *incorrigibly* terrible cafeterias. But above all, it is a faculty. It used to be said, when this country was much younger, that a log lying on the side of the road with a student sitting on one end and a professor on the other was a university.

That essence has not changed. It is the relationship between teachers and their students that gives a campus its own special genius. "Like a contagious disease, almost," William James wrote, "spiritual life passes from man to man by contact." Above all, a student should look for—and expect to find—professors who can bring to life the subject at hand.

What else should students find at college? They should discover great works that tell us how men and women of our own and other civilizations have grappled with life's relentless questions. What should be loved? What deserves to be defended? What is noble and what is base? As Montaigne wrote, a student should have the chance to learn "what valor, *temperance*, and justice are, the difference between ambition and greed, loyalty and servitude, liberty and license; and the marks of true and solid contentment."

This means, first of all, that students should find wide exposure to all the major disciplines—history, science, literature, mathematics and foreign language. And it means that they should be introduced to the best that has been thought and written in every discipline.

College is, for many, a once-in-a-lifetime chance to discover our civilization's greatest achievements and lasting visions. There are many great books, discoveries and deeds that record those achievements in unequaled fashion. There are many more that do not. A good college will sort the great texts and important ideas from the run-of-the-mill and offer the best to its students. And that offering will be the institution's vision of a truly educated person.

All students have different notions about where they want a college degree to take them. For some, it is law school or journalism. For others, it's public service. That's fine. College *should* be a road to your ambitions. But every student should take the time to tread the ground outside his or her major and to spend some time in the company of the great travelers who have come before.

Why? Put simply, because they can help you lead a better and perhaps happier life. If we give time to studying how men and women of the past have dealt with life's enduring problems, then we will be better prepared when those same problems come our way. We may be a little less surprised to find treachery at work in the world about us, a little less startled by unselfish devotion, a little readier to believe in the capacity of the human mind.

And what does that do for a future career? As Hamlet said, "Readiness is all." In the end, the problems we face during the course of a career are the same kind that we face in the general course of life. If you want to be a corporate executive, how can you learn about not missing the right opportunities? One way is to read *Hamlet*. Do you want to learn about the dangers of overweening ambition? Read *Macbeth*. Want to know the pitfalls of playing around on the job? Read *Antony and Cleopatra*. The importance of fulfilling the responsibilities entrusted to leadership? Read *King Lear*.

Even in the modern world, it is still that peculiar mix of literature, science, history, math, philosophy and language that can help mature minds come to grips with the age-old issues, the problems that *transverse* every plane of life. Students who bring to college the willingness to seek out those issues, to enliven the spirit and broaden the mind, will be more likely to profit in any endeavor.

From William Bennett, "The Lure of Learning," Reprinted by permission of the author.

 ## Vocabulary

As you think about this essay, these definitions may be helpful to you:
1. **sophisticated**   worldly, wise, knowing
2. **dictum**   a formal authoritative pronouncement of a principle or opinion
3. **incorrigible**   not capable of being corrected, permanently wrong, stubborn
4. **temperance**   moderation in action, thought, or feeling
5. **transverse**   set crosswise

 ## Discussion Questions

1. How did Bennett and his fellow students initially react to their philosophy class? How did their reactions change?
2. What does Bennett ask undergraduates to do in order to expose themselves to the same wonders of learning that he enjoyed?
3. According to Bennett, what gives each campus its own "special genius"? Have you found this in your classes? Describe.
4. What should students find at college in addition to good teaching?
5. What does the college experience do for a future career, according to Bennett?

 ## Suggestions for Your Journal

Did you decide to come to college because of the "lure of learning"? If so, how do you think that element arose in you? Have you always planned to attend higher education? Did your expectations for college fit the reality you have already found? Be specific in considering these questions, because the details of your experience may fade as time passes.

Have you begun to discover your institution's "vision of a truly educated person"? Write about that vision and the evidence you have already found for it.

The Value of a College Education

GetRichSlowly.org

This article comes from GetRichSlowly.org, a blog that is devoted to "personal finance that makes cents."

The Financial Value of a College Degree

Does earning a college degree make a difference to your future? Absolutely. The facts are striking. On average, those who have a college degree earn almost twice as much as those who do not. According to the U.S. Census Bureau:

> Adults with advanced degrees earn four times more than those with less than a high school diploma. Workers 18 and older with a master's, professional or doctoral degree earned an average of $82,320 in 2006, while those with less than a high school diploma earned $20,873.

> Workers with a bachelor's degree earned an average of $56,788 in 2006; those with a high school diploma earned $31,071. This flurry of numbers makes more sense when viewed in a table:

Education	Avg. Income	Increase
Drop-out	$20,873	—
High School	$30,071	48.9%
College	$56,788	82.8%
Advanced	$82,320	45.0%

Completing college is huge. Over a lifetime, a college degree is generally worth almost a million dollars. That's money that can be used for fun, for whatever. The financial benefits of a college education are significant, and they're very real.

Other Benefits of a College Degree

Obtaining a college degree isn't just about making more money. According to Katharine Hansen at Quintessential Careers, a college education is associated with other benefits, such as:

- Longer life-spans
- Greater economic stability and security
- More prestigious employment and greater job satisfaction
- Less dependency on government assistance
- Greater participation in leisure and artistic activities
- Greater community service and leadership
- More self-confidence

A college education also gives you a broad base of knowledge on which to build. It teaches you to solve more of life's problems. It gives you future reference points for discussing art, entertainment, politics, and history.

College offers other learning opportunities, too. Much of what I gained in college came from learning outside the classroom, from participating in clubs and other campus organizations. Many degree programs allow students to "test-drive" careers through internships and *practicums*.

I asked Michael Hampton, director of career development at Western Oregon University, what advice he would offer a student who is deciding whether or not to attend college. He replied:

> Unless you are going to be an engineer, architect, teacher, lawyer, the label on your degree does not matter. The degree is a check-mark (as opposed to the focus) in most job requirements. Many job ads will state: "Business, Communications or other degree required." Most folks have the "other." I have a BA in Speech, Telecommunications & Film. As a television newsphotographer, youth director, communications director, substitute school teacher, sports marketing manager, career programs coordinator, no one ever said to me: "You know what? We would like to hire you, but we're not sure what that label is on your degree."

> Honestly, at the University of Oregon, I was looking for an "easy" degree because I was not a book-smart student. I was able to take mostly film and television classes to earn a BA, so I signed up. The experiences I took advantage of (internships, volunteering, and part-time jobs) in college set me up to be marketable to employers. Again, the jobs I went after required degrees, but the label on the degree was not a barrier.

Here are some more prominent examples: What was Alan Greenspan's major? Econ, but he studied music first. What was Michael Jordan's major? Math, then Geography (dropped out to play professional basketball, later returned to earn his degree). What was Lisa Kudrow's major? Biology. What was Cindy Crawford's major? Chemical Engineering (dropped out for modeling career). What was Ted Turner's major? Classics (expelled for hanky-panky). What was former HP CEO Carly Fiorina's major? Philosophy. What was George W. Bush's major? History. What was Jay Leno's major? Philosophy.

If a student is struggling to get good grades, I encourage them to look at the course catalog and choose a major based on the likability of most of the classes they would have to take, their positive experiences with the professors in the major, and the number of credits they have already taken that are compatible. They should set themselves up to be successful. Getting through the pre-reqs is a major barrier for some. Combine some "fun" classes with the challenging required courses to try and make the experience more enjoyable.

While a college education statistically provides a better shot at obtaining wealth, it does not guarantee success. There are English majors who end up with convenience store careers. There are high school drop-outs who go on to run multi-million dollar corporations. But obtaining a college education improves your odds.

For some young adults, college can seem like a waste of time. (Or worse a waste of money.) Other things seem more important. I had friends who dropped out of school to pursue girlfriends across the country. I had friends who were convinced they could make more money by skipping college altogether. Student loans can be so enormous that they make a person lose sight of the fact that they're an almost guaranteed investment in the future.

I personally had problems finding a career path—I simply had no idea what I wanted to do. When I entered college, I wanted to be a religion major. Then I wanted to be a writer. Then I wanted to be a grade school teacher. Ultimately I earned a psychology degree, which has had little direct benefit to my life. But the education I obtained, my campus experience, and the contacts I made have been invaluable. A large part of who I am today was forged by my experiences in college. The value of a college education isn't just in the destination, but in the journey.

Provided by GetRichSlowly.org

Vocabulary

As you think about this selection, this definition may be useful to you:

1. **practicums**   A practicum is a college course, often in a specialized field of study that is designed to give students supervised practical application of a previously studied theory.

Discussion Questions

1. Most people suppose that getting a college education is worth while thanks to higher lifetime earnings, and the chart demonstrates this in detail. Were you surprised by the amount of difference earned with and without a degree, or with advanced degrees? What would you expect?

2. Assuming that the subject matter of the degree makes a difference (we usually expect engineers to earn more than librarians or kindergarten teachers, after all), the issue sometimes comes down to Which degree benefits me most financially?, and Do I want to earn *that* degree or one that might be worth less?

 ## Suggestions for Your Journal

Would you change your program simply in order to earn more money in your lifetime? What might make you compromise that decision? Imagine that you are already a multimillionaire. Would you still bother going to college? Why, or why not?

As you start your undergraduate program, you may already be thinking about going on to graduate or professional school. What post-baccalaureate education might you be considering? How will you decide whether to go on after the bachelor's degree?

The Evolution of Undergraduate Education

Derek Bok

Derek Bok is one of the most respected American academic leaders. He has spent virtually his entire career at Harvard University, where he began teaching law in 1958, served as dean of the law school from 1968 to 1971, and then accepted the responsibility of university president from 1971 to 1991. In 2006 he agreed to return as interim president for an appointment expected to last about a year. Bok is the author of many books, including *Our Underachieving Colleges*, published in 2006, from which the following excerpt is taken.

Until the Civil War, colleges in the United States were linked to religious bodies and resembled *finishing schools* more closely than institutions of advanced education. Student behavior was closely regulated both inside and outside the classroom, and teachers spent much of their time enforcing regulations and punishing transgressors. Rules of behavior were written in exquisite detail. Columbia's officials took two full pages merely to describe the proper forms of behavior during compulsory chapel. Yale turned "Sabbath Profanation, active disbelief in the authenticity of the Bible, and extravagant (personal) expenditures" into campus crimes.[1]

Most courses were prescribed in a curriculum that usually included mathematics, logic, English, and classics, with a heavy dose of Latin and Greek. In a typical class, students recited passages from an ancient text under the critical eye of the instructor. Although many colleges offered courses in the sciences, such as astronomy or botany, classes were taught more often by invoking *Aristotle* and other authorities than by describing experiments and the scientific method. By most accounts, the formal education was sterile. Many students felt that they learned much more outside the classroom in informal clubs and literary societies, where they engaged in debates, read modern literature, and discussed serious subjects.[2]

Despite their quaint ways, colleges before the Civil War were deliberately organized to pursue two important objectives: training the intellect and building character. The most influential defense of the prevailing model appeared in an 1828 report from Yale College, which held that the principal aim of college instruction was not to supply all the important information that students might some day use but to instill mental discipline.[3] According to the report's authors, a classical education was ideally suited to this purpose. Mental discipline was supposed to

---

[1]Laurence Veysey, *The Emergence of the American University* (1965), pp. 33–34.
[2]Frederick Rudolph, *Curriculum:* A History of the American Course of Study since 1636 (1977), p. 95.
[3]"Original Papers in Relation to a Course of Liberal Education," *American Journal of Science and Arts,* 15 (1829).

emerge from hours of demanding work translating ancient languages, disputing *arcane* questions in class, and solving mathematical problems.

Character would be forged by having undergraduates study classical texts, demanding strict compliance with the detailed rules of campus behavior, and requiring daily attendance at chapel. As a culminating experience, most colleges prior to the Civil War offered a mandatory course for seniors on issues of moral philosophy, often taught by the president himself. Ranging over ethical principles, history, politics, and such issues of the day, as immigration, slavery, and freedom of the press, this capstone course served multiple objectives. It set forth precepts of ethical behavior, it prepared students for civic responsibility, and it brought together knowledge from several fields of learning. For many students, it was the high point of an otherwise dull and *stultifying* education.

With the end of the Civil War, higher education began a period of unprecedented reform. Aided by federal land grants and by the philanthropy born of industrial fortunes, college presidents such as Charles W. Eliot, Andre White, William Rainey Harper, and Benjamin Gilman built new institutions and radically transformed old ones. Inspired by the great German universities, these leaders encouraged research, welcomed science, and introduced Ph.D. programs to build new cadres of scholar-teachers.

Undergraduate education soon felt the impact of these changes. The old classical curriculum gave way to offerings of a newer and more practical kind. Instruction in modern languages and literature continued to spread. Courses in physics, biology, and chemistry sprung up everywhere. Private universities introduced new programs in vocational subjects such as commerce and engineering. Public universities carried occupational training even further. According to Laurence Veysey, "such untraditional disciplines as pedagogy, domestic science, and various kinds of engineering were all becoming firmly established at a number of leading universities by the turn of the century."[4]

More radical still were the reforms at some of America's most prominent institutions. At Harvard, for example, President Charles W. Eliot not only rejected the old prescribed classical curriculum, he urged that *all* requirements be abolished, leaving students free to study whatever appealed to their interests. In the end, however, Eliot's vision proved too extreme to survive intact even at Harvard. Although no one wanted to return to the old, classical curriculum, most educators felt that the doctrine of total elective choice went too far in the other direction.

Religious orthodoxy also lost its grip on many colleges. *Nonsectarianism* was increasingly considered conducive to sound university governance. Faith was no longer thought central to the development of moral character. Compulsory chapel began to give way on many campuses, making religious observance little more than another option with a broad array of extracurricular pursuits.

Meanwhile, social clubs and fraternities flourished. Intercollegiate sports took hold, as football games attracted tens of thousands of raucous students and alumni. For many undergraduates, college was not a serious intellectual experience but an excuse for making social contacts and enjoying the good life.

[4]Veysey, p. 113.

As one dean of students, LeBaron Briggs, candidly admitted, "Social ambition is the strongest power in many a student's life."[5] In retrospect, it is likely that the casual attitude toward coursework reflected the spirit of the times more than the nature of the curriculum. Whatever the underlying causes, critics of the elective system seized on such carefree undergraduate behavior as a justification for imposing greater structure on the curriculum. By the early twentieth century both the extreme free-choice model embraced by universities such as Stanford and Cornell and the more rigid, traditional system still in place at Princeton seemed equally out of touch with the times.

By the start of World War II, college curricula were divided between two models. Most public universities offered a wide assortment of vocational majors along with the standard liberal arts concentrations, while achieving breadth through some form of *distribution requirement*. Most leading private universities tended to resist occupational majors (save for engineering and business). Patterns of breadth and depth were nourished by constant growth in the number of courses, made possible by the steady expansion of university faculties. Entirely new disciplines, with courses of their own, gave undergraduates a wider range of options from which to choose electives, fulfill their distribution requirements, or select a major.

In the aftermath of World War II, universities underwent further substantial changes. Encouraged by the GI Bill and later by the demands of an increasingly sophisticated economy, larger and larger numbers of young people crowded into colleges. Existing universities expanded, and new ones were founded. From 1945 to 2000, the number of B.A. degrees awarded annually rose almost eightfold, from 157,349 to approximately 1.2 million.

The rapid growth in the undergraduate population meant that higher education was no longer reserved for the elite but now attracted a majority of American youth. Student bodies became more diverse, as blacks, Hispanics, Asians, and other ethnic minorities entered private and public colleges alike. As applicant pools grew larger, the best-known institutions became highly selective, teachers' colleges evolved into multipurpose universities, and community colleges sprouted like mushrooms.

University faculties responded to these developments in various ways. Although the basic structure of the curriculum remained intact, with its provision for breadth and depth, the steady growth of new knowledge pushed aspects of science once reserved for graduate students back into intermediate and even introductory college texts. As researchers separated themselves into more and narrower specialties, colleges began developing interdisciplinary programs to focus on large societal issues, such as environmental problems or the impact of science and technology on society. Challenged by a more diverse student population many faculties launched other multidisciplinary ventures in fields such as women's studies, Afro-American studies, and ethnic studies. In response to America's new international prominence, and aided by significant outside support, other faculty members created research centers and interdepartmental programs aimed at understanding more regions of the world such as Western and Eastern Europe, Africa, and East Asia.

---

[5]LeBaron Briggs, *Routine and Ideals* (1904), p. 202.

As student numbers continued to rise and individual universities grew larger, colleges launched a variety of experiments to provide more individualized instruction, at least for portions of the student bodies. Honors programs were established for qualified students. Research internships offered opportunities for undergraduates to work in laboratories alongside experienced investigators. Freshman *seminars, group tutorials*, and small senior *colloquia* afforded students at least a modicum of personal contact with faculty members.

Meanwhile, advances in technology brought changes in the way professors taught their classes. In the 1950s, the spread of paperback books and photocopiers expanded the depth and variety of course materials far beyond the single hardcover text that had been the staple of most earlier college courses. Several decades later, the Internet brought an even wider array of readings within easy reach of students. Never before had such extensive intellectual resources been so readily available to enhance the undergraduate educational experience.

 ## Vocabulary

As you think about this essay, these identifications and definitions may be helpful to you:
1. **finishing school**   Until perhaps as late as the 1960s, with the rise of the modern women's movement, a "finishing school" was usually a small, elite private school for girls that emphasized cultural studies and prepared the students especially for social activities. Bok suggests that before the Civil War, the predominantly private, religious schools for men were more intended to polish young gentlemen than to educate young scholars.
2. **Aristotle**   A fourth-century B.C. Greek philosopher whose authority was considered unchallengeable until Galileo and other scientists began to question his writings. In early classrooms, if Aristotle said something was true, it was considered true, even if it contradicted the evidence of the real world.
3. **arcane**   secret, mysterious, or obscure, known only to those approved to learn secret knowledge, with the implication that such knowledge is not useful for daily living in the real world.
4. **stultifying**   so boring that it makes the listener become dull headed overall.
5. **nonsectarianism**   not affiliated with or restricted to a limited religious perspective.
6. **distribution requirement**   Usually a defined part of a structured curriculum. For example, in many colleges, no matter what you choose as a major, you may be required to take some courses in writing, mathematics, science, social science, and so on; that is, the required courses are "distributed" across the curriculum.
7. **seminars, group tutorials, colloquia**   All these terms refer to small classes of specific kinds, with a faculty member as teacher and a limited number of students. A seminar is usually a group of advanced students studying under a

professor with each doing original research and all exchanging results through reports and discussions. In a tutorial, a tutor, who is often a junior member of the faculty, coaches a student through a subject, normally without the original research involved in a seminar. A group tutorial is simply a group of students working together with a tutor. (In this usage, the modern notion of a computerized tutorial which takes a user through basic skills is not intended.) A colloquium (plural, colloquia) is not a full-term course but, instead, a single meeting (as short as an hour, as long as several days) at which specialists deliver addresses on a topic or on related topics and then answer questions.

 ## Discussion Questions

1. Many students today say that they share the sentiment that Derek Bok attributes to early students when he says, "Many students felt that they learned much more outside the classroom in informal clubs and literary societies, where they engaged in debates, read modern literature, and discussed serious subjects." Do you believe that you will learn as much, or even more, outside of classes than in them? What kinds of learning occur outside of class? How is that kind of learning valuable?
2. In talking about the history of why people have attended college in the past, Bok spoke about commerce—today we might say business—courses and engineering courses as "vocational subjects." The term "vocational" nowadays is commonly used to describe classes where students learn to become chefs, or real estate sales personnel, or hair stylists. What are the different uses and implications of this term?
3. Do you agree with former Harvard President Charles W. Eliot who, Bok tells us, not only rejected the old prescribed classical curriculum, but also urged that *all* requirements be abolished, leaving students free to study whatever appealed to their interests? Would you be happier if you were entirely without requirements? Would you learn as much?

 ## Suggestions for Your Journal

It is impossible to talk for long about the purposes of education without someone bringing up the idea that a college education should help to develop "character." What do you think is meant by this term? How might a college or university teach "character"? Is that why you enrolled in higher education?

Do some preliminary research into the history of your own college or university. Where in the general picture described by Derek Bok does your current school fit? When was it established? Was it originally a church-affiliated school? If so, is it still, and does that make a difference? How important is research, which Bok says came from a German model?

Unit Summary

In this unit you have examined many different perspectives about college as an American institution and its meaning and value to you as a student. The following questions can help you think about the viewpoints represented in these readings.

■ Summary Questions

1. What is a liberal education according to the authors in this unit? How will it prepare you to become a lifelong learner?
2. What are some general goals and objectives of higher education according to these readings? How do they compare with your personal reasons for being in college?
3. Many college students have traversed your campus in the past. What aspects of the history and traditions of your campus are most interesting and important to you?

■ Suggested Writing Assignments

1. Write an essay about your reasons for being in college. In it describe five goals you wish to accomplish during your first year.
2. How is college different from high school (e.g., teachers, assignments, classroom behavior, course content, learning expectations)? Write about your most difficult academic adjustment.
3. Interview a college teacher in whose class you have learned a great deal. Discuss learning from this teacher's perspective. How does this teacher think learning his or her subject matter can be useful in life?

■ Suggested Readings

Gardner, Howard. *Intelligence Reframed*, New York: Basic Books, 1999.

Hutchins, Robert M. "The Autobiography of an Uneducated Man." In Robert M. Hutchins, *Education for Freedom*, pp. 1–18. Baton Rouge: Louisiana State University Press, 1943.

Rudolph, Frederick. *The American University and College: A History*. New York: Knopf, 1962.

Thelin, John R. *A History of American Higher Education*, Baltimore: Johns Hopkins University Press, 2004.

Unit 2

What Can I Expect from College and How Will I Change?

What we anticipate seldom occurs; what we least
expect generally happens.

—BENJAMIN DISRAEL

What do you expect will happen to you during your college years? The college years are known for the personal and social changes that take place in individuals. New students are likely to notice, first, the academic challenges in the classroom and the social opportunities present at every turn. For many, the increased difficulty of college course work comes as a surprise and the social freedom, which may have been predictable, is more overwhelming than expected.

Furthermore, students usually expect that college will prepare them for a career and will accomplish this in some very specific ways. Students often expect a direct-line or one-to-one relationship between what they study in college and the job that follows graduation. Some direct relationships do occur in such fields as engineering, nursing and some technical school programs, but more often, college courses teach general knowledge and skills, not specific job tasks. Students who expect specific training may not see the relevance or importance of this more general instruction.

As time passes, they may become even more confused. For many first-year students, uncertainty about their future career and life is unsettling and worrisome. Their expectations for clear-cut decisions regarding their future may not be fulfilled.

According to many student developmental theorists, these unsettling feelings are common and can be considered normal. Most students need time to master certain developmental tasks that lead to a mature way of thinking and being. For example, as far as personal development is concerned, students need to cope with leaving home, perhaps for the first time. Often both parents and students find this transition difficult.

Some of the best features of college life are the opportunities to make new friends and to meet people who are different from yourself. Some students may find it easy to strike up new friendships, while others struggle with shyness and uncertainty. However, in time these relationships can become one of the most rewarding aspects of college life.

In classes, students are thrust into new experiences with demanding course work. They need to master rapidly moving and complex course content, and some will find they need help with basic learning skills. Academic freedom and the occasional need to drop a course may be new to many students. Some think they can succeed if they work harder, a strategy that doesn't always work. A student's expectations for academic success may take a few detours.

All these developmental concerns are in some sense predictable, as the essays in this section demonstrate. Gordon's essay outlining the theories of Perry and Chickering describes the importance of mastering the various developmental tasks. In the section "Senior's Advice to New Students," three college seniors reflect on their freshman year and pass on what they learned during that eventful time. The essay by Newman and Newman deals with the feelings of loneliness that some students may experience, especially as they begin college. Sears offers suggestions for ways to become personally effective in college, work, and life. Paying for college is a concern of most college students. Ellis suggests ways to manage your money so you can become more efficient in using the money you have.

Setting goals, both short-term and long-term, is an important element in the evolution of this highly personal process. Your expectations for what you want to receive and accomplish during the college years will probably change. It will be natural for you to expand and refine your expectations. The essays in this unit may give you some appreciation for the experiences and tasks that others consider important as you progress toward graduation.

The Developing College Student

Virginia N. Gordon

Virginia N. Gordon, who has been a college teacher and administrator, is best known as a researcher, academic advisor, and counselor for undecided students. She received her Ph.D. in counseling from the Ohio State University.

This essay describes two theoretical perspectives on how students change intellectually and personally during the college years. These theories are based on what students have experienced and related to researchers through personal interviews.

B y entering college you begin a very exciting and challenging period in your life. Although it may be difficult for you to imagine now, think about yourself on the day you graduate with a college degree. In addition to being a college graduate, what kind of person will you be? How do you expect to change during your college years?

After careful research, many theorists have described how students change and develop throughout the college experience. Social scientists who have studied college students have discovered some patterns and common themes in the way they change. One such theorist, Professor William Perry, of Harvard University, has studied how college students change intellectually and ethically. He developed a scheme to describe the development of the thinking and reasoning processes that takes place naturally as students mature and grow intellectually. Each phase of this development may be likened to a set of filters through which students see the world around them.

Dualistic students see the world in polar terms; that is, they believe that all questions have a right answer and, therefore, that all answers are either right or wrong. Such students are happiest when they find simplistic answers to their questions about the world, and they want to view their teachers and advisers as experts who can give them the right answer. They believe that hard work and obedience pay off. They depend on others to make important decisions for them. Many freshmen begin their college experience seeing through this dualistic lens.

As students develop, however, Perry says they become capable of more complex reasoning and dissatisfied with simplistic answers. They are moving into a *"multiplistic"* view of the world. They begin to see and understand cause and effect relationships. Diversity becomes legitimate because they realize that no one has all the answers. They believe everyone has the right to his or her opinion. They still, however, depend on others to make decisions for them. Some freshmen and sophomores view their experiences through this multiplistic lens.

Perry identifies the next phase, "relativism," as the time when students begin to synthesize diverse and complex elements of reasoning. They are able to view uncertainty as legitimate. They see *themselves* as the principal agent in decision making and acknowledge that they must not only make their own decisions, but also take responsibility for those decisions, regardless of how well or badly those decisions may turn out. Many juniors and seniors fall into this category of "relativistic" thinkers. Because the emphasis in Perry's system is always on how college students tend to think and reason, his theory is called a theory of *cognitive* development.

For Perry, the most advanced phase of cognitive development is one in which students make a commitment to a personal identity and its content and style. Each develops a sense of being "in" one's self, along with an awareness that growth is always transpiring, that change is inevitable and healthy. Students also make a commitment to a defined career area and are able to develop a lifestyle that is appropriate for them. Many students continue in this state of personal growth and development after college.

Through his theory of cognitive development, Perry helps us understand how students view, react to, and assimilate knowledge as they progress through college. It is important to recognize that while college experiences encourage and foster this development, non–college students also mature and develop in much the same way. (It is also important to remember that any theoretical model, no matter how carefully established, is just that: a model. Judgments about how individuals may be measured against a model require great care. And, as you see later, other models are also well established.)

Perry theorizes that growth occurs in surges, with pauses between the surges when some students might need to detach themselves for a while, while others even retreat to the comfort of their past ways of thinking. Ask five seniors to look back on how they have changed intellectually. While they will be able to reflect on their intellectual development in unique and personal terms, the patterns of growth that Perry describes will usually be evident. However, it sometimes takes courage to confront the risks each forward movement requires. Every student has the freedom to choose what kind of person he or she will become, but the forces of growth, according to Perry, will not be denied.

Developmental Tasks

Another theorist, Arthur Chickering, suggests that college students develop in an orderly way on many dimensions: intellectually, physically, psychologically and socially. He describes several developmental tasks, or "*vectors*," through which students move during their college years. A vector, according to Chickering, is a developmental task that (1) has specific content, (2) shows up at certain times in our lives, and (3) takes two to seven years to resolve. The process is ongoing throughout our lives, and even though we may resolve a task once, it may resurface later. These tasks build on each other; how we resolve one may affect the ones that follow. While these tasks develop in order, they may also be concurrent, so we may be dealing with several at one time. The seven developmental tasks that Chickering has proposed are described next.

1. Achieving Competence

The first task is achieving competence. College students need to achieve competence in several areas: intellectually, physically, and interpersonally. Chickering likens this to a three-tined pitchfork, since all three happen simultaneously.

Intellectual competence involves the skill of using one's mind in "comprehending, analyzing and synthesizing." It means learning how to learn and acquiring knowledge. Most students enroll in college in order to develop intellectual competence. They begin to develop good study habits and the skills of critical thinking and reasoning. They will be able to appreciate and integrate many points of view in their thinking. Ideally, they will enjoy learning for its own sake and feel the excitement of entering new realms of knowledge. Physical competence involves manual skills as well. The recreational value of, and prestige associated with, athletic skills or the creative value of arts and crafts are important to many students. More and more we are concerned that lifelong fitness is important. Recreational skills and interests that one develops in college continue throughout life. Colleges provide many physical facilities for students who seek to develop competency in this area.

Probably the greatest concern of many students is how to develop interpersonal and social competence. They feel a need for communication skills, such as listening and responding appropriately, so they can relate to others individually or in groups. Learning the social graces and how to interact with peers is an important task that most students accomplish early in their college years. Much of this learning happens as a result of observation, feedback from other students, and experience.

When these three competencies are achieved, students feel a *sense* of competence; they sense that they can cope with whatever comes. They are confident of their ability to achieve successfully whatever they set out to do. They respond to new challenges by integrating old learning with new. The task of developing competence is especially important during the freshman year.

2. Managing Emotions

Two major emotional impulses that need to be managed during college are sex and aggression. Maturity implies that legitimate ways have been found to express anger and hate. Sexual impulses are more insistent than ever. Students feel pressured to find answers to questions concerning interpersonal relationships. They move from being controlled by the external rules of their heritage to control by internal norms of self. (Students from rural areas may have different sets of rules, for example, than inner-city students.) Many students are still controlled by the external norms of their peers. Exaggerated displays of emotion are not uncommon: in the past, for example, college students initiated panty raids or held contests for swallowing the greatest number of goldfish.

People often feel boredom, tension and anxiety as normal emotions while their impulsive feelings need to be controlled. Becoming aware of positive emotions such as sympathy, yearning, wonder and awe is also important. Eventually, students learn to be controlled by their own internal set of norms. Achieving competence in the management of emotions means moving from an awareness of the legitimacy of emotions, to acting on them, to controlling them internally.

3. Moving Through Autonomy Toward Interdependence

Another important task for new college students during the first months of college is to achieve independence. A student may be hesitant to try certain new experiences or to approach new people. Such a student is trying to become independent but, as Chickering says, is like a "hog on ice," a little shaky at first. For probably the first time in their experience, many students may be living with no restraints or outside pressures, with no one to tell them when to study or to be home by 11 o'clock. As they act on their own, they may flounder at first. Beginning students may wonder, for example, why they have so much free time. They attend classes for only three or four hours a day and then may squander the rest of the day—until they realize the importance of quality study time.

The student who achieves *emotional* independence has learned to be free of the continual need for reassurance, affection or approval. Such a student has learned to deal with authority figures and feels comfortable with professors or other very important people on campus. There is less reliance on parents and more on friends and nonparental adults. Achieving *instrumental* independence means students can do things for themselves that parents used to do, such as washing the laundry or managing money. They are able to solve problems and use resources on their own.

When the student finally comes to recognize and accept *inter*dependence, the boundaries of personal choice become clearer and the ranges within which one can give and receive become more settled. Autonomous students feel less need for support from their parents and begin to understand that parents need them as much as they need their parents. They begin to see their parents for what they are: middle-aged people with weaknesses just like themselves. Becoming autonomous is a very important task for freshmen to accomplish.

4. Developing Mature Interpersonal Relationships

Developing mature relationships means that students become less anxious and less defensive, more friendly, spontaneous and respectful. They are more willing to trust and are more independent. They develop the capacity for mature intimacy. They can participate in healthy relationships that incorporate honesty and responsiveness. They finally realize that perfect parents don't exist and that Prince or Princess Charming is not coming to sweep them off their feet. They also have an increased tolerance for people culturally different from themselves. They have acquired increased empathy and altruism and enjoy diversity. They are able to develop mature relationships with many types of people.

5. Establishing Identity

The fifth vector, according to Chickering, is establishing identity. This task is really the sum of the first four vectors: developing competence, managing emotions, developing autonomy through interdependence, and developing mature interpersonal relationships. Success at achieving identity will often hinge on how these former tasks have been accomplished. Studies suggest that students generally achieve a coherent, mature sense of identity during their sophomore or junior years.

In addition to these inner changes, students need to clarify their conceptions of physical needs, personal appearance, and sex-appropriate roles and behavior. They identify a personal lifestyle that is theirs. Once such a sense of identity is achieved, other major vectors may be approached. Establishing an identity is the hinge on which future development depends.

6. Developing Purpose

Developing purpose is the vector related to career choice. The questions to be faced for this vector are not only "Who Am I?" but also "Where Am I Going?" Interests tend to stabilize; vocational exploration becomes a serious task. A general orientation toward a career area is achieved first, and then more specific career decisions are made. Students begin to formulate plans and integrate vocational and lifestyle considerations into those plans. An initial commitment to a career goal is made with the move into adulthood.

7. Developing Integrity

Students also need to clarify a personally valid set of beliefs that have some internal consistency. This happens in three stages, according to Chickering. Their values are first (1) humanized, then (2) personalized, and then (3) their beliefs and actions begin to suit each other. During childhood, students assimilate their parents' values. In college, students begin to examine these inherited values to see if they fit them personally. Some values may be rejected while others may be retained. The student's task is to personalize these values by achieving behavior consistent with them and being willing to stand up for what he or she strongly believes. Such a degree of commitment leads to congruence between one's beliefs and values and one's actions. Standards for assessing personal actions are set and are used as guides for all behavior.

Working through these seven developmental tasks is crucial to the college student's successful passage into mature adulthood. How will you be different on graduation day? I hope that you will have no regrets about missed opportunities to become involved in your own development. The college environment offers an almost unbelievable assortment of opportunities in and outside the classroom. There are many resources, including people, who stand ready to challenge and support you. As you move into the world you will be willing to assert the convictions and values you carefully (and sometimes traumatically) learned during your college years. Knowing that everyone moves through these passages of development and that change is inevitable can help you see the more difficult times as periods of growth. In this way you will be able to react positively and productively.

Vocabulary

As you think about this essay, these definitions may be helpful to you:
1. **dualistic**   consisting of two irreducible elements or modes; a way of thinking that sees issues as black or white, rather than as shades of gray
2. **multiplistic**   numerous or various
3. **cognitive**   involving the act of knowing, including both awareness and judgment
4. **vector**   a course or direction
5. **instrumental**   serving as a means, agent, or tool; in this essay, instrumental independence is the ability to live and work on your own

Discussion Questions

1. What aspect of student development does Perry's scheme address? What is its primary thesis? Do all students fit these patterns?
2. How does a dualistic student view the world?
3. How does Perry describe commitment, which he considers the most advanced phase of cognitive development? How do you reach commitment?
4. What are the seven developmental tasks of college students as proposed by Chickering? Which are most relevant to first-year, traditional-age college students?
5. What, says Chickering, is required to develop an identity? How are the last two tasks of developing purpose and integrity related to identity?

Suggestions for Your Journal

Sketch your own intellectual development from the time you were a child until now. Where do you think you fit into Perry's scheme? Have you ever consciously experienced a period of intellectual growth? How would you describe it?

Which of Chickering's developmental tasks have you completed? Which will be the most difficult to master?

Seniors' Advice to New Students

The following three essays were written by college seniors eager to offer advice to students who are starting their life as college students. In retrospect, these seniors share some of their first-year experiences and offer suggestions that can help you become a personally involved and academically successful student.

The Stakes are Low

BEN BERNSTEIN

Ben Bernstein is an International Relations Major at Brown University.

The first few months of college were pure agony. I remember two moments specifically. The first occurred a week into school when my roommate, whom I'll call Jimmy, announced that to beat the late summer heat wave, he was going for a swim in a nearby river. Totally impressed with his daring and rugged sense of adventure, I wished him good luck and counted myself lucky for being matched with such a cool roommate.

The second event took place three weeks later. My room had started smelling like the bathroom in hell and I had no idea why. I was embarrassed to invite my few friends over to watch baseball and drink beers because I thought they might suspect me of a lack of proper toilet training.

Jimmy, still the coolest guy in the world, was rarely around—in addition to his regular swimming trips, he had joined the rugby team and was seemingly always at practice. One day, in a burst of curiosity, I decided to look for more information on his river. Mystery solved. It turned out that Jimmy had been swimming in toxic sewage for the last three weeks. When he hung his bathing suit up in our room, the stench made itself right at home.

Soon, I started noticing other things about Jimmy. He rarely showered. He talked loudly in his sleep. One day he decided to make a mural of empty record covers on our ceiling, which looked awesome for two hours—until they crashed down on our heads while we were sleeping. Our conversations about politics and music were less exciting than contentious as the frustrations over shared living space spilled into every aspect of our relationship. Suddenly, the person who I had described in a phone call hom during orientation as "like a brother" was more and more like a toxic tornado.

Two months into college, Jimmy and I were barely on speaking terms and while there was no animosity, we had both made a genuine commitment to avoidance. I had to make new friends and find a new roommate for the next year.

One could find a million little lessons in this story—from "maintain good relations with your roommate" to "don't swim in raw sewage"—all of which I imagine are simply too specific to be truly valuable when thinking about the broader college experience.

Instead, I'll pass on the advice that my dad gave me when I spoke to him anxiously on Parent's Weekend, which occurred a week or so after the sewage discovery. After I'd recounted the story, he laughed and told me that the stakes were low.

Ultimately, I ended up making new friends, losing some of them, making more new ones, and even reconnecting with old ones. The university is a place where change is a rare constant and remembering that and internalizing the idea that no situation is permanent is the most fundamentally healthy action one can take at college.

Before I arrived at school, I had ambitions as an Ultimate Frisbee player. After working hard all summer on my throws, I got to school, spent a few months practicing with the team and realized that it wasn't the place for me, or in the words of the team captain, "you aren't fast enough." It was demoralizing, but I reminded myself that the stakes were low.

Perhaps inspired by the success I'd had investigating my roommate's toxic river, I started writing for the newspaper. This activity stuck, for whatever reason, and by junior year I was writing a regular investigative campus issues column and interviewing student leaders and university big shots like the chancellor and president. However, even within my time at the newspaper, there was turbulence and change. I'd started out reviewing music and movies until one day, after a strong disagreement with an editor, decided I needed a different section. A chance encounter with a friend who worked in the fundraising office led me to a story on alumni contributions and after that I started exploring other campus issues like wasted funds for a new fitness center and the origins of a controversial student group.

My college experience, and that of most of my fellow students, was not a primarily academic endeavor. I learned, I hope, to write persuasively, articulate my ideas clearly and think critically. But I am unconvinced that these skills are the real legacy of four years of college. The truly significant learning and growth at college takes place in a more social sphere, through deep participation in student groups and intensive interaction with one's peers.

Within that severe social environment, then, my advice to incoming freshmen is to understand and internalize the idea that no single event, relationship or situation at college is necessarily permanent. Instead, the beauty of the college experience is its potential for change and evolution in a short period of time. As a freshman, the best thing you can do is to keep all of this in perspective. Work hard on projects you enjoy, ditch the ones that bore you, stay physically healthy and if your room starts to smell like the monkey cage at the zoo, find out where your roommate has been swimming.

Reprinted by permission from Ben Bernstein.

Four Pieces of Advice

JENNIFER ROSELLA

Jennifer Rosella is an Elementary and Special Education Major at Providence College.

Just four short years ago I was in your position, a college freshman embarking on a new journey with new classes, new people, and a new living situation. I was far from home for the first time and trying to adjust to everything at once was overwhelming. Now, as I approach my college graduation, I cannot believe how fast those four years of college have gone. Looking back, being a college freshman was stressful at times, but it was also one of the most exciting times of my life. I can truly say that college has been a great experience and I have learned so much more than I ever thought possible. As you begin your own college experience, I wish to share with you four pieces of advice I've learned along the way.

The first and probably the most important advice I can give you is to get involved. You've probably heard this before, but it is most definitely true. Signing up to become involved in campus activities such as clubs, sports, or community service allows you to meet new people, find new interests, and continue what you love to do. Don't be afraid to sign up for something that you may have never done before. I found that college is the perfect time to challenge yourself and learn more about who you are. If you've always wanted to be on a sports team, sign up for intramurals. If you want to volunteer at a hospital or help build a house with Habitat for Humanity, sign up. Most clubs and organizations in college are very open to anyone who has an interest, even if you don't have any prior experience.

My freshman year I found the opportunity to join the Irish Dance Club. Irish dancing was something I had always wanted to do but never really tried. When I went to the first meeting, I was surprised at how open the members were to anyone with or without experience. This openness was something I found in all the organizations I joined. Through my participation in the Irish Dance Club, I not only made many new friends, but gained some great memories.

If I hadn't gotten involved outside the classroom, I would have missed out on some of the best social experiences I had as a first-year student. I've learned that being open to new things and new people and taking on responsibilities outside of your normal course load can provide endless benefits and can make you a better-rounded person. Truthfully, most of your learning will come from these experiences because they will challenge you to discover new skills and abilities you never thought you had.

Another piece of advice that I had to learn the hard way was to manage my time wisely! Time management is an essential skill for all college students, but it is not always easy to practice. The more you are aware of how much you need to do, the better you will be at gauging the amount of time you will need to do it. Find a system that will work for you, whether it is a calendar, planner, to-do list, or a combination of the three. Start assignments well in advance, and don't hesitate to talk with your professors about your progress. Writing papers the night before they are due will certainly not result in your best quality work and will definitely provide unnecessary stress. The key to success in managing your time is to be aware of what needs to be done, make a plan, and stick to it.

Another big challenge of my freshman year was to make a decision about a major. Personally, I came to college thinking I knew exactly what I wanted to study and then wound up changing my major three times! I could not make up my mind because I had so many interests and my college offered so many courses that I wanted to take. This brings me to my third piece of advice: unless you really know what you want to do in college, don't rush to make a decision. Deciding to be undeclared in the beginning allows you time to explore the different programs your school has to offer. You may take a class in college that was never offered in your high school and find that you love it. Take advantage of the resources on your campus as you explore, such as your academic advisor, faculty in your areas of interest, or a counselor in your Career Services office. After I explored and researched my academic interests, I chose the strongest and used the other as a minor.

The last piece of advice that I offer is to develop healthy habits! Exercising regularly, eating healthy, and getting a good night's sleep were three of the most important things I learned to do for myself. Pulling all-nighters or choosing French fries and pizza every night in the dining hall may seem like good decisions at the time, but they will inhibit your ability to perform well and may set you on an unhealthful path. If you want the chance to be the most successful, take care of yourself. You will also avoid developing bad habits that will be hard to break later.

These pieces of advice that I pass on to you have been a tremendous help in my getting the most out of my four years in college. As you embark on your own college journey, I hope that you will remember this advice from a senior who has been there! Your freshman year only happens once—make the most of it.

Reprinted by permission from Jennifer Rosella.

Things I Wish I Knew as a Freshman

ANDREW GORDON-SEIFERT

Andrew Gordon-Seifert is a Music and History Major at The Ohio State University.

I'm sure you heard before you became a freshman that college work is more difficult than high school and that most students are often confronted with new and challenging experiences. To some extent, both were true for me. I was away from home, the course work was harder and more time consuming, and for the first time I had to make definite decisions about what I wanted to do with my life. While my freshman year proved to be successful in many ways, there were many things I wish I had done differently.

After a long and tedious college application process, I was naturally relieved when I made my final decision. Of course the prospect of leaving home was scary but it didn't really hit me until my first night, when I realized that I was 600 miles from home and didn't know anybody. My first year, I struggled with finding my place at the university academically and socially. At first I spent my free time in my room playing Xbox and searching the Internet for useless facts on sports and history. The vast amount of knowledge that accrued from my reading turned me into the sports guru of my dorm floor. People would come to me asking questions like "Who was the Super Bowl MVP in 1972?" and "Who won the AL Cy Young award in 1986?" and somehow, I'd always have an answer. While this gained me a great deal of respect amongst the sports fans on my floor, it didn't really give me any sense that I was making good use of my time in college.

This leads me to the first thing I wish I had known as a freshman: getting involved in campus organizations and clubs is one of the most productive things you can do. At my university one of the first things you get at orientation, along with a student handbook and a buckeye nut, is a t-shirt saying "GET INVOLVED!" For some reason, perhaps my inclination to question authority, I ignored this advice. My junior year I joined a music fraternity and quickly realized the mistake I had made in not joining earlier. I became part of a group of students who cared about what they did and actively promoted what they believed. We did community service, hosted social events, played music and hung out together.

One of the best parts of going to college is that you can easily find people who share your interests. As I discovered, being involved allows you to feel you are a part of campus life while making really close friends. Besides, colleges and universities have almost infinite resources, so why not take advantage of them? Another great aspect of belonging to an organization is that it offers an opportunity to take a leadership role. Not only does leadership experience look good on a resume or a grad school application but it is also a way to build skills that you can use for the rest of your life.

Another thing I wish that I had dealt with better during my freshman year was organizing my time. Freshman year offers an excellent opportunity to revolutionize the way you approach your academic and personal life. In my case I should have adopted much better time management skills. Being a double major in music and history has its benefits but if you are not organized, your life can become a living hell. At 1 AM, when I'd be doing theory homework, analyzing listening examples and trying to grasp 30 pages of reading on historical method, I wished that I had planned my work better. I certainly wasn't alone either: I lived in a music major dorm so we had the same classes and assignments. On Sunday nights from about midnight to one in the morning it would become clear that almost everyone had waited till then to do the assignment and you would hear a loud "What the [heck] is this!?" and other exclamations I'd rather not repeat. While this was amusing at the time, it was not amusing at the end of the term when I would be up until four in the morning completing term papers. The physical and mental toll that getting three hours of sleep a night for a week took on me, forced me to learn that I needed to carefully plan ahead for all of my assignments.

Along with time management I wish that I had better organized my life and my planner. I'll never forget one Tuesday during exam week when I started chatting with a friend and she said: "What did you think of the music history exam?" This question came as quite a shock considering I was convinced that the exam was the next day. It turns out that if I had kept the syllabus or written the exam dates in my planner I would have realized that in the battle of word of mouth against the syllabus, the syllabus always wins. Luckily I was able to make up the exam but I don't think that many professors would have been so generous. Since then, I have made a detailed exam schedule at the beginning of each quarter to ensure that I never miss an exam again.

Overall I have learned a great deal from the mistakes I made as a freshman and have used what I learned to my advantage ever since. After all, college is a time for learning and self-improvement. I feel that if I had just gotten involved sooner, managed my time and organized my schedule more efficiently, I would have had a much easier freshman year. It would have greatly reduced the stress of an already difficult time and would have given me the tools to be a more effective student a lot earlier. Although many aspects of the first year in college can be challenging, I look back on it as a time when I "grew up" in many positive ways.

Reprinted by permission of Andrew Gordon-Seifert.

 ## Discussion Questions

1. What recurring themes do you detect in these senior students' essays? Do any of the experiences described by these seniors sound familiar to you? If so, which ones and why?
2. All of these seniors emphasized the importance of becoming involved in out-of-class activities early in the freshman year. According to them, what are some of the advantages of becoming involved immediately?

 ## Suggestions for Your Journal

What themes in these senior essays are most relevant to your experiences as a freshman so far? What advice do you feel you might follow? Why? What other issues are you encountering as a new student that are not mentioned in these essays? How are you resolving these issues?

Tips on Becoming Personally Effective

Susan Jones Sears

Well known for her work in counselor education, Susan Jones Sears is a professor emerita in the College of Education at the Ohio State University. In this essay, she offers some practical tips for becoming a competent and successful student.

Whether you are a new college student or a more experienced one, you are probably impressed with the number of talented and highly skilled individuals in your classes—individuals who seem to know more than you do and who are motivated, bright, and dedicated. With increasing competition in the classroom and the workplace, individuals have begun searching for a psychological edge, an advantage to help them excel and be recognized as competent students and workers. Think about the concept of personal effectiveness—personal behaviors and skills that result in enhanced performance in college, at work, and in life. As you begin your college career and prepare for the work world, you can benefit from reflecting upon what it takes to excel.

What are the ingredients of success? During the last two decades, hundreds of books have been written with the intent of helping people improve themselves and increase their chances for success. Techniques for improving your personality, learning to communicate more effectively, and managing stress are all familiar topics to readers who avail themselves of the self-help books in their local bookstores or on the Internet. In the early 1980s, those interested in improving their performance read *Peak Performers* by Charles Garfield; in the latter 1980s and early 1990s, they read *The Seven Habits of Highly Effective People* by Stephen Covey. In the 2000s, Philip C. McGraw is the latest self-help guru.

Today, many books on coaching are generating a lot of attention and discussion. Professional athletes and actors have used the services of coaches for decades, and now ordinary individuals are hiring coaches to give them advice and offer strategies on how to improve their personal and professional lives.

If you study high achievers or personally effective individuals, you begin to see that they function at higher levels not because of a single talent but, rather, because certain factors, taken together, result in greater accomplishment. Individuals who know what they want to do in life, who have a vision, a game plan, or a purpose or goal, are more successful than those who do not. If you have a sense of purpose, you will naturally attract those who are going in the same direction. What is your purpose or goal in life? What are you trying to achieve? Maybe you want to find a major or a career that you will enjoy and [that will] bring you fulfillment, or maybe you want to travel to learn about other cultures. Take a few minutes to think about your goal or purpose for the year.

Replacing Distractions with Energy Boosters

Petty annoyances are often small irritants, but they tend to become real hassles when they are not dealt with. They drain your energy and distract you from your quest for success. Perhaps something around the house or apartment is broken, but you can't seem to get around to repairing it. Or your roommate is a "night owl" and you are not.

Maybe one of your own bad habits is annoying you! Your notes are disorganized and scattered, and when it is time to study for a test, you procrastinate. Or maybe a friend has a habit of making fun of you or putting you down when you make even a small mistake. You have tolerated it but find yourself getting angrier each time it happens. Many of us tolerate petty annoyances and really don't realize how much they are irritating us, wearing us down, and draining our energy. Write down a list of the things you are putting up with or tolerating that are draining your energy. Now set aside a day within the next week to tackle some of these petty annoyances. Try to eliminate everything on your list that you can.

Some annoyances take time to eliminate. If you are having difficulty in a relationship and want to rebuild or repair it, you probably can't do it in a day. But at least you can begin. When you succeed in working through the annoyances that bother you the most, you should reward yourself by indulging in some favorite activity.

Simplifying Your Life

One way to attract something new in your life is to make space—get rid of the clutter, toss out old notes, clothes, and memos, and sell those old books and CDs. Ask yourself: "Have I used this in the past six months?" If your answer is no and it isn't a seasonal item, toss it. If you don't know where to start, take one part of a room at a time. Give your usable items to a local charity. Someone will appreciate what has been cluttering up your space. Getting rid of things you do not need can invigorate you and create the sensation of starting anew.

Once you have rid yourself of the clutter in your life, look at your schedule. If your schedule is packed with stuff to do, people to meet, and places to go, it may be time to simplify. People who are too busy can miss opportunities because they don't notice what is going on around them and don't have time to think. Consolidate your credit cards so you don't spend so much time paying and keeping track of bills. Turn your cell phone off. Before you say yes to a social event, make certain it is really something you want to do.

Managing Your Time Effectively

Do you attend classes, study as hard as you can, and then run to your part-time or full-time job? Do you find yourself complaining that there aren't enough hours in the day? If you feel pressured for time, perhaps you should take a week and track your time in one-hour increments. Keep a notepad in your pocket or bookbag and write down what you are doing each hour from the time you rise until you go to bed. Writing just a few words will allow you to keep track of how you are spending your time. At the end of the week, quickly calculate how much time you spend on major life activities such as attending classes, studying, talking on the phone, sleeping, watching television, listening to CDs, hanging out with your friends, e-mailing or instant messaging. Are you surprised by how you spend your time? In what areas do you think you are wasting your time? How can you reschedule your time so you will use it more effectively?

Learning to Say No

Are you overcommitted with work and social obligations? Do you find yourself participating in activities that don't really interest you? Perhaps you need to learn to say no. Women in particular are brought up in our society to please and to be liked. As a result of this kind of socialization, they find it harder to say no when asked to do favors or take on extra work. Some fear that saying no will turn off their friends, but in reality it doesn't. Often your friends and colleagues respect you more when they learn they cannot take advantage of you. Learning to say no is one way of getting control of your time and your life.

Managing Your Money Well

During the last 20 years, it has become acceptable to have debts. Your parents probably saved money before they purchased a cherished item, whereas you may find it easy to simply charge the cost to your credit card. The costs of immediate gratification (charge it now) can be high. First, the interest rate on debt is high. Second, too much debt can lead to stress that can drain your energy, making it difficult for you to be your best and attract the people and opportunities you want. Instead, if you pay off the balance on your credit cards each month, you will feel lighter, more free, and in control of your life.

Building a Strong Network of Friends

Part of your success in life and work is having some close friends with whom you can laugh, love, and celebrate your and their successes. Be aware of the people around you, and get to know those who are particularly interesting. With our increased mobility, we sometimes have to create our own communities, a circle of friends with whom we feel comfortable and supported. Some create this circle of friends at college or at work, and others find opportunities to create friendships at church or in clubs. Be proactive and create your own network of friends.

Making Time for Yourself

Life can become boring if we do not have something to look forward to. Taking a walk, talking to friends, taking a hot bubble bath, or listening to your favorite music are just a few examples of activities that might be pleasurable and inspiring to you. Taking time for yourself is an important way to keep balanced in today's hectic world. Think about the activities that you really look forward to doing, and then how can you change your schedule to include them in your daily life.

Identifying and Managing Stress

If you are to become truly effective, you must begin to identify the sources of stress in your life and learn to manage stress at work, school, and home. Stress can be either a positive or a negative force. It is negative when it interferes with your ability to function at your optimal level. It is positive when it enhances your performance or your effectiveness. That is the key to stress management.

What does the term *stress* really mean? According to psychologist Donald Meichenbaum, you experience stress when you appraise an event (a demand on you, a constraint, an opportunity, or a challenge) as having the potential to exceed the resources you have available. You may think it's too hard, too frightening, or too challenging. Stressors or events that can create anxiety vary greatly from individual to individual. Three classifications are:

- *external* physical stimuli, such as heat, cold, crowding, loud noises
- *interpersonal* difficulties with others
- *internal* stimuli, such as our own thoughts or feelings

Although stressors are specific to individuals to some extent, universal categories of stressors are environmental stressors, life stress events, and daily hassles.

Environmental stressors include things such as noise, crowding, commuting time, worry about crime, traffic and pollution, economic difficulties, isolation, restricted leisure opportunities, and job insecurity. These often are a function of where you live and sometimes your socioeconomic class.

Life stress events are major occurrences that create stress and require people to change and adapt. Holmes and Rahe identified 43 life events that cause significant stress and assigned each event a weight, using what they called "life change events." Events that call for a greater amount of change and adaptation are assigned a higher number of life change units. For example, the death of a spouse is assigned a very high weight. Holmes and Rahe used their instrument, the Social Readjustment Rating Scale, to measure the amount of life stress a person was experiencing. They found that too many life stress events forced the body to adapt and change so much that those stresses weakened the immune system.

In fact, researchers have made connections between life stress events and both physical and mental illness. Evidence has shown that life stress events contribute to emotional disorders, heart disease, accidents, and other conditions. Whether individuals who experience stressful life events subsequently become ill, however, also depends on their personal vulnerability, as well as the amount of social and emotional support available to them.

Daily hassles (for instance, physical appearance, concerns about weight, too many things to do, and losing or misplacing things) are also stressors. Until the early 1980s, little research had been done on the effect of minor but more common daily hassles. Since then, researchers have paid considerable attention to studying effects of hassles on health. Hassles seem to vary depending on age and, to some extent, the circumstances in which people find themselves. Some common daily hassles for students are:

Taking tests or exams
Worrying about not meeting academic deadlines
Not knowing how to study effectively
Taking hard and demanding classes

Strategies for Managing Stress

Preventive approaches such as relaxation training are important to any stress management program. The term *relaxation training* refers to any technique whose purpose is to decrease the negative symptoms the human body experiences under stress. If individuals can be taught to relax, they should be able to produce voluntarily an alternative physiological response to offset the negative stress symptoms. For example, if a stress reaction results in increases in muscle tension, blood pressure, or heart rate, the voluntarily induced state of relaxation can reverse these increases.

Engaging in a healthy lifestyle goes a long way in managing stress. Individuals who experience the physiological effects of stress are endangering their health. If they also are practicing unhealthy habits that weaken the body's ability to resist stress, their level of stress may increase. Clearly, if you are stressed, you should practice good eating habits, use alcohol only moderately if at all, not smoke, and get regular exercise.

Accepting and Adapting to Change

Change is anything that causes us to shift from old and familiar ways or situations to ones that are new, different, and often challenging. More than a decade ago, Alvin Toffler talked about "waves of change" that are accelerating at a faster and faster pace. The rate of change in today's world is greater than any other time in our history. Global competition, almost unbelievable advances in technology, particularly communication technologies, and a knowledge and information explosion all contribute to this fast-paced change. Learning how to adapt and adjust to change is a critical skill that can be learned.

In times of rapid change, you must be able to adapt quickly. Below are several suggestions on how to adapt to change rather than ignore or resist it:

• Withhold judgment and tolerate ambiguity or uncertainty until you see the results of whatever changes you are experiencing.

- Be flexible and try new approaches.
- Stay current about changes and trends in your field and try to understand their potential impact.
- Anticipate the new skills needed in your field and acquire them.
- View change as part of a natural process of growth.
- Look to the future; don't glorify the past beyond its worth.
- Scan your environment and reassess your goals regularly.

Think about the changes that have occurred in your life in the last 18 months. How did you respond? For example, did you try to avoid change at all costs, complain about the change, reluctantly change, or see change as an opportunity and develop ways to deal with it? At times, change can create situations in which you feel you have little or no control over events going on around you. When that happens, we usually experience anxiety or stress. Although we cannot always control what is happening in life, we can control our reaction it. We can decide how to react to change so it does not overwhelm us.

The personal characteristics and skills outlined above can give you the psychological edge in school, work, and life in general. As you establish your educational and career goals, developing these habits, attitudes and skills can enhance your success in all areas of life.

Works Cited

Covey, Stephen. *The Seven Habits of Highly Effective People*. New York: Simon and Schuster, 1989.

Garfield, Charles. *Peak Performers*. New York: Avon, 1986.

Holmes, T. H., and Rahe, R. H. "The Social Readjustment Rating Scale." *Journal of Psychosomatic Research*, 11(2), 213–218, 1967.

Meichenbaum, Donald. *Stress Inoculation Training*. New York: Pergamon Press, 1985.

Toffler, Alvin. *The Third Wave*. New York: William Morrow, 1980.

From Susan Jones Sears and Virginia N. Gordon, BUILDING YOUR CAREER: A GUIDE TO YOUR FUTURE, 3ed, (Upper Saddle River, NJ: Prentice Hall, 2002). Reprinted with permission from Pearson Education, Inc. Upper Saddle River, N.J.

 Discussion Questions

1. What does becoming a "personally effective student" mean to you? Does being a competent college student differ from being a competent high school student? If so, how?
2. Which of the author's suggestions for improving your daily life would be the most difficult for you to accomplish? (For example, do you have trouble saying no when friends ask for a favor?)
3. What are some stressors in your life, and what can you do to alleviate them?

Suggestions for Your Journal

Reflect on your ability to accept and adapt to change. Since you began college, what changes (for example, in your daily routine, in the classroom, in your relationship with your parents) have been the most difficult to deal with? The easiest?

What has surprised you the most about how being a college student has changed your life?

Loneliness

Barbara M. Newman and Philip R. Newman

Barbara and Philip Newman are the authors of many books on human development. They are especially well known for *Development through Life: A Psychosocial Approach*, now in its eighth edition. Barbara Newman is professor and chair of the Human Development and Studies Department at the University of Rhode Island. Philip Newman is a lecturer in the same department.

Some students may experience feelings of loneliness as they enter a new and foreign college environment. The authors describe loneliness as a common college experience and suggest that friendships can play a key role in overcoming it.

College brings new opportunities for friendship, but it also brings new experiences of isolation and loneliness. Many college students leave the comfort and familiarity of their support system at home for a new environment. Others break ties with old friends who have gone to work or entered the military right after high school. The early weeks and months of college are likely to bring deep feelings of isolation and loneliness. These feelings are intensified because students usually approach the transition to college with such positive anticipation. They often do not even consider that this change will bring any sense of *uprootedness* or loss.

Loneliness is a common experience of college life. An estimated 25 percent of the college population feel extremely lonely at some time during any given month. These feelings are likely to be most noticeable during the freshman year because of the sharp contrast between the structure of high school life and the independence expected of students in college. However, loneliness can be a theme throughout the college years. The process of becoming an individual brings with it a new appreciation for one's separateness from others. As young people discover their own uniqueness, from time to time they are bound to feel that no one else really understands them.

Your parents may also experience periods of loneliness. They miss the physical presence of a person they love. They miss the daily interactions. Now and again, they may yearn for things to be more like they were and wish to be less separate.

Loneliness can be classified into three categories: *transient*, situational, and chronic.[1] *Transient loneliness* lasts a short time and passes. College students may feel this kind of loneliness when their friends are out on dates and they are alone in the dorm. This type of loneliness may occur when a student is the only one to take a certain position in a discussion; the only black student in a class; or the only one working out in a large, empty gym.

---

[1] These categories are adapted from J. Meer, "Loneliness," *Psychology Today,* July 1985, pp. 28–33.

Situational loneliness accompanies a sudden loss or a move to a new city. Students commonly experience this kind of loneliness when they first come to college, especially if they are away from home. Most of us are *disoriented* when we move to a new town. Going to college is no different. Despite the many new and wonderful facets of college life, most young people experience situational loneliness due to the loss of the supportive, familiar environment of their homes and communities.

Your parents may undergo situational loneliness because of the loss of your presence. Even though they have planned and saved for this opportunity, they may experience intense loneliness following your departure. Rather than trying to create a myth that no one is feeling lonely, parents and college students can help each other through this time by admitting their loneliness and doing their best to reduce it. Frequent telephone calls, letters, and visits home in the first few months can ease the feelings of loss.

Chronic loneliness lasts a long time and cannot be linked to a specific event or situation. Chronically lonely people may have an average number of social contacts, but these contacts are not meaningful in helping the person achieve the desired level of intimacy. Chronically lonely people often seem reluctant to make contact with others. There appears to be a strong relationship between social skills and chronic loneliness. People who have higher levels of social skill, including friendliness, communication skills, appropriate *nonverbal* behavior, and appropriate response to others, have more adequate social support and experience lower levels of loneliness.

You may not recognize that you suffer from chronic loneliness until you are away at college. While children are living at home, parents are usually able to provide the amount of social support their children need. At college, children may find it extremely difficult to replace the level of trust and closeness that were provided by family members and high school friends.

Inadequate friendship relationships may actually interfere with your academic performance as well as your physical and mental health. Substantial research evidence supports the relationship between inadequate social support and *vulnerability* to illness. People who are part of a strong social support system are more likely to resist disease and to recover quickly from illnesses when they occur. Their general outlook on life is more optimistic.

A college student's circle of friends plays a key role in keeping the young person integrated into the social environment. Friends look in on you when you are sick; they make sure you have an assignment if you miss class; they invite you to join them if they are going to a party, a special lecture, or a campus concert. Friends worry about you and remind you to take care of yourself. Friends monitor your moods and prevent you from becoming too preoccupied or too discouraged. Friends value you and support your emerging identity. They understand the importance of the questions you are raising, and they encourage you to say what's on your mind. Building and maintaining satisfying friendships are key ingredients to feeling at home and succeeding in college.

Vocabulary

As you think about this essay, these definitions may be helpful to you:
1. **uprootedness**   in psychology, a sense of being displaced
2. **transient**   passing through with only a brief stay or sojourn
3. **disoriented**   having lost a sense of time, place, or identity
4. **nonverbal**   involving minimal or no use of language
5. **vulnerability**   openness to attack or damage

 ## Discussion Questions

1. What factors may trigger loneliness in a college student?
2. What are the three categories of loneliness described by the authors?
3. How does transient loneliness differ from chronic loneliness?
4. Why are students with little or no social support more vulnerable to illness?
5. What is the hardest part of maintaining a friendship?

 ## Suggestions for Your Journal

Did you experience situational loneliness when you started college? How did it feel? Do you know students who are lonely? How can building and maintaining friendships be helpful in overcoming loneliness? How can you as a friend help another student through lonely times?

Three Paths to Financial Freedom

Dave Ellis

Dave Ellis is an author, nationally known lecturer and founder and past president of College Survival, Inc. Over the past 16 years he has facilitated workshops on topics ranging from becoming a more effective college instructor and creating individual life plans.

"I can't afford it" is a common reason that students give for dropping out of school. "I don't know how to pay for it" or "I don't think it's worth it" are probably more accurate ways to state the problem.

Money produces more unnecessary conflict and worry than almost anything else. And it doesn't seem to matter how much money a person has. People who earn $10,000 a year never have enough. People who earn $100,000 a year might also say that they never have enough. Let's say they earned $1 million a year. Then they'd have enough, right? Not necessarily. Money worries can upset people no matter how much they have.

Most money problems result from spending more than is available. It's that simple, even though often we do everything we can to make the problem much more complicated. The solution also is simple: *Don't spend more than you have.* If you are spending more than you have, then increase your income, decrease your spending, or do both. This idea has never won a Nobel Prize in economics, but you won't go broke applying it.

There is a big payoff in making money management seem more complicated than it really is. If we don't understand money, then we don't have to be responsible for it. After all, if you don't know how to change a flat tire, then you don't have to be the one responsible for fixing it. It works the same way with money.

There are three main steps in money management:

- First, tell the truth about how much money you have and how much you spend.
- Second, commit to spend no more than you have.
- Finally, apply the suggestions for earning more money, spending less money, or both.

For many people, making more money is the most appealing way to fix a broken budget. This approach is reasonable, and it has a potential problem: When their income increases, many people continue to spend more than they make. This means that money problems persist, even at higher incomes. You can avoid this dilemma by managing your expenses no matter how much money you make.

If you do succeed at controlling your expenses over the long term, then increasing your income is definitely a way to build wealth. Among the ways to make more money are to focus on your education, work while you're in school, and do your best at every job.

Focus on Your Education

Your most important assets are not your house, your car, or your bank accounts—they are your skills. As Henry Ford said, "The only real security that a person can have in this world is a reserve of knowledge, experience, and ability. Without these qualities, money is practically useless." That's why your education is so important. Right now, you're developing knowledge, experience, and abilities that you can use to create income for the rest of your life. Once you graduate and land a job in your chosen field, continue your education. Look for ways to gain additional skills or certifications that lead to higher earnings and more fulfilling work assignments.

Work While You're in School

If you work while you're in school, you can earn more than money. You'll gain experience, establish references, and expand your contacts in the community. And regular income in any amount can make a difference in your monthly cash flow. Many students work full-time or part-time jobs. Work and school don't have to conflict, especially if you plan carefully and ask for your employer's support.

On most campuses, there is a person in the financial aid office whose job is to help students find work while they're in school. See that person. In addition, check into career planning and job placement services at your school. Using these resources can greatly multiply your job options. Most jobs are never advertised. In fact, a key source of information about new jobs is people—friends, relatives, coworkers, and fellow students. In addition, make a list of several places where you would like to work. Then go to each place on your list and tell someone that you would like a job. She might say that she doesn't have a job available. No problem. Ask to be considered for future job openings. Then check back periodically.

Another option is to start your own business. Consider a service you could offer—anything from lawn mowing to computer consulting. Students can boost their income in many ways, such as running errands, giving guitar lessons, walking pets, and house sitting. Charge reasonable rates, provide impeccable service, and ask your clients for referrals. Self-employment during higher education can blossom into amazing careers. For example, David Filo and Jerry Yang started making lists of their favorite Websites while they were graduate students. They went on to create Yahoo!, which became the world's most popular site.

Do Your Best at Every Job

Once you get a job, make it your intention to excel as an employee. A positive work experience can pay off for years by leading to other jobs, recommendations, and contacts. See if you can find a job related to your chosen career. Even an entry-level job in your field can provide valuable experience. Once you've been in such a job for awhile, explore the possibilities for getting a promotion—or a higher-paying job with another employer. No matter what job you have, be as productive as possible. Look for ways to transfer your evolving skills to the workplace. The following examples can stimulate your thinking.

Develop Financial Literacy

Your first job after college may require you to prepare budgets, keep money records, make financial forecasts, and adjust income and expenses in order to meet an organization's financial goals. The ability to handle such tasks successfully is called financial literacy. To get the most from your education, create a detailed plan for gaining this form of literacy.

Think about the ways you will be handling money in your chosen career. If you plan to become an architect, for example, you'll need to estimate costs for a building project, request bids from contractors, and then evaluate those bids. Find out more by interviewing people who work in your field and asking them about how they handle money on the job. After listing the financial skills that you need, consider which courses you will take to develop them. You might benefit from classes in business management or accounting. Also look for work-study assignments and internships that help you to develop financial skills.

Learn Spreadsheet Software

With spreadsheet programs such as Microsoft's Excel, you can enter data into charts with rows and columns and then apply various formulas. This makes it possible to create budgets, income reports, expense records, and investment projections. Master this software now and you'll have a marketable skill to add to your resume.

Keep Records of Your Financial Success

Throughout your career, keep track of the positive outcomes you produce, including financial successes. Summarize these results in a sentence or two and add them to your resume as well.

Consider Income and Expenses Related to Your Career Choices

Your career plan can include estimates of how much money you'll earn in various jobs in your field. In addition, think about the possible expenses involved in your career choice. If you're planning a career that requires graduate school, for example, then consider how you will pay for that education. Perhaps advancement in your career calls for additional certifications or coursework. Examples are continuing education credits for teachers and board certifications for nurses and physicians. Start thinking now about how you'll meet such requirements.

The expertise you develop now in monitoring money, increasing income and decreasing expenses can help you succeed during and after college.

 ## Discussion Questions

1. Discuss Ellis' statement that "most money problems result from spending more than you have." What other situations might cause money problems for students?
2. In what ways can students increase their income beyond what the author suggests? In what areas can they decrease their spending?
3. What does Ellis mean by advising you to "focus on your education"? Do you agree?
4. Do you think every student should "work while in college" as Ellis suggests? Why or why not?
5. What level of income do workers earn in the jobs you are considering after graduation? What kind of life-style could you have with this type of income?

 ## Suggestions for Your Journal

How would you rate yourself as a money manager? Why? Have you changed about money matters since becoming a college student? If so, in what ways? If you want to improve your spending habits, how and where would you cut? What type of courses would you like to take to prepare you to be a more competent money manager during and after college?

Unit Summary

The readings in this unit discussed many aspects of college life and its effect on students. Although adjusting to college may take some time, the challenge and excitement of being a student makes this experience unique and memorable.

■ Summary Questions

1. How do the expectations about college expressed by the readings in this unit differ from your own? How are they similar?
2. How can the college experience help you in your intellectual, personal, and career development?
3. If you were not attending college, how would your life be different? Evaluate the differences.

■ Suggested Writing Assignments

1. Write a brief essay on how you have changed since your first day in college. How do you expect to change by the time you earn a degree?
2. Describe one experience that you have had with taking control of your situation in life. How did you manage the change?
3. Describe one of your own college experiences that was also described by an author in this unit. Some examples are loneliness, stress, roommate relationships, classroom experience, and money management. Compare your experience with that author's account.

■ Suggested Readings

Bernstein, Mark, and Yadin, Kaufman. *How To Survive Your Freshman Year*, 2nd ed. Atlanta: Hundreds of Heads Books, 2006.

Chickering, Arthur W., and Linda Reisser. *Education and Identity*, 2nd ed. San Francisco: Jossey-Bass, 1993.

Gilligan, Carol. *In a Different Voice. Cambridge*, MA: Harvard University Press, 1982.

Nist, Sherrie, and Jodi Holschuh. *College Rules*. Berkeley: Ten Speed Press, 2002.

Unit 3

How Can I Succeed Academically?

'Tis education forms the common mind.
Just as the twig is bent, the tree's inclined.

—ALEXANDER POPE

Academic success can be defined from many perspectives. Some measure it by grade-point average (known commonly as GPA) or by "accume," which is short for cumulative point-hour ratio. A student with a 3.5 GPA, for example, is usually considered more successful academically than a student with a 1.9. Academic success is also defined by one's accumulation of knowledge. Students who, when tested, can successfully throw back to their instructors the facts and concepts they have memorized may be considered academically successful. Still others define success by the salary and prestige of the job they are able to acquire at the end of their senior year. Some students may consider what they have genuinely learned to be the true measure of their academic success. Learning how to learn is a skill that can be used for a lifetime. Successful students will always be intensely involved in their own learning.

Regardless of how a student measures academic success, certain activities in which students engage are essential to the learning process. Among them, reading and writing are two of the most critical. Some first-year students find themselves ill prepared in these basic skills. Most new students who understand the value of these activities work hard to improve their reading and writing skills throughout their college years.

Some other skills closely associated with academic success are:

Communication Skills. These include being able to communicate ideas and concepts effectively in a prepared presentation or in the conversational give-and-take of a committee meeting. Such skills are important in the classroom and marketable in the workplace.

Writing Skills. Students who can express themselves well in writing have a highly marketable skill. The ability to write clear and persuasive reports, proposals, and similar important documents is essential in every work environment.

Organizational Skills. Students need to set goals and priorities and to organize their time and energy accordingly. Self-discipline plays a key role in how students balance their academic life with other personal and social demands.

Analytical Skills. Learning to think critically and logically is important to academic success. Identifying problems and solving them creatively are central to accomplishing many academic tasks.

Research Skills. Students need basic research skills to fulfill many academic assignments. Defining a problem, formulating pertinent questions, using appropriate resources to study the problem, and employing a variety of research methods to solve the problem are all part of the research process that students use constantly.

Computer Skills. These skills include the ability to use a computer and its software to accomplish practical tasks.

The authors in this unit would certainly agree on the importance of the six categories of skill listed above. Newport offers suggestions for improving learning, reading, and writing skills. Pauk and Owens offer practical ways for managing time, an important skill that students need to succeed. Schein, Laff, and Allen emphasize the importance of academic advising. Minnick provides some ways for thinking about elective courses, which are all the classes you take that are not stipulated as some requirement. Gold suggests punctuality, and Brown requires regularity in attendance to class. All these readings can have a bearing on your thoughtful approach to course selection and establishing good academic habits.

How to Win at College

Cal Newport

Cal Newport graduated Phi Beta Kappa from Dartmouth College. He has published articles on the topic of student success in the *Wall Street Journal* and *Business Today* magazine. He is currently enrolled in the computer science Ph.D. program at MIT and lives in Cambridge, Massachusetts.

What does it take to be a standout student? How can you make the most of your college years? Here are just a few of the many college-tested strategies described in the book, *How to Win at College* (2005).

Don't Do All of Your Reading

You will be assigned a lot of reading in college. Probably more reading than seems humanly possible for any one person to complete. Social science and humanities courses will taunt you with seemingly short academic articles that turn out to riddled with Byzantine sentence structures and devilishly complicated logic. Science courses will siphon your time, and help you develop a life-long hatred of bar charts, with a steady stream of ultradense technical material. And just to keep things sporting, professors will periodically slip entire books into the syllabus, often giving you a week or so to finish them. Sound bleak? It doesn't have to be. All you need to remember is one simple rule: *Don't do all of your reading.*

To a hardworking student, ignoring assigned reading probably seems blasphemous. But as unusual as this may sound at first, covering every page of reading listed in a course syllabus is rarely necessary. Here is what you should do instead:

For reading that covers the topic of an upcoming lecture, it's often sufficient to just skim the main points ahead of time, and then fill in the gaps during class by taking very good notes. Students are sometimes afraid of skimming, but you shouldn't be. You need to master the skill of covering hundreds of pages of text very quickly. The secret is to read chapter introductions and conclusions carefully and then skim everything else. Make tick marks next to sentences that catch your attention—this is faster than highlighting. Don't get bogged down trying to understand the significance of every paragraph. Instead, note only the passages that seem to obviously support the thesis. You will definitely miss some key points, but your professor won't. So pay attention in class when the work is discussed, and you will pick up the arguments that you overlooked. Come exam time, your lecture notes, plus a review of the sentences you marked, will bring you up to speed on the material.

When multiple books are assigned as background for a paper, find out early exactly what your paper topic will be, and read only the material you need to develop your specific thesis. Skip optional readings. With all due respect to your professors, there are better uses for your limited time.

For science courses, you will typically be assigned one or two chapters of dense technical material to review for each class. These assignments almost always cover the exact same topics that the professor will detail in lecture. Skim these chapters quickly so you know what to expect, but put the bulk of your energy into concentrating in class. Science courses don't test you on your reading. They test you on the concepts taught in the classroom. Your goal as a science student should be to come away from each lecture understanding what was covered, and feel comfortable about applying it. If you find yourself falling behind the professor's chalkboard heroics, ramp up the amount of preparatory reading you are doing until you are able to comfortably follow along. In general, reading in science courses should consume very little of your time. Put your attention where it matters: class lectures and homework problems.

This approach to completing class work is admittedly an acquired skill. At first you should err on the side of caution, doing as much reading as possible. But as you gain a feel for your professors, and the structure of your courses, you can begin to back off on your assigned reading until you find that perfect balance between being prepared and being efficient. If you have ever wondered how top students can accomplish so much work in such limited amounts of time, this rule is a large part of the answer.

Start Long-Term Projects the Day They Are Assigned

College students dread long-term projects. Why? Because we are really bad at them. At this very moment, at college campuses across the country, students are convincing themselves that just because it's possible to complete long-term projects in one frenzied night of panicked work, they should follow such a plan. You don't have to be one of these people.

The lure of procrastination is powerful, but you can conquer it by employing one very simple technique: When assigned a long-term project, finish some amount of work toward its completion that very same day. This doesn't have to be a major chunk of work. Thirty minutes is enough. Do something simple: jot down a research schedule on your calendar; sketch out an outline; check out and skim the introduction of several relevant books; write a series of potential thesis statements. This is all it takes.

Once you have accomplished something, no matter how small, you realize that starting your project early is not actually all that bad. In fact, it feels good. You are a step ahead of your entire class, and it was easy to do. This sensation is powerful. Believe it or not, it actually makes you look forward to completing more and more work ahead of schedule, until, before you know it, you'll be finished—and it won't be four forty-three A.M. the morning the project is due.

Of course, this approach is not a miracle cure for completing long-term projects on time. Big college assignments are still really hard, and you'll still need to work diligently in order to complete them. However, for whatever psychological reason, doing some work the day a project is assigned seems to have a near-miraculous effect on reducing the tendency to delay. So give this rule a try. There is no reason to let long-term projects force you to scramble like a maniac at the last minute. Start small and start immediately.

Ask One Question at Every Lecture

Keeping alert throughout a long lecture is not always easy to do. Especially if the class is early in the morning or held right after a hearty lunch and it begins to take all of your effort to stop your eyes from closing. And just like that, the lecture has slipped by without you learning anything. If you want to succeed at college, you have to do whatever you can to prevent this from happening to you. Fortunately, one of the most effective ways to stay engaged and interested during a lecture is also very easy to do: Make sure that you always ask at least one question at every lecture.

The night before, when you are doing the reading that will be covered in lecture, jot down a quick list of questions that seem relevant. Then, once in class, follow the professor's material carefully, modifying and honing your questions as appropriate. Finally, when you have a question that is meaningful and will clarify an important point of the discussion, ask away. The key is to stay involved while, at the same time, not acting like the obnoxious kid in the front row who asks random questions every thirty seconds or so.

This approach not only helps you clarify the material and reinforces your understanding, it also keeps your attention focused and ensures that you stay alert. It's a powerful technique for resisting the urge to drift off into a boredom-infused stupor. One or two good questions a class are enough to keep the professor happy, but not enough to solicit the annoyance of your classmates. Take the time to ask at least one question at every lecture. It's simple, and will redefine your classroom experience for the better.

Study in Fifty-Minute Chunks

According to conventional wisdom on college campuses, the most effective way to tackle a large amount of studying is to: (1) pile all your books, notes, and review sheets in front of you; (2) study until you collapse; (3) awaken several hours later wondering where you are; (4) consume large quantities of caffeine; (5) repeat. *Do not do this.* When you do school work, be it reading, taking notes, working on a lab, or memorizing verbs, try to do everything in fifty-minute chunks. Take ten-minute breaks in between each fifty-minute chunks. This is key for any successful student.

Why fifty minutes? For one thing, there are compelling scientific rationales. Those who study cognition can draw maps of memory retention over time, and demonstrate how periods of roughly fifty minutes, divided by short breaks, will maximize the amount of material you can successfully learn and remember in a given sitting. But just as important, breaking down all your work into distinct known periods of time provides structure for your studying. If you have five hours of reading to do, that stack of books in front of you can seem hopeless. How can you focus on the first chapter when there are so many to follow? But if you only have to stay focused for fifty minutes at a time, then the impossible suddenly seems possible. Five work chunks don't seem so bad. You could do three before dinner and two after, or whatever seems easiest and suddenly your assignment is approachable. Not to mention that you are learning the materials in the most effective way possible for the human brain. You never want to approach any large amount of studying or reading or note-taking without some sort of structure. Using fifty-minute chunks is a great addition to any such structure.

Use Three Days to Write a Paper

There are two types of papers assigned at college: long ones and short ones. Long papers are typically of the research variety. They require quite a bit of time to complete because you have to track down sources, generate original theses, and master complicated new ideas. These papers are really hard. Fortunately, the vast majority of papers assigned at college are short papers. These range from actually being short (2–4 pages), to being not so short (5–10 pages), to being downright evil (11–20 pages). Whatever the length, the defining features of a short paper are that you typically have only a week or two to write them, and they usually deal with material you covered in class and your readings (not original research).

A good rule is to always use three days to write your short papers. This doesn't mean spending three days working on the paper; it means spending three days actually writing. Before your fingers first hit the keyboard, you need to finish any necessary preparation. Go back through your readings and notes and figure out what you want to say. Make an outline of your points, write out your thesis with crystal-clear clarity, and have the sources you need to quote readily available. This is the easy part. Preparing information for a paper is much less painful than actually writing. And for a short paper you are not covering anything you haven't seen before, so this prep work can be accomplished in one or two sittings.

Once you have your ideas and materials organized, it's time to spend three days writing. The first day is the hardest. If possible, make the first day a weekend day, or a weekday when you don't have many obligations. On this first day try to power through your outline and build a rough draft of the entire paper. This first draft will take a while to write as you will be consuming and organizing a lot of thoughts all at once. It will also be long. Probably much longer than your assigned page limit. Don't worry; its length will be brought back under control shortly. Also, don't worry about crafting a perfect prose; you will fix all of that later. Just get all of your ideas down in some sort of coherent manner.

Your second day should be much easier than your first. Go back through your massive rough draft, tighten up your wording, cut out excess arguments, and add support where it seems to be glaringly missing. The goal of the second day is to pare your prose down into lean and mean arguments. No sentence should be wasted. Don't worry about the nitty-gritty details of fixing all grammatical mistakes and perfecting sentence structures. The second day is all about making your argument compelling.

Finally we come to the third day, which is the easiest. Make another run through your paper, this time really polishing the details of your arguments where they might still feel a little thin. Make sure all your support is clearly defined and advances your thesis. Check that all your sentences read well, that the ideas flow logically, and look for any remaining grammatical mistakes. Go back and rework your introduction and conclusion to make them exactly match the final form of your paper. Print out and edit your writing with a pencil at least twice. There is something about reading text on a computer screen that makes it easy to overlook stupid mistakes. Then, finally, go through and make sure your citations are properly formatted, add a cover sheet if needed, check your margins, and handle any other administrative details demanded by your professor.

All too often, students try to combine all three days into one. This is a horrible idea. It's painful to try to combine so much intense concentration into one drawn-out experience, and it produces lackluster papers. By approaching your paper fresh on two separate occasions after you complete your rough draft, you will really hone your arguments and produce the type of polished writing that can easily receive an A.

There is, however, one exception to the three-day rule. When working with the aforementioned "evil" papers (fifteen plus pages), three days may not be enough time, but the concept of breaking up the work into three chunks still applies. Just expand the size of these chunks. For example, for a really long paper you might stretch your rough-draft-writing phase out over three days, and the argument-polishing phase out over two days. What is important is preserving the idea of always separating the paper-writing process into three distinct segments. Successful students don't spend much more time working than their peers, they just spend their working time smarter. Take three days to write your short papers—your mind, your body, and your professors will thank you.

 Discussion Questions

1. What do you think of Newport's advice about not doing all your reading? Which suggestions do you find helpful? With which suggestions do you disagree?
2. Do you think Newport's idea about starting long-term projects the day they are assigned a good one? Why or why not?
3. Can you relate to the author's suggestion that you should be prepared to ask at least one question at every lecture? Why do or why don't you think this is good advice?

4. Have you ever studied in fifty-minute chunks as Newport advises? If so, how has it worked for you? If not, why do you think it might or might not be worth trying? Explain.

5. Newport describes in detail his method for writing short projects. How does it compare with how you are currently approaching writing projects? How are they different or the same?

 ## Suggestions for Your Journal

How would you rate the efficiency of your study skills? How have your study habits changed since you began college? What areas do you think you need improvement? What ideas in this essay would you like to try?

Using Time and Space Effectively

Walter Pauk and Ross J. Q. Owens

Walter Pauk was the director of the Reading Study Center at Cornell University and over the years has published more than 100 books, including eight editions of *How to Study in College,* considered by many to be the gold standard for sound study advice. Ross Owens has written numerous articles on Internet-related topics and is an accomplished computer programmer.

Time is a precious and irreplaceable *commodity*. As she lay on her deathbed, Queen Elizabeth of England (1533–1603) reportedly said, "All my possessions for a moment of time." How you use time can determine your success or failure in college. If you use time wisely, you'll prosper. If you use it poorly, you'll fail the job you came to do. That's why the management of time is the number-one skill to master in college.

Although many people waste time needlessly and habitually, you needn't put yourself in the same position. You can gain extra time by reclaiming lost time, by sticking to a schedule, and by staying organized, which will help you use your time more efficiently.

All of us have claimed that we don't have enough time to accomplish what we need to do. But the fact is that everyone is allotted the same amount of time: twenty-four hours a day. Many of us allow a lot of this time to go to waste by failing to realize it is available in the first place. In addition, it's often our day-to-day habits and activities we no longer notice, that save time or waste it. You can put your time to better use by pinpointing areas of "hidden" time and cultivating time-saving habits.

Finding "Hidden" Time

There's a lot of valuable time in your day that is being overlooked, simply because you didn't realize it was time you could use. For those who flush tiny slivers of soap down the drain or toss small scraps of cloth into the wastebasket, there are others who combine these slippery bits and pieces into a whole new bar or stitch discarded shreds into a comfortable quilt. Think of all the time you spend standing in line or even waiting for a traffic light to change. If you could find ways to make use of this "hidden" time, you could almost certainly add hours to each week.

Carry Pocket Work

Many situations may leave you with a few moments of unexpected free time—a long line at the bank or supermarket, a delayed bus or train, a wait at the doctor's

57

office, a lunch date who arrives late. If you make a point to bring along a book, a photocopied article, index cards on which you've written key concepts, vocabulary words or formulas, you'll be able to take advantage of otherwise frustrating experiences.

Use Your Mind When It's Free

Some activities may afford an overlooked opportunity for studying if you're prepared. For example, if you're shaving, combing your hair, or washing dishes, there's no reason you can't be studying at the same time. Since many of us tend to "zone out" in such situations, they are excellent opportunities to use time that might otherwise be squandered. Attach small metal or plastic clips near mirrors and on walls at eye level. Place a note card in each clip. Do a problem or two in math or master some new vocabulary words as you eat a sandwich at work.

Record Study Information

Another way of using hidden time is by listening to information you have recorded on audiocassettes or MP3 files or burned onto CDs. Recorded information enables you to keep studying in situations where you're moving about or your eyes are otherwise occupied, such as when you're getting dressed or driving. In addition, recorded information can provide a refreshing change from written material.

Employ Spare-Time Thinking

You can make the most of the moments immediately before or after class by recalling the main points from the last lecture as you are heading to class or by quickly recalling the points of a just-completed lecture as you're leaving class.

Use Your Subconscious

At one point or another, you have awakened during the night with a bright idea or a solution to a problem that you had been thinking about before bedtime. Your subconscious works while your conscious mind is resting. If you want to capture the ideas or solutions produced by your subconscious, write them down as soon as you wake up; otherwise, they'll be lost. Many creative people know this and keep a pad and pencil near their beds. For example, Nobel Prize winner Albert Szent-Gyorgyi said, "I go to sleep thinking about my problems all the time, and my brain must continue to think about them while I sleep because I wake up, sometimes in the middle of the night, with answers to questions that have been eluding me all day."

Changing Your Time Habits

Habits, by their very nature, are things we do routinely without even thinking. Most of us are unaware of our habits unless someone or something draws attention to them. A good way to take inventory of your time habits is by keeping a daily activities log. From the time you wake up to the time you go to sleep, note all your major activities, the time you started and finished each, and the time each activity consumed. With your day itemized on paper, you can gain a clearer picture of where your time is being spent and where it's being wasted. Once you have concrete evidence of a daily activities log before you, you can begin to eliminate your time-wasting habits and develop or reinforce the time-saving ones.

Defy Parkinson's Law

Parkinson's Law says that work expands to fit the time allotted. To avoid running out of time, work Parkinson's Law in reverse: For each task, set a deadline that will be difficult to meet, and strive to meet that deadline. Each time you achieve your goal, reward yourself with some small but pleasant activity. Take a break. Chat with a friend. Stroll around the room. Have a special snack, such as a bag of peanuts (keep it in your desk, to be opened only as a reward). If you fail to meet a deadline, don't punish yourself. Just hold back your reward and set another goal. Positive reinforcement is powerful in effecting a change in behavior.

Obey Your Alarm Clock

How many times do you hit the snooze button on your alarm clock before you finally get out of bed? Even one time is too many. Set your alarm for the time you want to get up, not for time you want to start getting up. If you can't obey your alarm, you'll have a hard time sticking to your time schedule. After all, it doesn't even buzz.

Limit Your E-mail and Internet Time

As marvelous as they both can be, e-mail in particular and the Internet in general can be tremendous "time sinks," swallowing up hours in a typical day. Rather than checking it constantly, designate specific times during the day when you read and send e-mail. It's true that e-mail has sped up communication, but it's a rare message that can't wait a few hours before being read or sent. The same applies to any Web surfing you may do, whether for schoolwork or pleasure. Time has a tendency to fly by as you click from one link to the next. You can help keep things under control by setting a timer when you surf and returning to your studies when the timer goes off.

Take "Time Out"

Reward yourself with regular short breaks as you work. Learning in several small sessions, rather than one continuous stretch, increases comprehension. In one study, students who practiced French vocabulary in three discrete sessions did 35 percent better on an exam than those who tried to learn the words in one sitting. So take a breather for ten minutes every hour, or rest for five minutes every half-hour. Whichever method you choose, keep your breaks consistent. This way, you will study with more energy and look forward to your regular rests. When you return to your desk, you'll find that you feel more refreshed.

Listen to Your Body

All of us are subject to *circadian rhythms*. That is, we have periods when we are most wide awake and alert and other periods when we're sluggish or drowsy. In general, we're sleepiest a few hours before dawn and twelve hours later, in mid-afternoon. In keeping with these natural cycles, we're widest awake about every twelve hours, usually at mid-morning and again in mid-evening. Knowing this can help you plan the day's activities more strategically.

1. *Schedule cerebral tasks for mornings and evenings.* Reading, writing, problem solving and other "thinking tasks" should be done when you're likely to be most alert.
2. *Save active behavior for mid-afternoon.* Fieldwork, lab work, exercise, and errand running are best done at this time of day when more sedentary activities may make you feel drowsy. If you're not a heavy coffee drinker, a cup of coffee might get you through the afternoon slump.
3. *Resist the temptation to sleep in on the weekends.* Changing your sleep schedule on the weekends can have a chain reaction effect on the following week. You may find yourself feeling jet-lagged on Monday or Tuesday if you sleep in on Saturday or Sunday.
4. *Read in the morning; review in the afternoon.* Scientists have discovered that short-term memory peaks at about nine o'clock in the morning and that long-term memory is strongest at about three o'clock in the afternoon.

Sticking to a Schedule

A time schedule is a game plan, a written strategy that spells out exactly what you hope to accomplish—during a day, a week, or even the entire term—and how you plan to do it. Committing yourself to planning and keeping to a schedule can seem a bit frightening at first, but following a schedule soon becomes a source of strength and a boon to your life.

Most people understand the supreme importance of time and the value of sticking to a schedule, yet many of us continue to waste time needlessly. Why? Perhaps it is because we are human beings, not machines. Learning to use time wisely after years of wasting it doesn't happen by simply flipping a switch. Controlling your time is ultimately a matter of developing the right mindset. If the dying words of Queen Elizabeth and the compelling evidence in this essay haven't been enough to convince you to change your time-wasting ways, perhaps the following tidbits about time will finally make things click.

Seven Valuable Tidbits about Time

1. One of America's greatest composers, jazz giant Duke Ellington wasn't ashamed to admit that "Without a deadline, I can't finish nothin'."
2. Be a *contrarian.* Go to the library when almost nobody is there. Get into the dining-hall line before the crowd. Get the reserved books before the line forms. The time you save will add up quickly.

3. Make decisions wisely by asking, "What are the alternatives?" Make a list of the alternatives and then put pluses and minuses alongside them. Learn this process. It will save lots of time.

4. Don't spread yourself thin by attempting to become an "information junkie." This scattershot approach takes up a great deal of time and can still leave you feeling stressed and dissatisfied. Just make sure that you gain a firm grip on your own field.

5. When you're really through studying, spend an extra fifteen minutes studying just an extra bit more.

6. If the thought of saving time sounds sensible but uninspiring, ask yourself this simple question: What do I want to save time for? Suddenly the efficient use of time may take on a significance that it never had before.

7. A Sanskrit proverb puts everything in proper perspective:

Today well lived.
Makes every yesterday a dream of happiness.
And every tomorrow a vision of hope.
Look well therefore to this day.

From Pauk/Owens, HOW TO STUDY IN COLLEGE, 9E. © 2008 Wadsworth, a part of Cengage Learning, Inc. Reproduced by permission. www.cengage.com/permissions.

Vocabulary

As you think about this essay, these definitions may be helpful to you:

1. **commodity**   an economic good
2. **circadian rhythms**   rhythms occurring in approximately 24-hour periods or cycles
3. **cerebral**   relating to the brain or intellect
4. **contrarian**   a person who habitually takes a contrary position or attitude

Discussion Questions

1. Pauk and Owens list several ways to find "hidden time" in your day or week. Which of these have you tried? How much time did it save? How did you use the time that was saved?

2. What specific suggestions do the authors give for changing your time habits? Which ones seem the easiest to implement? The most difficult?

3. How much time a day do you spend answering and sending e-mail and on the Internet in non-coursework? Which of the authors' suggestions for controlling time spent this way could you use? How?

4. Do you use positive reinforcement during your study time? If so, what kind of positive reinforcement works best for you? If you haven't used it, would you consider trying it? Why or why not?

5. Which of the "Seven Valuable Tidbits about Time" are you already using? Which ones are you interested in implementing? Why?
6. Some people may find that some of the suggestions in this essay are unrealistic. Do you? If so, how might you adapt or replace them for the same objective of making your time work for you?

 ## Suggestions for Your Journal

Write about your concept of time and how it affects your life as a student. What are your strengths in managing your time? In what areas do you need to improve your time management? Of the many tips in this essay, which ones do you already practice? Which ones, if any, could help you make better use of your time? Will your concept of time change after you graduate? In what way?

Want Good Advising?
Take the Initiative!

Howard K. Schein, Ned S. Laff, and Deborah R. Allen

This essay was written for the *Daily Illini*, the student newspaper at the University of Illinois at Urbana-Champaign. The authors hoped that by introducing basic advising tricks to undergraduates, they would become active members of the campus community and learn how to use the university better. The authors are professional academic advisors in a variety of higher education settings.

What is good academic advising? In its broadest sense, academic advising should involve an assessment of your personal values, a plan for attaining intellectual fulfillment, an investigation of career direction, and a look at the real world from objective and subjective positions. In a large sense, academic advising should lead you to ask: "What does all this mean to me?" Advice givers and their resources should help you learn how to answer this question.

Good academic advising is aimed at giving you the skills to answer the key question: what does this all mean to me? It's like all good educational experiences and all well-taught courses. It's a process that helps you learn to plot your path through college. It should help you orchestrate courses, resources, and other opportunities into an educational experience personally fit for you and one that seduces you into becoming personally involved in and responsible for your own learning.

The only thing you are going to get from your college programs catalog is a bare scheme of curricula, and its presentation will hardly tell you what you need to know. On most large campuses, for instance, you can study literature though several departments, such as English, Chinese, French, Russian and comparative literature. However, do any differences exist between these tracks, and if they do, what are they? Do they offer different opportunities to utilize the resources of the campus, and will your career marketability be affected if you choose one track over another? For that matter, what does a person with a bachelor's degree in literature do after graduation?

Consider another example: Is the best route into medical school through traditional science? What nontraditional programs offer a route that is more attractive and offers better alternatives than the standard pre-med curricula? If such programs exist, how do you find out about them? You won't be able to answer these questions by consulting your college programs catalog. More important, you don't want to wait until your last year of college to begin to search out the answers.

So what do you do?

First, you need to understand the role of advising and advisors in your academic life. You are responsible for the academic choices that affect your education. Don't assume that the advice you receive represents the only, correct, or beneficial alternative for you. All that academic advisors can do, at their best, is advise from the perspective of their personal and professional experiences, but their professional experiences do not necessarily give them a comprehensive view of your institution. For example, departmental advisors know about their own department's requirements, but they aren't paid to know every detail of the campus. Still, many have underground networks of people who can give them information about nondepartment opportunities, and you can access this information, but only if you take the time to sit, talk, and ask. Remember that when you talk with an advisor you are receiving consultation. Advisors are not there to tell you what to do; they are to give you information to help you make a decision. The appropriate synonym for "advise" is "recommend" not "command."

Second, faculty and professional advisors are not the only advisors with valuable recommendations. Take advantage of parents' and friends' knowledge and pay attention to information you read, see, or hear. You cannot make a good decision until you learn how to determine what's going on around you.

Third, large universities can be big, impersonal places, and they will stay that way if you sit back and expect to maneuver through your degree like a customer moving through a buffet line. Smaller schools have their own problems: How do you maximize the relatively few resources available? Think about the difference between getting a degree and getting an education: The two are not necessarily the same, and how you pursue these options will determine whether you become a victim of the system.

If you receive inadequate services and support, you may not have made the effort to discover the offerings at your college. You need to find and create your own community, consisting of deans and faculty members, counselors, residence hall staff, and advisors with whom you can talk on a casual and personal basis and who can give you the inside road map to your campus. This will take time and effort, but the benefits will be worthwhile. With a good set of personal contacts, you will discover that most of your academic goals can be accomplished, and you can open up fields of study for yourself that are hidden beneath the surface of curricular requirements.

Finally, it's up to you to know the rules, requirements, and resources of your campus. If you don't understand the reason for a requirement or a rule, or if you have unanswered questions, you need to ask for assistance, and you need to keep on asking until you get answers that make sense! Each college differs in how it handles rules, exceptions to rules, the substitution of courses to meet requirements, and other such issues. Don't assume that you know everything about any rule, constraint, or restriction until you check the information, and then double-check it. Many times you will find the hidden loopholes that allow department heads and deans to make exceptions to rules, and often you will find someone who will help you accomplish your objective. However, you will never know about these possibilities if you sit passively and make assumptions about the information you think you know. If you are not active, the system, with absence of malice, is going to do a number on you.

From "Want Good Advertising? Take the Initiative" by Howard Schein, Ned S. Laff, and Deborah Allen. NACADA Monograph Series, Number 11. Reprinted with permission from the National Academic Advising Association (NACADA).

 ## Discussion Questions

1. What do the authors consider good academic advising?
2. The authors use literature as an example of the wide range of course topics that could be taken within fields of study that are offered on a campus. Name some courses in other academic disciplines that would be interesting to take to broaden a business major. What courses would broaden a psychology major? An education major?
3. What do the authors say is the role of advising and advisors in students' academic life?
4. What are four steps that students can take to ensure they are getting the best possible academic advice?

 ## Suggestions for Your Journal

What are your expectations from academic advising? What happened the last time you visited your advisor? Did the exchange answer all your questions? Why or why not? What can you do to take better advantage of your advisor's knowledge of the curricula and campus and community resources?

Fourteen Ways of Looking at Electives[1]

Thomas L. Minnick

Thomas L. Minnick is Special Assistant to the Vice Provost of Minority Affairs and former associate dean of University College at The Ohio State University, where he completed his bachelor's, master's, and doctoral degrees in English. He is a specialist in the English Bible and the writings of William Blake. In this essay, he encourages you to think before you schedule your electives so that they can complement your required course work by helping you to achieve some of your goals for college study.

Electives are what is left over for you to take once you deduct all your required courses.

Typically, a college degree is made up primarily of several kinds of requirements. These may include courses required of all students, no matter what degree they may have decided to seek; such university-wide requirements are often called "core" or "general education" requirements. They are likely to include some basic mathematics, one or more courses in college-level English composition, and several courses distributed among the social sciences, sciences, and humanities. Does everyone at your institution need to take some history? Then history is probably a general education or "core" requirement for your institution, whether you are working toward a bachelor's degree at a university with an extensive graduate program or toward an associate's degree at a community college.

Additionally, you are likely to have to complete some courses that everyone in your degree program needs to take. For example, students working toward a degree in engineering, no matter what area of specialization, all typically need to have at least a year of college physics, mathematics through differential equations, some basic course work in engineering graphics, mechanics, and chemistry. Similarly, business students are all required to study economics (both "micro" and "macro"), accounting, statistics, marketing, finance, and the like. Requirements shared by everyone aiming toward a specific degree are usually called "program requirements" or "degree requirements."

A third kind of required course work is that which you complete for your major. Major requirements might include an introductory survey course (or a series of them), usually taken by first- or second-year students while they learn the dimensions and variety of the major field. English majors are likely to be required to take a survey of American literature and another of British literature, for example. In some colleges they may be required to have a course in research methods for English majors. And some majors require that everyone in the program complete

---

[1]With apologies to Wallace Stevens. (Gentle reader, Wallace Stevens wrote a thoughtful poem entitled "Sixteen Ways of Looking at a Blackbird." You might enjoy it.)

a senior year "capstone" course that puts—or attempts to put—all their previous major work into a *coherent* perspective.

Once you add up all these kinds of requirements (general education, college, and major), you are likely to find that there are still some classes you need to take to complete your degree. At the university where I work, which follows the quarter system and sets 196 quarter credit hours as the minimum for an undergraduate degree, the university-wide general education core and the college/ program requirements usually total about 100 credits. Major programs vary dramatically but average about 45 credit hours. Deduct 145 from 196 and you get 41 credit hours (or eight to ten classes) that are not specified. For these, which are "electives," our students can take just about anything they like. This essay is about some ways you can use these extra classes to your advantage.

1. To explore possible majors. Many students enter college without knowing what they want to study for a major. An undecided student can use elective hours to explore several possible major programs, usually by taking the appropriate introductory survey classes. Do you think you might like Forestry? Sign up for a basic introduction to the field and find out through that class whether you really have an interest and/or an aptitude for it.

2. To serve as a cushion. This use of electives is closely related to (1) above. Suppose you started college as an engineering major and then discovered that you lack the commitment or the focus to be an engineer, so you change programs to business. You will probably have taken some classes in your first term (engineering graphics, for example) that are not required in your new major. Electives allow you to move from one major to another without losing useful credits: in this example, the engineering graphics class will still count toward graduation, and it served the purpose of helping you make a sound decision on a new major. Electives give you flexibility—within reasoned limits—to change from one program to another without losing credits or unduly prolonging your degree work.

3. To develop a focus or cluster outside your major. Perhaps you don't really want to be limited to a single concentration. If your college does not provide for dual majors or minors, or if you don't want to complete *all* the work for a second major but would like an additional focus to your degree, electives can provide the way. Imagine that you have decided to major in Elementary Education but you also have an interest in the History of Art. Using your electives, you can build your own concentration in art history by taking the courses in that area that attract you. In this way you may be able to select your art history classes more freely than a formal major might allow—limiting yourself to national schools (American painting) or individual styles (contemporary art) that you really like, while official majors may need to follow a strictly prescribed *regimen* of courses.

4. To explore your career options. Nationally, one of the most frequently selected electives is the career exploration course. Such courses usually fall into one of two categories—fairly general in approach and scope, or quite specific. A general approach can help you assess your personal characteristics, such as your interests, abilities, values, and goals. It can also help you explore educational and occupational fields that might match your personal interests and strengths.

Some courses include information about techniques for writing your résumé and for presenting yourself effectively in job interviews. These general career courses can teach you career decision-making strategies that will be useful throughout your life. The other, more specific type of career course is often limited to specific career opportunities in the area (or areas) related to the department teaching the class: "Careers in Agriculture" would be such a course that focuses on, and discusses in very specific detail, the career options available to people with a specific kind of education. Such a course typically provides very helpful information about specific employers who look for and hire graduates with a particular educational and career background. Career information courses—whether general or specific—can help you enhance your understanding of who you are in relation to your academic major and related career opportunities and, in so doing, prepare you for the work world.

5. To enhance your marketability. A popular use many students make of their electives is to build a business focus—even if they are not pursuing a business degree. Suppose you are an English major who likes and knows something about computers. By adding several advanced computer science courses to your English major, you become more competitive for job offers that want a liberally educated student with added skills. Your focus might take the form of several courses from a single department (a number of marketing classes, for example), or several related classes from a variety of departments (a marketing class, a course in beginning accounting, a class in business management, a course in personnel issues). A business major might like to take classes in the language and culture of a specific part of the world in order to be better prepared to do business with that part of the globe.

6. To develop a talent you have neglected. Are you good at singing or playing a musical instrument? Perhaps you don't want to major in that area, but it would be a shame to give up that *expertise* or let it *languish* while you complete your undergraduate studies. Take a class in singing, or join one of your college's choral or instrumental groups. Register for drawing or painting, or making pottery, or creating art on the computer. Sign up for a basic photography class. Electives can allow you to pursue and develop interests and talents that you do not plan to turn into a major, but that you should not neglect. Because the credit you earn with electives counts toward your graduation, you do not need to feel that courses you take just because you want to are wasted.

7. To get, or stay, fit. I am often surprised by the number of college students I talk with who participated strenuously in high school sports. Both men and women find physical exercise and competition to be challenging and exciting. Yet often, when such students get to college, they neglect their interests in being fit, largely, I think, because they equate college courses with "serious" work and sports with play. However, getting fit and staying fit are lifelong activities that help you to work and think better. They also promote a healthful lifestyle because people who have worked to keep fit as a rule avoid destructive activities like drinking alcohol to excess and smoking. If your college has a good physical education facility and offers you courses in activities you have never tried, take a few elective credits to learn and practice some of these activities—oriental martial arts, for example, or caving, or whitewater rafting, or working out on the high ropes. And all these physical activities can be great for helping to cope with the stress of college work.

8. To develop skills in leisure time activities. Once you begin your career, your work will take up much of your life, but it will always be important for you to make time for enriching activities—especially when you are away from the stimulus of a learning environment. Develop the habit of reserving time for thoughtful entertainment. Electives may provide just the opportunity you need to learn more about theater, fine art, music, and similar interests. Do you like jazz? Check your school's course catalogue to see if there are classes in American music, or nonwestern music, that might help you to better understand the origins and history of jazz. Do you like attending plays? Take an introductory theater course, or take an acting class and try out your talents in a learning setting, or sign up to help build scenery and earn college credit while learning more about the technical details of putting on a performance.

9. To learn to help others. Most universities provide courses, often for modest amounts of credit, in such helpful skills as first aid and cardiopulmonary resuscitation (commonly abbreviated to "CPR"). These skills can help you in getting summer work. More important, knowing how to help others in an emergency can actually save a life—maybe even your own. Less dramatic but also very helpful are opportunities to provide tutoring and similar assistance to others at your university or in your neighborhood. Interested? Ask your adviser if there is a program where you can tutor underprivileged kids or read a textbook for a blind student or help in adaptive physical education for handicapped students. These experiences can teach you a great deal about yourself and may provide some of the greatest personal rewards of your college experience.

10. To learn life skills that will be useful later. For example, many business schools provide a "service course" (so named because they teach it as a service to students from outside their own college) about basic financial matters, like establishing credit, managing your income, buying a home, planning for financial independence, selecting basic insurance, and the like. Courses in family financial planning for nonbusiness majors are likely to accentuate the practical and introduce theory only when absolutely necessary. Many other departments offer the chance to learn material that will have lifelong practical value. Basic courses in public speaking and communicating effectively in small groups apply to almost every later career; go to the Communications Department to find them. Most sociology departments offer a class in the varieties of modern marriage, or the sociology of the family—with obvious utility for later experience.

11. To learn to understand and appreciate different cultures. Studying other cultures can help you prepare for working with people from those cultures in your life after college. The rest of your life will be spent in the 21st century, and experts predict that there will be *no* majority culture in America in your life. Many American cities in the south and west—Dallas, Los Angeles, Miami—already have no dominant majority group, only larger or smaller minorities. Even if you plan to live in a largely *homogeneous* small town, chances are you will be doing business with, or your children will need to do business with, the larger multicultural world. If you find that a little frightening, take a class in dealing with other cultures and you may find it exciting instead. Check with the appropriate language departments, and you are likely to find some classes taught in English that will help you understand the patterns and values of cultures different from your own.

12. To learn study and time-management skills. Most two- and four-year colleges now provide organized help for students who need better study habits. This need is not restricted to students who did less than well in high school. Often, good students could earn better than average grades in high school with only modest investments of study time—and have consequently developed weak study habits that need to improve in the face of more difficult, more rapid college instruction. Would you like to read with greater comprehension? Could you manage your time better than you do? Check with your advisor for information about classes that teach effective study skills, time management, and related learning skills. Even if these are offered *without* credit, and so are not technically "elective hours," consider them carefully, because they can greatly improve the quality of your work as a student.

13. To develop leadership skills. Usually students turn to their extracurricular experiences (student government, interest clubs, other campus associations) for training in leadership. But there is a significant body of writings about various leadership qualities and styles, and your institution is likely to offer at least one credit-bearing class in leadership. Such courses are often taught as "laboratory courses"—that is, you get practical training in a hands-on way. If you are aiming toward a professional career in a management position, you ought to get some experience in leadership, and such a course may be your best route toward it.

14. To take some courses just because you will enjoy them. In the best of all possible worlds, every class you take would be one that you love to attend, and I hope that many of your required courses—in general education, in classes that relate to your degree program, and certainly in your major—fit this description. But in the real world we are bound to spend our time in, you may find yourself required to take some classes you enroll in only because they are required. If you anticipate that such a course is coming up next term, you may successfully balance it with an elective class that you take just because you want to take it: perhaps you've already had the instructor, and you really enjoyed his or her previous course, or perhaps you've always had a hobby of reading about a specific area, so taking a course in it as an elective would help round out your knowledge of that field.

How can you select classes for Use Number 14? I encourage my advisees to imagine that they have just won the lottery (tonight at $35 million!) and have spent a chunk of it having fun—traveling the world, buying your parents a mansion and each of your friends an expensive car. Eventually, you tire of doing nothing, however nicely you can now afford to do it, and you realize the permanent attraction of learning. In such a case, what courses would you take? Assuming you do not financially *need* a degree, you could just take the classes you want. If you were free in this way, what classes would you sign up for? Make a list of them, then sign up for them as electives!

Vocabulary

As you think about this essay, these definitions may be helpful to you:
1. **coherent**   consistent
2. **regimen**   a systematic plan
3. **expertise**   the skill of an expert
4. **languish**   to be or become weak or enervated
5. **homogeneous**   of the same or similar kind or nature

Discussion Questions

1. How are electives defined in this reading? How do they fit into the general structure of degree requirements?
2. What kind of electives can enhance your chances of finding a satisfying career?
3. Through what kind of electives can you acquire skills and knowledge that may be useful for your future leisure-time activities?
4. Although taking extra courses in your major is not listed as a way to use elective hours, would this be a good way to increase your mastery of the subject? Why or why not?
5. How can you expand your understanding and appreciation of other cultures through electives? Why is this a particularly good use of electives today?

Suggestions for Your Journal

What has been your impression of the function of electives in the curriculum? Which of the 14 reasons for selecting electives appeal to you the most? Why? Look at the list of courses in your college's catalogue. If you could select any courses to take just for fun (and not worry about a grade), which would you choose? Why? What does this tell you about your choice of major?

Please! It's Only Seven Minutes Late, Professor

Joel J. Gold

This essay describes Professor Joel J. Gold's "solution" to overdue student papers. However, after recounting a student's experience with a late paper to his classes, he was the recipient of one class's payback.

Toward the bottom of the large *pseudo*-wooden door of my faculty office is a small hand-lettered sign that reads: PAPER SHREDDER. An arrow points to the space under the door where students are always sliding things, such as late papers and requests for letters of reference. My colleagues see the sign and make little jokes, but most of them don't really know the story behind it.

It began simply enough a few years back, when I was telling a class about the next essay. Allowing myself to be jollied away from the usual deadline of class time on Thursday, I told them the papers could be submitted by 5 P.M. Friday, but no later. At 5 o'clock, I would leave and turn on the paper shredder, so that anything slipped under the door later would be automatically shredded.

Now it should be obvious that in these *straitened* times no garden-variety English professor is going to have a paper shredder at his disposal. They all grinned back at me, and I figured we understood each other.

By 4:50 on Friday, all but three papers had been turned in. In a few minutes I heard someone running down the hall, and a young man thrust his paper at me. "Plenty of time," I said. He looked almost disappointed that he was not the last. At 4:57 the next-to-last paper arrived. "Am I the last one?" the young woman wanted to know. Again disappointment.

Well, now it was 5 o'clock, and one paper was still out. It was possible that it would not arrive, but the student was one of my conscientious overachievers. She was probably triple-checking her footnotes. I decided to wait.

I shut my door. I turned out my light. Then I pulled a chair up behind the closed door, gathered a couple of sheets of old copier paper in my hand, and sat down to wait. At seven minutes past, I heard footsteps hurrying toward my office. Whoever it was stopped right outside. And panted for a few seconds. Then the paper began to come in under the door. There in the dark, I was ready.

With exactly the degree of pull you get when you try to make change for a dollar in one of those airport change machines, I tugged slightly and evenly at the proffered paper. For a moment, the person on the other side gripped the paper more tightly. Then, probably surprised at herself, she let go. Her paper was mine.

I took the copier paper I had been holding all this time and began as noisily as I could to tear it into bits and pieces. There was dead silence on the other side of the door. Then I said aloud. "Chomp, chomp, CHOMP." Audible gasp outside.

"Please!" she said. "It's only seven minutes late." The thought of what it might look like outside that door to a passerby got me giggling. (I know, I know. It was unworthy of me. But I pictured a stricken young woman, talking to the door: "Please, door, it's only seven minutes late.") Perhaps the muffled giggling or the implication of the "Chomp, chomp, CHOMP" had just registered, but I heard the closest thing to a "Humph!" I have heard in real life before she stalked off down the hall. I suppressed my giggling, collected my papers and my *composure*, and went home.

She wasn't in class the next time it met, and I told the story—without names, of course. The class loved it. "Chomp, chomp, CHOMP!" they kept repeating throughout the hour.

I told the story again the following semester and the one after that—you can get a lot of mileage out of a good story. Students began to ask me about the paper shredder, and that's when I decided on the sign for the bottom of the door.

For a couple of semesters it was Our Joke. But you know how it is—sooner or later the old retired gunslinger is going to have to draw one more time. One of my students actually had the nerve to say, "You're always telling us about what you did to other classes, but you don't ever *do* anything about it." Now it was my turn for a "Humph!"

So amid the groaning about the deadlines for papers in my course, "The Comic Spirit," was born the idea for One More Twist. Essays were due Friday by 5 P.M. "And then the paper shredder," they chortled. "And then the paper shredder," I said.

When 5 P.M. came, and six papers were still missing, I gathered up what I had, turned out the lights, and went home. That weekend I spent much of my spare time tearing paper—all kinds of paper—into tiny bits and dropping them into a brown paper sack.

On class day, I secreted my nearly full shopping sack inside a large book bag and went upstairs. I *surreptitiously* pulled it out and hid it in my reading stand, planning to *discourse* on the papers at the end of the period.

It worked out even better. Halfway through the period, as I was shifting from *Northanger Abbey* to *Alice in Wonderland*, one of my anxious worrywarts raised his hand. "When," he wanted to know, "will you be giving back the papers?"

"I'm glad you asked me that," I said, quite sincerely. The students were now all waiting for the answer, not paying much attention to my hands, which were reaching in behind the reading stand to move the sack into position.

"Those of you who turned your essays in by 5 o'clock last Friday will get them back at the end of next week." A slight groan: They had hoped it would be sooner. They always do. "For the rest, those who slid them under the door some time after 5 P.M.—and I'm afraid I don't know how many of you there actually were. . . ." By now, they were hanging on every word. The sack was in ready position. "But those of you who turned your paper in late (I had lifted the sack high above the desk) should come up after class (I turned the sack upside-down and thousands—thousands—of little shreds of paper were fluttering down over the reading stand, the desk, the floor) and identify your papers. If you can."

There was an explosion of laughter, stamping feet, pandemonium, as the shower of confetti continued for several seconds. They could not believe that a university professor would do anything so idiotic.

"Now," I said, in my best professional rhythms, "let us consider the scene in which Alice finds the caterpillar sitting on a mushroom."

At the end of the period, while I tried to get as many of the tiny bits of paper into the wastebasket as I could, I saw a few of my students in the doorway, pointing at the debris. They were apparently explaining to friends and passersby what had just happened in the classroom. And I don't think they were discussing the Mad Hatter or the March Hare. At least not directly.

I knew that somewhere down the road the old gunslinger would probably have to draw one last time, but I reckoned I was safe for a couple more semesters.

I didn't have quite that much time.

Given everything else that had gone on in my honors satire class, I might have known they would be the ones. I had, of course, recounted to them the story of the paper shredder.

The day I realized just how closely they had been listening was the day their papers were due. As I unlocked my office door, I saw on the floor a few hundred strips of shredded paper. Without quite understanding what had happened, I gathered up the scraps and carried them to my desk. There, I found that the segments could be fitted together and deciphered. I appeared to be in possession of 10 or 11 (it was a little hard to tell) essays on ". . . andide and Saint Joan," "The Innocents in *Volpone* and *Can . . . ,*" and "Satiri . . . *Travels.*" Page numbers helped me piece parts of essays together. Then I realized that the scraps were all on copier paper. On a hunch, I went to see the departmental secretaries. Grinning widely, they handed me a large envelope filled with the originals.

Those wags in the honors class had copied their essays, shredded the copies, slid them under my door, and given the originals to the secretaries to whom, obviously, they had explained the whole scam.

And up on Boot Hill, the old gunslinger's tombstone reads: Those Who Live by the Shredder, Die by the Shredder.

Joel J. Gold, "Please! It's Only Seven Minutes Late, Professor". Reprinted by permission of the author.

 ## Vocabulary

As you think about this essay, these definitions may be helpful to you:
1. **pseudo**   false
2. **straitened**   hard up, short of money
3. **composure**   calmness of mind, bearing, or appearance
4. **surreptitiously**   secretively, as if afraid of being caught
5. **discourse**   verbal exchange of ideas

Discussion Questions

1. What happened to the student who turned in her paper seven minutes late?
2. How did Gold get even with the class that began to doubt his story about the paper shredder? What was their reaction?
3. How did one class "get even" with the author? How did Gold react to their prank?
4. What policies do your professors have about late work? Should there be a campus-wide policy on this issue? Why or why not?

 Suggestions for Your Journal

Have you ever turned in a late assignment? What was the result? What do you think is a fair reaction to students who turn in papers late? How would you react to Gold's policy if you were in his class?

Under what circumstances do you think it is acceptable for you to turn in a paper late? If you turn your assignments in on time and others turn in theirs late without penalty, have you been treated fairly? Why?

Why I Don't Let Students Cut My Classes

William R. Brown

William R. Brown is professor of English at the Philadelphia College of Textiles and Science. In this essay, he presents his opinions on why students cut classes and describes how he arrived at his no-cut policy in his course. The positive results from enforcing his policy are also described.

Last year I announced to my classes my new policy on absences: None would be allowed, except for illness or personal emergency. Even though this violated the statement on cuts in the student handbook, which allows freshmen cuts each term up to twice the number of class meetings per week and imposes no limit for upperclassmen, my students didn't fuss. They didn't fuss even after they discovered, when I e-mailed or sent warning notices through the mail to students who had missed classes, that I meant business.

Part of their acceptance of the policy may have resulted from the career orientation of our college, but I don't think that was the main reason. After I explained the policy, most seemed to recognize that it promoted their own academic interests. It was also a requirement that virtually all of them would be obliged to observe—and would expect others to observe—throughout their working lives. It had to be Woody Allen who said that a major part of making it in life is simply showing up.

I told my classes about recent research, by Howard Schuman and others, indicating that academic success is more closely tied to class attendance than to the amount of time spent studying. I shared my sense of disappointment and personal *affront* when I carefully prepare for a class and a substantial number of students do not attend. I think they got the message that the policy is not arbitrary—that I care about their learning and expect them to care about my professional effort.

I don't claim to have controlled all the variables, but after I instituted the no-cut rule, student performance in my classes improved markedly, not so much in the top rank as at the bottom. In fact, the bottom rank almost disappeared, moving up and swelling the middle range to such an extent that I have reassessed my evaluation methods to differentiate among levels of performance in that range. The implications of so dramatic an improvement are surely worth pondering.

Additional benefits of the policy have been those one would expect to result from a full classroom. Student morale is noticeably higher, as is mine. Discussions are livelier, assignments are generally turned in on time, and very few students miss quizzes.

The mechanics of maintaining the policy kept me a little busier than usual, especially at first, but the results would have justified a lot more effort. I called or e-mailed notes to several students about their cuts, some more than once. I eventually advised a few with *invincibly* poor attendance to drop my course when it seemed that an unhappy outcome was likely. They did.

No doubt this kind of shepherding is easier in a small college. But it can work almost anyplace where a teacher cares enough about the educational stakes to make it work. The crucial element is caring.

At the first faculty meeting of the year, I confessed what I was doing. After all, I was defying college policy. I told my colleagues—at least those not cutting the meeting—that it rankled me when I had carefully prepared a class and a fifth, a quarter, or a third of the students didn't show. I thought my classes were good, and I *knew* Faulkner, Austen, and Tolstoy were good. What had been lacking in my classes, I said, was a significant proportion of the students. I told my colleagues that I believed my problem was not unique but was true of college classes everywhere, and that I was doing something about it.

Although no one seemed to attach much importance to my ignoring college policy, few of my colleagues gave me active support. Some were agreed that a 25 percent absence rate in a college class was not alarming. Others felt that college students must take responsibility for their studies, and that we should not feel liable for their losses from cut classes. One implied that if students could bag a lot of classes and still pass the course, it reflected badly on the teacher.

If professors have enough drawing power, another said, students will attend their classes. (How do you *parry* that?) Still another pointed out that if the professor covers enough material, there will be no time to waste taking the roll. In a large lecture, someone said, who knows who is there and who isn't? After the meeting, one *wag* told me I should consider using the acronym PAP for my "professional attendance policy," but congratulated me on at least evoking an interesting discussion in a faculty meeting, something rare indeed. It was easy to conclude that most of them preferred not to see a problem—at least their problem—in spotty class attendance.

Why do students cut so frequently? I can cite the immediate causes, but I first want to note the enabling circumstance: They cut because they are allowed to. They cut because of the climate of acceptance that comes from our belief that responsibility can be developed only when one is free, free even to act against personal best interests. That this is a misapplied belief in this case can be easily demonstrated. When substantial numbers of students do not attend, classroom learning is depreciated, student and teacher morale suffer, and academic standards are compromised. Students who miss classes unnecessarily are hurting more than themselves. With our *complicity*, they are undermining what colleges and universities are all about.

Students cut for two general reasons. They have things to do that appear more important than the class, or they wish to avoid what they fear will be painful consequences if they attend. In regard to the first, nursing an illness or attending family weddings or funerals are good excuses for missing a class. But other excuses—the demands of outside jobs, social engagements (including recovering from the night before), completing assignments for other courses—are, at best, questionable.

The other general reason is more disturbing and perhaps less well recognized. A few years ago, I asked several classes what they most disliked about the way courses were taught, and the answer was plain—anything that produced sustained tension or anxiety. I believe cutting is often a result of that aversion. The response of students to feelings of personal inadequacy, fear of humiliation, or a threatening professorial personality or teaching style is often simply to avoid class. This response feeds on itself, as frequent absences make attending even more threatening.

But what accounts for frequent cutting where the teacher tries to make the material interesting, knows the students by name, and approaches them with respect, help, and affability? I accept that question as unanswerable. I simply tell my students: Attend my classes regularly or drop the course. That's the rule.

William R. Brown, "Why I Don't Let Students Cut My Classes," reprinted by permission of the author.

 ## Vocabulary

As you think about this essay, these definitions may be helpful to you:
1. **affront**   an insult
2. **invincibly**   incapable of being overcome or subdued
3. **parry**   to evade, to shove aside
4. **wag**   joker, smart-aleck
5. **complicity**   association with or participation in

? Discussion Questions

1. What, according to Brown, does research indicate about academic success as related to class attendance?
2. What happened after the author instituted his no-cut rule?
3. What benefits did he see after enforcing the policy?
4. What reaction did he get from his colleagues?
5. Why, according to Brown, do students cut classes?

Suggestions for Your Journal

Have you ever cut a class? If so, what were the consequences? If you put yourself in the place of your instructor, how would you be affected by students cutting your class? Do you think students appreciate a teacher who cares enough about them to institute such a policy? For what reasons would you cut a class? Can you answer Professor Brown's "unanswerable" question about why some students cut classes, even when all the positive aspects of the course are in place?

Unit Summary

The writers in this unit offer many perspectives on how to be a successful student. One defining purpose of college is to learn about our intellectual and cultural heritage. To be intensely involved in learning requires great concentration and many skills. The readings in this unit have offered many suggestions for accomplishing this.

■ Summary Questions

1. How do the readings in this unit suggest you can become a successful student?
2. What tasks or strategies described in the readings could you adopt to improve your own attitudes or behaviors toward your academic work?
3. What skills do you hope to acquire in college to help you in your future work and in living in general?

■ Suggested Writing Assignments

1. Write a brief essay describing the qualities of a successful student and why you selected those qualities.
2. Select one reading in this unit and write about your personal experience with the academic concern it describes.
3. Several authors in this unit write about various approaches to learning. Describe how your own approach to learning is the same as or different from the ones they describe.

■ Suggested Readings

Arthur, John. *A Concise Guide to College Success: Carpe Diem*. Upper Saddle River, NJ: Prentice Hall, 2003.

Lawrence, Gordon. *People Types and Tiger Stripes*. Gainesville, FL: Center for the Application of Psychological Types, 1982.

Pauk, W. *How to Study in College*, 9th ed. Boston: Houghton Mifflin, 2008.

Robson, James B. *Beginning College 101: How to Achieve Real Success in College*. South Plainfield, NJ: College and Future Company, 2001.

Unit 4

How Should I Expect to Learn?

I am not young enough to know everything.

—JAMES M. BARRIE

The act of learning is so ingrained in our everyday life that we usually take it for granted. However, as psychologists who study learning professionally can demonstrate, learning is a complex process that operates differently for many people. Learning can be defined in many ways. It is not only the acquisition of knowledge and skills by instruction or study; it is also an accumulation through experience. Although students enter college after years of "learning," many find that college learning offers new and exciting challenges.

A great deal of research on how people learn has provided important insights and tools to enhance our understanding of the process. David Kolb, a business professor, has suggested that the demands of different academic disciplines require students to use different learning styles or approaches. Howard Gardner takes a multifaceted view when he discusses eight "intelligences," which he describes in terms of a set of abilities, talents, and mental skills. Daniel Goleman writes about "emotional intelligence," which includes both personal competence and social competence. Goleman suggests that emotional intelligence will be especially important in the future workplace where emotional competencies will be increasingly essential for excellence in every job.

Many researchers believe there is a relationship between the knowledge that exists in the mind and the situations in which it was acquired and used. Successful learning also depends on the individual's past experiences and attitudes toward the learning process. Perhaps the most important factor in successful learning, however, is the motivation or desire to learn.

This unit offers many perspectives about learning. Gardner identifies five different types of "minds" that are critical to the tasks of the future. Siebert and Gilpin provide insights into students' varied approaches to learning. They point out that the learning circumstance or situation for one person may require a different approach than for another. Hellyer, Robinson, and Sherwood offer tips on how to use your memory. Schein, Laff, and Allen emphasize the importance of using faculty in and out of the classroom. Problem solving is an important skill that is often taken for granted. To complete this unit, Albrecht offers insights into this important process.

Minds Viewed Globally

Howard Gardner

Howard Gardner has been called one of the one hundred most influential public intellectuals in the world. A MacArthur Fellowship recipient, he is the Hobbs Professor of Cognition and Education at the Harvard Graduate School of Education.

For several decades, as a researcher in psychology, I have been pondering the human mind. I've studied how the mind develops, how it is organized, what it's like in its fullest expanse. I've studied how people learn, how they create, how they lead, how they change the minds of other persons or their own minds. For the most part, I've been content to describe the typical operations of the mind— a daunting task in itself. But on occasion, I've also offered views about how we *should* use our minds.

While making no claims to have a crystal ball, I concern myself with the kinds of minds that people will need if they—if *we*—are to thrive in the world during the eras to come. The larger part of my enterprise remains descriptive—I specify the operations of the minds that we will need. But I cannot hide the fact that I am engaged as well in a "values enterprise": the minds that I describe are also the ones that I believe we *should* develop in the future.

Why the shift from description to prescription? In the interconnected world in which the vast majority of human beings now live, it is not enough to state what each individual or group needs to survive on its own turf. In the long run, it is not possible for parts of the world to thrive while others remain desperately poor and deeply frustrated. Recalling the words of Benjamin Franklin, "We must indeed hang together, or, most assuredly, we shall all hang separately." Further, the world of the future—with its *ubiquitous* search engines, robots, and other computational devices— will demand capacities that until now have been mere options. To meet this new world on its own terms, we should begin to cultivate those capacities now.

Because I am speculating about the directions in which our society and our planet are headed, political and economic considerations loom large. I balance these scholarly perspectives with a constant reminder that a description of minds cannot escape a consideration of human values. With these "minds," as I refer to them, a person will be well equipped to deal with what is expected, as well as what cannot be anticipated; without these minds, a person will be at the mercy of forces that he or she can't understand, let alone control. I'll describe each mind briefly and explain how it works.

The *disciplined mind* has mastered at least one way of thinking—a distinctive mode of *cognition* that characterizes a specific scholarly discipline, craft or profession.

Much research confirms that it takes up to ten years to master a discipline. The disciplined mind also knows how to work steadily over time to improve skill and understanding—in the *vernacular*, it is highly disciplined. Without at least one discipline under his belt, the individual is destined to march to someone else's tune.

The *synthesizing mind* takes information from *disparate* sources, understands and evaluates that information objectively, and puts it together in ways that make sense to the synthesizer and also to other persons. Valuable in the past, the capacity to synthesize becomes ever more crucial as information continues to mount at dizzying rates.

Building on discipline and synthesis, the *creating mind* breaks new ground. It puts forth new ideas, poses unfamiliar questions, conjures up fresh ways of thinking, and arrives at unexpected answers. Ultimately, these creations must find acceptance among knowledgeable consumers. By virtue of its anchoring in territory that is not yet rule-governed, the creating mind seeks to remain at least one step ahead of even the most sophisticated computers and robots.

Recognizing that nowadays one can no longer remain within one's shell or on one's home territory, the *respectful mind* notes and welcomes differences between human individuals and between human groups, tries to understand these "others," and seeks to work effectively with them. In a world where we are all interlinked, intolerance or disrespect is no longer a viable option.

Proceeding on a level more abstract than the respectful mind, *the ethical mind* ponders the nature of one's work and the needs and desires of the society in which one lives. This mind conceptualizes how workers can serve purposes beyond self-interest and how citizens can work unselfishly to improve the lot of men. The ethical mind then acts on the basis of these analyses.

One may reasonably ask: Why these five particular minds? Could the list be readily changed or extended? My brief answer is this: The five minds just introduced are the kinds of minds that are particularly at a premium in the world of today and will be even more so tomorrow. They span both the cognitive spectrum and the human enterprise—in that sense they are comprehensive, global. We know something about how to cultivate them. Of course there could be other candidates. I considered candidates ranging from the technological mind to the digital mind, the market mind to the democratic mind, the flexible mind to the emotional mind, the strategic mind to the spiritual mind. I am prepared, however, to defend my quintet vigorously.

We will need to cultivate these five kinds of minds in the future if we are to have the kinds of managers, leaders, and citizens needed to populate our planet. To approach my brief sharply:

- Individuals without one or more disciplines will not be able to succeed at any demanding workplace and will be restricted to menial tasks.
- Individuals without synthesizing capabilities will be overwhelmed by information and unable to make *judicious* decisions about personal or professional matters.

- Individuals without creating capacities will be replaced by computers and will drive away those who do have the creative spark.
- Individuals without respect will not be worthy of respect by others and will poison the workplace and the commons.
- Individuals without ethics yield a world devoid of decent workers and responsible citizens: None of us will want to live on that desolate planet.

No one knows precisely how to fashion an education that will yield individuals who are disciplined, synthesizing, creative, respectful, and ethical. I have argued that our survival as a planet may depend on the cultivation of this pentad of mental dispositions. Indeed, without respect, we are likely to destroy one another; without ethics, we return to a Hobbesian or Darwinian world, where the common good is nowhere to be seen. But I firmly believe that each human faculty should also be justified on noninstrumental grounds as well. As a species, we human beings have impressive positive potentials—and history is replete with individuals who exemplify one or more of these kinds of minds: the discipline of a John Keats or a Marie Curie; the synthesizing capacities of Aristotle or Goethe; the creativity of a Martha Graham or a Bill Gates; the respectful example of those who sheltered Jews during the Second World War or who participated in commissions of truth and reconciliation during more recent decades; the ethical example of ecologist Rachel Carson, who alerted us to the dangers of pesticides, and of statesman Jean Monnet, who helped Europe move from belligerent to peaceful institutions. Education in the broadest sense should help more human beings realize the most impressive features of the most remarkable representatives of our species.

Vocabulary

As you think about this essay, these definitions may be helpful to you:
1. **ubiquitous**   widespread
2. **cognition**   a process that involves conscious mental activity
3. **vernacular**   normal spoken form of a language
4. **disparate**   fundamentally different
5. **judicious**   exercising sound judgment

Discussion Questions

1. What reasons does the author give for choosing these five minds? Are they valid?
2. Do you agree that these five minds are the most important for people to cultivate? What others would you add?
3. Which of these five minds do you think is the most difficult for people to cultivate? The easiest? Why?

4. The author claims that "our survival as a planet" will depend on how well we cultivate these five minds. Do you agree with this statement? Is it overstated? Why or why not?
5. What other examples of people, besides the ones the author gives, can you think of that represents each of these five minds?

 ## Suggestions for Your Journal

To which of these five minds do you personally feel the strongest connection? What evidence do you have? Which of the five minds do you feel is the most difficult for you to cultivate? What specific steps can you take now to increase your capacities in each of these five "mental dispositions"?

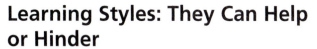

Learning Styles: They Can Help or Hinder

Al Siebert and Bernadine Gilpin

Al Siebert is a psychologist with more than 20 years of teaching experience in adult education. Bernadine Gilpin started college at age 35 after rearing five children. She has more than 15 years' experience as a teacher, administrator, and counselor.

Siebert and Gilpin believe that understanding how one learns best can help make studying and learning easier. This essay points out how mismatches between teaching and learning styles may cause difficulties and makes suggestions for recognizing and overcoming this common problem.

Researchers wanting to understand all aspects of success in college asked: "Why do some students do well with one instructor but not another?" Their research uncovered a simple truth about academic life: The way some people teach does not always match up with the way other people learn.

Other research looked at why students show wide differences in the time of day and the circumstances best for learning. This research identified an important truth about studying and learning: The learning circumstances best for one person may not be good for another.

Research findings and experience have identified the following important differences in how people learn.

Auditory versus Visual Styles

Have you ever noticed that someone can read a note you've left him, but the message doesn't get through to his brain? Or that you can tell a person something, but it doesn't register unless you write it down for her? That's because people differ in how information gets into their conscious mind.

Some people learn best by listening. Information doesn't stick well unless they hear it. Other people learn best by reading. They must see something before they believe it and remember it. Some people learn best by doing. What is your natural style?

Do you remember best what is said to you or what you read?
Do you prefer television or newspapers as your source of news?
Would you rather hear an expert talk on a subject or read what the expert has written?
When you purchase new equipment, do you read the instruction manual carefully or do you rarely read manuals?

Is reading the college catalog your main way of learning about your program and classes, or do you merely skim the catalog and go see an advisor who tells you everything you need to know?

Based on your answers to these questions, which learning style do you prefer, auditory or visual?

Everyone learns both ways, of course. It is not an either/or situation. Yet the differences between people are sometimes extreme enough to cause problems. If you have a visual learning style, you operate mainly on the basis of what you read. You may have difficulty with an instructor who believes that telling people what and how to learn is sufficient.

Auditory Learning Style

If you have an auditory style, you will probably do well with an instructor who says everything to learn and do. You may have difficulty with a visually oriented instructor. Such an instructor hands out a written statement about what to do to pass the course without discussing it and assigns textbook material and outside readings that are never discussed in class.

The solution, if you have an auditory style in a class taught by a visually oriented instructor, is to:

1. Find classmates who will tell you what they learned from the textbook readings.
2. Dictate the main points from the reading assignments and handouts onto CDs and then listen to the CDs.
3. Consciously work at improving your ability to acquire information visually. (Note: For professional help, go to the reading improvement center or the office of disability services at your college.)

Visual Learning Style

If you learn best visually, you may be in trouble with an instructor who doesn't use handouts, emphasizes class discussion, and doesn't write much on the blackboard. The solution with a verbally oriented instructor is to:

1. Take good notes on what the instructor and your classmates say. After class fill in sentences and compare notes with other students.
2. Ask the instructor for suggested articles or books that will let you read the information you need to understand better.
3. Consciously work at listening and remembering what the instructor says. TIP: One woman wrote to us saying that she types her lecture notes immediately after each class.
4. If you are confused about a point, ask the instructor to tell you again and write down what you hear.

External versus Internal Learning Styles

Psychologists have done extensive research on a significant personality variable. It is called the "external and internal *locus of control.*"

Externally oriented students believe information when it comes from an authority or expert. Information or suggestions from other sources aren't trusted as accurate.

If you prefer to get the guidance from expert sources and your instructor enjoys being an expert, then you have a good match. The more you need an instructor who tells the class exactly what to learn, the better you will do with this type of instructor. If you need clear guidelines from instructors but take a course from someone who provides little direction, you may flounder. You may be sitting in class waiting for the instructor to tell you what the answer to a problem is, only to have him or her ask the class, "What do you think?" After the class talks for a while, the instructor may refuse to say what the right answer is. He or she might say, "You may be right," or "There is some truth to that."

Some students react negatively to classes in which the instructor encourages discussion and encourages students to develop their own views and answers. These students protest, "I didn't pay good money to sit and listen to a bunch of uninformed people express their opinions. I can get that in the coffee shop." This attitude is legitimate. It is also narrow-minded.

The word *education* means to "draw out of." It does not mean "shovel into." A good education teaches you to think for yourself. It teaches you to ask good questions and then how to find the answers on your own. A good education does not give you a diploma for learning how to seek out an expert for any question you have. It teaches you how to both listen to authorities and come to your own conclusions.

Self-motivated, internally oriented students appreciate an instructor who allows them freedom to follow their own paths. Such students get upset with instructors who tell them exactly what they must learn, and in what way. For them, too much course structure is *abrasive.* They feel handicapped more than helped. Such reactions are legitimate and narrow-minded.

In every field of study, certain basics must be mastered. There are basic terms and concepts that must be understood. There are some techniques fundamental to the mastery of the subject even though the reasons may not be given.

Being Both Internal and External in Learning

Students who get the most out of school are able to follow the tightly controlled steps used by some teachers and, at the same time, organize their own learning experiences when in a class taught by someone who gives few guidelines. Can you learn to do both?

Differences in Temperament

Isabel Myers and her mother Katharine Briggs developed a test to measure four dimensions of *temperament* identified by psychotherapist Carl Jung. Myers–Briggs tests are probably the most popular personality tests in the country because many people benefit from seeing how differences in temperament explain misunderstandings among people.

This means that differences in *how* you and an instructor think are more important than differences in *what* you think. Here's how the four temperaments influence your learning style.

Extroversion versus Introversion

Instructors and students vary widely in how friendly they want to be and how much emotional distance they need to have. A friendly, *extroverted* instructor enjoys after-class contact with students. He or she will ask students to coffee or out for pizza. If you are similarly friendly, you will have a great year.

If you are a more *introverted* person, however, you may suffer from too much personal attention and closeness. You would much rather have a quiet, tactful instructor who respects your need to be left alone. Such an instructor understands how embarrassing it is to be called on to talk in class or to be openly praised for getting a high score on an exam.

On the other hand, if you are an extroverted person with a more introverted instructor, you may find it puzzling to have him or her pulling away from you after class. After all, what are instructors for if not to be available for students? Yet your desire to be friendly may cause the instructor to stare at you and make excuses to get away. After that, you may feel avoided.

When it comes to studying, the introverted person needs a private, quiet place where everyone stays away. The extroverted person likes to study in the kitchen, in a student lounge, or with classmates. Don't hesitate to tell friends, relatives, and classmates with temperaments different from yours what you need.

Thinking versus Feeling

Descriptions of this dimension of temperament match up closely with left-brain/right-brain research findings. The left brain is where the speech center develops in most humans. The left brain is where you remember words, use logic, and think analytically. It gives you your ability to think rationally and unemotionally. The left brain thinks in a linear fashion. It is time oriented.

The right brain carries your memory for music. You think visually, emotionally, and irrationally in the right brain. It is the source of creativity and intuition. Right-brain thinking follows emotional logic. Using it, you can visualize and think in patterns, jumping from one spot in a pattern to another without apparent logic or reason.

If you tend to be left-brained, you will be well matched to an instructor who gives you thorough, unemotional listings of facts, data, analytic explorations, hypotheses, logic, evidence, numbers, definition of terms, and rational conclusions.

If you tend to be left-brained and get an instructor who teaches in a right-brained way, you may find the course to be a bewildering experience. You may experience the instructor as weird, too emotional, disorganized, and a bit nutty.

If you tend to be right-brained with a left-brained teacher, the course will be painful for you. You'll feel like a thirsty person handed a glass of water only to find it is filled with sand.

To resolve personality conflicts such as these, avoid indulging in the attitude, "If only other people would change, my world would be a better place for me." When you have a mismatch, you can try to find someone (perhaps even the instructor) who will translate the material into a form you understand better. More important, however, make an effort to gain more use of your other brain.

The situation may not be easy at first, but it does give you a chance to add another dimension to yourself. And isn't this why you're in school?

You do not have to give up your more natural and preferred way of thinking, feeling, and talking. What you can do is add more to what you already have.

Sensation versus Intuition

Sensation-oriented people like to be sensible. They are guided by experience. Intuitive people like fantasy. They are creative dreamers. According to David Keirsey and Marilyn Bates, authors of *Please Understand Me*, differences on this dimension cause the widest gulf between people.

The sensation-oriented student is practical, wanting facts and evidence. An intuitive instructor can fill the lecture hour with hypothetical explanations, theories, concepts, and a long list of views held by others.

A sensation-oriented instructor gives practical instructions on what to do. An intuitive student wants to know what the underlying theories and concepts are, and asks "but what if?"

What to do about this sort of conflict? Stretch your understanding. Ask for what you need. Try to minimize the judging dimension of the next pair of traits.

Judging versus Perceiving

If you remember Archie Bunker from the television series "All in the Family," you have seen an excellent example of the judging temperament. Such people make up their minds quickly. They judge others and situations as good or bad, right or wrong.

The perceiving style is to observe without judgment. Such people can watch world events, movies, and sports events without taking sides or having an opinion.

A judgmental style instructor believes that the purpose for being in college is to work hard to become qualified for an occupation where hard work will get you ahead. The instructor works hard, expects the same from every student, and privately judges students as good ones or bad ones.

A perceiving instructor looks for ways to make learning fun, tries to minimize office work, and sees all students as learners. This instructor is frustrating for a judging style student who wants serious homework and wants to know how he or she compares to the other students.

Practical Suggestions

What do you do when a teacher is less than ideal? Do you get distressed? Complain?

By now we hope you have realized that finding a really good match between yourself and an instructor does not happen all the time. In fact, if you are an experienced victim, then the college will provide you with many chances to be upset, complain to classmates, and criticize instructors you judge to be imperfect.

As an alternative to being a victim, we have the following suggestions:

1. Before registration ask around to find out about various instructors. If you have a choice between instructors, you'll know which one to choose.
2. Try to get as much out of every course as you can, regardless of who your instructor is or how much the teaching style does not fit your preferred learning style. Be open to try a new way of learning.
3. When you have difficulty understanding what is happening in a course, make an appointment to talk with the instructor. Be prepared to ask for what you want.
4. If you still have problems, go to the office or center that teaches studying and reading skills. The specialists there can be very helpful.

Learn to Appreciate Human Differences

When you experience conflicts with others at school, at work, or in your family, question your attitudes about what other people should be like. If you experience an irritating difference, use that as an opportunity to learn more about human nature. You might as well, because you won't change other people by criticizing them!

We humans are all born with different temperaments and different ways of functioning in life. That is simply the way things work.

Do You Know Where and When?

Several final suggestions: If you grew up in a large family you may study best in a noisy place with lots of people around. Experiment with locations to see what works best for you.

Time of day is another learning style difference. If you are a morning person, get up and study for an hour before others get up. Leave chores for evening when your brain is disengaging. If you are an evening person go ahead and study until one or two in the morning.

The better you know yourself, the more skillfully you will manage your learning style and the easier it will be to succeed in college!

Al Siebert and Bernadine Gilpin, "Learning Styles: They Can Help or Hinder," from THE ADULT STUDENT'S GUIDE TO SURVIVAL AND SUCCESS: TIME FOR COLLEGE ©1992. Reprinted by permission of Practical Psychology Press.

Vocabulary

As you think about this essay, these definitions may be helpful to you:
1. **locus of control**   center of self-control, by either internal or external influences
2. **abrasive**   causing irritation
3. **temperament**   characteristic or habitual inclination
4. **extroverted**   being predominantly influenced by what is outside of the self
5. **introverted**   being wholly or predominantly concerned with one's own mental life

 ## Discussion Questions

1. What is a learning style?
2. What is the difference between the auditory and visual style of learning?
3. How does temperament affect your approaches to learning?
4. What aspects of learning does the left brain control? What aspects does the right brain control?
5. What four temperaments can influence your learning style? Describe them and how they affect the way you learn.

 ## Suggestions for Your Journal

Analyze how you learn best. Are you more visual or auditory? Have you ever experienced a class in which the instructor's teaching style did not work with your best learning style? If so, what happened?

Do you think a student who does not learn well with a certain teacher's style should switch instructors or learn to adapt? What suggestions given by the authors for learning more effectively pertain to you?

The Power of Memory

Regina Hellyer, Carol Robinson, and Phyllis Sherwood

The authors of this essay are English teachers at the Raymond Walter College of the University of Cincinnati. Regina Hellyer is director of the reading program, Carol Robinson teaches English composition, and Phyllis Sherwood is the director of the writing lab.

Everyone forgets something sometimes. And almost everyone wishes he or she could remember more. You probably already have some methods to help you remember. What do you do to jog your memory? The classic (and probably the corniest) way to remember something is to tie a string around your finger. Today Post-It Notes have become a popular means of sparking memory because they are conveniently sized and adhere to most surfaces. All memory begins with the senses because the five senses are the channel through which all information comes. However, although you are bombarded by vast numbers of sights, sounds, touches, tastes, and smells each moment of the day, only certain impressions and information actually go into your short- or long-term memory.

Many people make this complaint: "I have a terrible memory. I just can't remember anything!" Such a statement is not only exaggerated, it is usually untrue. Most people's memories are not bad; they are just not as well trained as they could be. Everyone uses some memory strategies. But whatever memory devices you already use, you may want to add to the power of your memory by adopting some of the following techniques: observation, association, clustering, imaging, and mnemonics.

Observation

Much of your ability to remember hinges on careful observation. *Observation* involves a *conscious* effort to pay attention, be alert, listen attentively, and notice details. If, for example, you have ever lost track of your car in a public parking lot, it was probably because you did not make a conscious effort to pay attention or to notice landmarks. Likewise, you need to employ basic observational skills both in the classroom and in your studying before you can apply any other memory techniques. When you are listening to lectures, taking notes, and studying textbooks, you must make a conscious effort to notice and remember pertinent information. For example, when you are taking notes in class, besides recording the obvious—information on the chalkboard or a *Power Point presentation*—you should be noticing the teacher's body language, his or her vocal emphasis, and transitions and organizational cues. Careful observation of these details allows you to determine

94

what information is of major or minor importance and what you should empha-size in your notes, that is, what is important to remember.

Association

The second memory technique, learning by *association*, is based upon a simple principle: Learning something new is always easier if you can associate or con-nect it with something you already know. For example, if you are just beginning to use a computer, you might not understand what is meant by "windows" until you realize that windows on computers are very similar to windows in buildings: When you look into them, you can see what exists in the computer and in the environment. Or, in a biology class, if you are learning about the structure of neurons in the brain, you might associate one part of the neuron, the dendrites, which grow as you learn new information, with the roots of a tree, which grow when they are watered.

Clustering

Clustering, the process of grouping a large number of ideas into subgroups, is another handy memory device. This technique is based on the fact that you can remember several groups of five or so items more easily than a large number of separate items. If you have thirty items to learn, try to organize them into groups. For example, you might try clustering new terms you have to learn.

Clustering can also be useful as a method for prewriting or organizing an essay or research paper. If your ideas, information, or material cannot be arranged chronologically (relating to time, from first to last) or spatially (relating to area, from top to bottom, side to side, etc.), you can cluster to find categories or group-ings that will provide you with a logical method of organization.

Imaging

Imaging, or using a pictorial representation of something, can be an excellent way to remember a fact, process, definition, or concept. For example, most of us know the geographical shape of Italy because its image resembles a boot. However, draw-ing the geographical outline of Switzerland, Italy's close neighbor to the north, would prove challenging for most people, since its shape does not easily conjure up a picture.

You may already be drawing pictures in your notebooks to reinforce ideas, definitions, or other material you need to learn. If you have not done so yet, try this method with something that you are having trouble remembering. You do not have to be a great artist. Stick figures are fine. These pictures are for your eyes only, so however they look, you will know what the picture is sup-posed to represent, and the picture will be imprinted on your mind because *you* drew it!

Mnemonics

Mnemonics is a general category of memory devices; mnemonic devices include songs, ditties, and other catchy techniques to help you remember. Mnemonic devices take the form of acronyms, made-up sentences, rhymes or songs, and physical manipulations.

Acronyms

Acronyms are a kind of mnemonic device formed from the first letters of items you are trying to learn. The first letters are arranged to spell a word. People have used acronyms for ages, but in this era of rapidly increasing information, they are becoming more and more prevalent. For example, you are all familiar with Light Amplification by Stimulated Emission of Radiation printers and Light Amplification by Stimulated Emission of Radiation surgery, but you call them laser printers and laser surgery. The acronym *laser* (originally in capital letters) and other words like *radar, sonar,* and *scuba* have become so familiar that you may forget that they were acronyms.

In college, an acronym can act as a trigger to help you remember information. For example, if you have to learn the names of five Great Lakes, it is easy to remember HOMES—standing for Huron, Ontario, Michigan, Erie, and Superior. Likewise, some people remember the colors of the spectrum in their proper order by making each color part of the name "ROY G. BIV" (red, orange, yellow, green, blue, indigo, and violet). Another acronym that is useful to know is SAGE—a "wise" way to remember the four different kinds of context clues: synonyms, antonyms, general sense of the sentence, and examples.

Sentences

Making up sentences or phrases, either nonsensical or serious, can be an effective way of learning and remembering material. The spellings of difficult words can often be learned easily with mnemonics. For instance, saying "A Rat In The House May Eat the Ice Cream" is an easy way to teach a child how to spell *arithmetic* because the sentence is silly (making it memorable), and the first letters of the words, taken together, spell *arithmetic*. For adults, mnemonics can be applied to remember more difficult or confusing spellings. For example, do you spell attendance with an *ance or ence*? It's easy to remember the correct spelling if you think of attending a dAnce. Likewise, FeBRuary is a very cold month—brrrr! A sentence mnemonic to learn the letter keys of a standard keyboard on a computer is "The quick brown fox jumped over the lazy dogs." If you type this sentence, you will have practiced using all the letter keys of the three major rows on a standard keyboard.

Jingles or Rhymes

Jingles and rhymes are popular mnemonics because they help you learn through rhythm and sound. Probably the first "learning" song you encountered was the

ABC song. Another popular jingle shows how to remember which months have thirty days and which ones have thirty-one. "Thirty days hath September, April, June, and November, all the rest have thirty-one; excepting February alone, which hath but twenty-eight in fine, till leap year gives it twenty-nine."

Another rhyme that you might find useful if you are taking chemistry is "-*ate*, I ate; *ide*, I died." This rhyme helps you remember that cyan*ates* are harmless chemicals, whereas cyan*ides* are extremely poisonous—an important distinction to know.

Physical Techniques

Physical participation can also act as a mnemonic. This can mean simply putting something in a particular place, like putting letters that need to be mailed under your car keys, or acting out a process. Instead of the "Thirty Days" poem for remembering the days in the month, perhaps you learned the knuckle method. This method names the months chronologically, counting January on the first knuckle, February in between, March on the second knuckle, April in between, etc. Knuckle months have thirty-one days; in-between-knuckle months have thirty. Unfortunately, this method does not give you a clue about how many days are in February; you are on your own to figure that out. Nevertheless, this example illustrates that mnemonic devices can include physical components, and the more senses you use to learn something, the more easily you will learn and remember.

Although mnemonic devices made up by others can be very helpful, you may want to make up your own mnemonic devices—you will really own them, and they may be even easier to remember than devices that are provided for you. All the memory techniques described in this essay can help you remember difficult concepts and material that can empower you to be a successful college student.

 ## Vocabulary

As you think about this essay, these definitions may be helpful to you:
1. **mnemonics**   assisting or intended to assist in memory
2. **acronyms**   an abbreviation formed from initial letters
3. **antonyms**   words of opposite meanings

 ## Discussion Questions

1. Do you agree with the authors that there is no such thing as a "bad" memory but just an untrained one? Why or why not?
2. The authors suggest you pay attention to the means of nonverbal communication used by your teachers. What important information can you pick up from this?

3. What are the differences between the memory techniques of observation, association, clustering, and imaging? Describe some learning situations where you might use each technique.
4. What mnemonic devices do the authors suggest you use to help you remember? Which ones work best for you? Why?

 ## Suggestions for Your Journal

How would you rate your ability to remember the material required in your courses? Do you use different memory devices in different courses, or do you use the same devices in all courses? Do you use different memory devices in your life outside the classroom than the ones you use in your courses? What steps can you take to improve your memory?

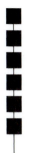

How Do I Find Out What Faculty Are Doing?

Howard K. Schein, Ned S. Laff, and Deborah R. Allen

This essay was written for the *Daily Illini,* the student newspaper at the University of Illinois at Champaign-Urbana, to inform students about how to access faculty resources. The authors are professional academic advisors with wide experience in many areas of higher education.

Faculty members are the moving forces of higher education. You want to pick their brains. You want their ideas, their commentaries on your ideas, and their advice. If you are building a field of study, faculty members are the experts. However, sometimes they don't seem very accessible. How do you find these people, and what do you say once you have located them? Some tips for the curious follow.

Your college's web site or books that list course schedules are academic catalogs. Small gems and good bargains are frequently hidden in the small print. Faculty members teach under their departmental sponsorship, even if their course titles are far afield from their departments' major focuses. International relations may be a natural for a political science department, but at one school, for example, a former ambassador has an appointment in the sociology department. By carefully looking through all course offerings, you may find interesting classes in unexpected places.

Faculty members show off their true interests in upper level courses and in special-topics seminars. Departments go potluck when assigning instructors to introductory courses, so if you want to know who specializes in specific areas, look at upper division and graduate level offerings.

Keep a special eye out for seminar courses, too. Although you may not take courses offered by the specialists of interest for credit, you may be able to sit in on the class. You will find the faculty members' expertise and cross-disciplinary interests in these courses. For instance, when you discover the course in geography of world conflict, your perspective on international relations may take a different bent, especially if your interest is national security policy. You may find that your interest in international relations, when tied to special-topics courses in communications, physics, and economics, makes up an appropriate field of study.

Once you have identified the courses and professors of interest, you need to go through the process of generating a field of study. Suggestions for getting started on planning your tailor-made education follow.

Contact the professors of the identified courses to talk over your interests and expectations for their courses. Get the current course descriptions and look over the reading lists. Ask these professors to identify other people who are working in your areas of interest.

Many departments publish listings of the faculty members' interests. At larger schools, these lists are often part of the promotional package for prospective graduate students. These lists are usually available on departmental Web sites or through the departmental secretary. By the way, the secretary usually knows much more about the faculty's work than most students realize!

Check out all upcoming seminars and lectures. You'll usually hear an informative talk and find out who on campus is involved in your areas of interest.

Once you begin to get a sense of who's doing what, think about how their work fits in with your plans. Then, see these professors during their office hours or write brief e-mails or make quick phone calls to make appointments with them. In your meeting, talk with the faculty member about how to make your program of study substantive. You need to find out if ongoing groups of faculty members and students meet to discuss the topics in which you are interested. They may be meeting through informal lunches, study groups, or Friday afternoon coffee breaks; a faculty member can invite you to these seminars. In your meeting, you can also find out about independent study opportunities with them or their colleagues.

Make use of your elective hours to get into the special-topics courses you've identified, create special-topics courses with the faculty you've discovered, or convince faculty members to lead an independent study project with you. In these special-topics courses, you will be asked to think, apply the tools you have learned, and produce your own work: Your education truly begins in these environments. Faculty members are usually willing to teach under such arrangements as long as they know that you are serious.

Find out about ongoing research projects in your areas of interest and try to get involved in these projects. If the lead researchers know that you want to learn and find you to be energetic and able to contribute through good efforts, they'll listen to you. Faculty members won't usually turn away good help. Here's an approach that seems to work: "Professor B, I've been reading some of your articles on international economic development in Latin America. I'm interested in your theory on the interaction of cultural patterns and economic growth. I'd like to work on this problem with you." If you tie into an ongoing research project or independent study, you learn how people define the critical problems in their areas, how they learn to ask the questions to find solutions to those problems, and what it takes to come up with workable answers. Regardless of your field, such skills are critical to your success when you graduate from college.

Keep in mind that you cannot accomplish your goals in a vacuum. You must integrate your current knowledge into your educational plan. You also must increase the amount of information you get and learn to think about how it pertains to you. For example, in addition to reading the major national newspapers and magazines, pick up the trade journals and papers that the professionals read.

Don't wait until your senior year to take the initiative to learn outside of class; and if you are a freshman, do it now.

"How Do I Find Out What Faculty Are Doing?" by Howard Shein, Ned S. Laff, and Deborah Allen. From NACADA Monograph Series, Number 11. Reprinted by permission of the National Academic Advising Association (NACADA).

 ## Discussion Questions

1. Why do the authors say, "Faculty members are the moving forces of higher education"?
2. How do the authors suggest you use the course catalog to find course offerings that might appeal to you?
3. How can you find faculty members who have expertise in an academic area for which you have an interest? What should you do before making contact?
4. What is the difference between a "major" and a "field of study"? If you would like to put together a "field of study," what are some steps that the authors suggest you take?
5. Do you think the authors' suggestions for approaching faculty members are good ones? What other ways would you approach faculty members if you wanted to study with them?

 ## Suggestions for Your Journal

Describe a positive experience you have had with a faculty member and how it enhanced your academic work. If you have not had a direct, one-to-one contact with a faculty member, how can you initiate one? Have you ever considered asking a faculty member in an area of strong personal interest if you could study or do research with him or her? If so, what was the result?

How to Become an Expert Problem Solver

Karl Albrecht

Dr. Karl Albrecht is a management consultant, executive advisor, futurist, researcher, speaker, and prolific author. He devotes much of his effort to finding and developing promising new concepts for both organizational and individual effectiveness.

> *No problem can be solved from the same consciousness that created it.*
>
> *We must learn to see the world anew.*
>
> —ALBERT EINSTEIN

According to a news report, two burglars broke into the basement of a building in Vang, Norway, below a hardware store. Apparently they found it too difficult to get through the door at the top of the stairs leading to the store, so they had to settle for whatever they could find in the basement.

One of the things they found was an old safe, which looked very promising. Having some skill at safecracking, they rigged up a small charge of plastic explosive, pressed it into the crevice around the safe's door, and hid behind a wall while they detonated it, presumably expecting the door to come off so they could get away with some cash to show for their efforts.

Unfortunately, the safe didn't contain any cash: it contained explosives. The basement of the building—and the burglars—were demolished. Investigators surmised the details of the episode from what was left of the crime scene. One might wonder about the problem-solving process used by these two *benighted* delinquents—what assumptions they were making; what options they considered; indeed, what they defined as "the problem" they were intending to solve.

In keeping with our habit of specifying simple definitions for the key terms and ideas we're trying to think about, here's a very basic definition:

Problem: A state of affairs you have to change in order to get what you want.

You're dissatisfied with some part of reality; you're not getting what you want; what you want to happen is not happening; you think you see an opportunity to make things better, but you don't know yet how to go about it. So you go into some kind of a special thinking mode—a mental process you hope will enable you to figure out how to change the state of affairs so you can get what you want. That's problem solving.

If your educational experience has been fairly typical, somewhere along the way they taught you about the "problem-solving process." They probably told you "there are five steps in problem solving"—or six, or seven, according to the favorite method espoused by the teacher or the school. The method probably involved steps like "define the problem," "gather information," "identify options for solving it," "select the best option," and maybe "take action" based on the solution you chose. They might have also included an extra step, such as evaluating results to see whether the solution actually worked.

Here's a trick question: *When did you last use that five-step problem-solving process?* Is that really how your mind works? Do you sit down and say, "Now I'm going to solve Problem X. Let's see, the first step is to define problem X"?

It's very likely that Problem X is interwoven with various other things you have to think about and decide on; it's less likely that you get to attack it in a step-wise process. You may have been thinking about various aspects of it well before you officially declared it a problem. You may have partly solved it intuitively even before you began to deal with it consciously. Problem solving tends to be a much messier process than we'd like to believe. However, understanding that intrinsic messiness, and using it to our advantage, can make us much more skillful problem solvers than if we tried to follow a formal step-wise method every time.

Not many years ago, as I was pondering the problem-solving process for the umpteenth time, I had a sudden realization—sort of a "blinding flash of the obvious." I'd been teaching and touting the standard problem-solving process for decades (I used a six-step model), and I *realized it's not actually the way I problem solve.* Nor is it the way most skillful problem solvers whom I've observed problem solve.

> *Effective problem solving is not a series of steps; it's an adaptive process that unfolds based on the nature of the problem that's being solved.*

I began thinking more carefully about the flow of mental processes that come into play in various kinds of decision-making and problem-solving situations. I finally found myself pushed to the conclusion that the "five-step process" we all had to learn was basically a convenient intellectual fiction—something we tell ourselves in order to support our belief in a logical, rational world. When you give up on the idea that all thinking has to be logical and rational, not only do you have more fun, but you become a much better problem solver.

A more accurate description of the flow of mental processes involved in a typical problem-solving experience might look something like the following:

- You sense that something's wrong—you become aware of the symptoms; or someone tells you something's wrong; or several people agree to declare something "a problem." You bring the problem to a conscious level—yours or that of a group of people who are concerned about it.
- You get more information—you ask a few questions; explore the symptoms further; what, if anything, has been done so far to try to solve it?
- You reflect on some possible solutions—what actions might possibly solve it? Which options seem most promising? Are there options no one has yet thought of?

- You get more information—how did this problem get to be a problem? What caused it or allowed it to happen? Who's affected by the problem? Who has a stake in seeing it solved? Are there people who don't want to see it solved?
- You search more vigorously for options; you, and others if it's a team problem-solving effort, put on your explorer hats and stretch the boundaries of what might be possible. You try to get a fresh perspective; look for more connections and possibilities.
- You gather more information—what are the limits or constraints you have to consider? What kinds of options are ruled out once you understand the nature of the problem in more detail? Has anyone else solved this kind of problem, or some variation of it? If so, what can we learn from their experience?
- You restate the problem—based on a clearer understanding of the situation, the possibilities, and the constraints, now you have a more concise understanding of the outcome that's desired.
- "Et cetera, et cetera, et cetera," as the King of Siam liked to say. Eventually you work your way to a solution.

At first glance, this hypothetical flow of mental process might sound confused and disorganized—and in a way, it is. The sample process just described doesn't follow the standard five-step recipe we all learned, but it's actually more like the natural process by which we move from problems to solutions. It's what information scientists call a *heuristic thinking process:* what you do at each point in the process will depend on everything you've learned so far.

Heuristic thinking, in addition to being a very natural thinking process, is a fairly clever way to think. We think of it as "seat-of-the-pants" or "trial-by-error" learning. We can define it as:

> *Heuristic thinking: arriving at a result by intelligent guesswork rather than by following a pre-established formula.*

For the technically minded, heuristic thinking can be contrasted with *algorithmic thinking,* which follows a fixed, step-wise process. An algorithm is a step-wise formula, with pre-defined branching procedures.

Suppose we think of solving any problem as a *learning process;* you "learn" your way to a solution by increasing your understanding at every stage of the journey. Let's call it a "learning journey." Rather than slavishly trying to follow a pre-determined set of steps or an algorithm, we use our natural wisdom—our common sense together with our capacity to learn, discover, and conclude, to navigate from symptoms to solutions. We shift our focus from reliance on the "five steps" to trusting our own natural intelligence.

Heuristic thinking and problem solving don't have to be completely random or instinctive. We can *augment* its natural, exploratory, discovery-based patterns with a conscious process of managing our mental strategies as the problem unfolds before us. One useful way to think about the problem-solving process is by considering the various kinds of mental processes we can engage in along the way to the solution. Let's call these patterns or processes *mindzones.*

A mindzone is a mental "territory"—a place you go in your mind for a particular kind of thinking. Here are five useful mindzones that can come into play when you're in your problem-solving mode:

- *The Neutral Zone.* This is the central playing field for the thinking process where ideas meet, and the place to which participants in a group discussion keep returning to evaluate their progress toward a solution.
- *The End Zone.* This is the goal line—the place we'll be when we have the solution basically scoped out and we're ready to define all the details.
- *The Data Zone.* This is the land of evidence: facts and figures; basic "truths"; logical conclusions we can pretty much depend on; assumptions we agree to make (and test for accuracy); speculations we agree to consider (and test for validity); hypotheses, properly identified (and tested); opinions, properly characterized as opinions; expert judgments; reports we will consider as valid.
- *The Ozone.* This is the "option zone," the "outer space" of thinking, idea generating, brainstorming, and harvesting possible options that might become ingredients for a solution.
- *The Judgment Zone.* This is the place for critical evaluation, where ideas, options, possibilities, and prospective solutions are subject to impartial and impersonal scrutiny. Here judgment is permitted and officially required; the only acceptable activity in this zone is *convergent* thinking.

One reason why so many people are not more skilled in problem solving is that they tend to muddle up their thinking processes by mixing mindzones willy-nilly. Instead of becoming conscious of the process of moving from zone to zone, many people simply wander through the process.

> *"Get your facts straight first. Then you can distort them as much as you please."*
>
> —MARK TWAIN

To paraphrase the Biblical verse, there's a time for judging and a time to refrain from judging; a time to gather evidence and a time to put the evidence to use; a time to consider far-out ideas and a time to come back down to earth and see which ones have promise. Expert problem solvers can typically navigate through these five mindzones with ease and fluency. So can you.

   Vocabulary

As you think about this essay, these definitions may be helpful:
1. **benighted**   unenlightened
2. **augment**   to make greater or larger
3. **convergent**   to come together and unite in a common interest or focus

Discussion Questions

1. Do you agree with Albrecht's definition of a "problem"? How would you define a "problem"? Name a problem you are currently facing and discuss how it might involve something you want.
2. Have you ever been taught the "Five- (or Six or Seven) step" problem solving method? If yes, when was the last time you used it? Did it help you solve the problem? Describe your experience.
3. Have you ever confronted a decision situation that you could not resolve? Why couldn't you decide? What happened as a result?
4. Considering the author's definition of heuristic thinking, do you ever use "intelligent guesswork" when you problem solve? If so, describe a decision you made using this thinking process. If not, how would you apply this mode of thinking to a decision situation you are currently confronting?
5. Using Albrecht's concept of "mind zones," give an example of how you might have used this process in thinking through a decision you made in the last month. What "zone," if any, might be the most difficult for you to navigate?

 Suggestions for Your Journal

What thinking processes do you go through when you are faced with a decision? Do you consider yourself an effective decision maker? In what way? Consider an important decision you will need to make in the near future. Using Albrecht's mindzones process, describe how you will follow his steps to solve the problem. How is this process different from how you have made decisions in the past? Has reading this essay changed your mind about how you make important decisions? How might it be different if you were in a group decision-making experience?

Unit Summary

The writers in this unit describe the learning process from many different perspectives. Because learning is the central mission of the college experience, understanding learning is essential to college success. The readings in this unit have offered an overview of different learning approaches from which every student can benefit.

■ Summary Questions

1. What specific approaches to learning do the readings in this unit describe? Which ones would you like to experience in more depth? Why?
2. What tasks or strategies described in the readings could you adopt to improve the learning skills needed in your academic work?
3. What implications for your own lifelong learning are suggested in these readings?

■ Suggested Writing Assignments

1. Write a brief essay describing the way you learn best. Do you have a preferred learning style? Is college "learning" what you expected? In what ways?
2. Select one reading in this unit and write about how your personal experience has been the same as or different from what the writer describes.
3. Has the use of the Internet influenced how you learn? If so, in what ways?

■ Suggested Readings

Brown, Neil, and Stuart Keeley. *Asking the Right Questions: A Guide to Critical Thinking*. Upper Saddle River, NJ: Prentice Hall, 2001.

Gardner Howard. *Multiple Intelligences*. New York: Basic Books, 1993.

Goleman, Daniel. *Emotional Intelligence*. New York: Bantam, 2006.

Kolb Learning Styles. http://www.businessballs.com/kolblearningstyles.htm.

Unit 5

What About Technology?

The information revolution has changed people's perception of wealth. We originally said that land was wealth. Then we thought it was industrial production. Now we realize it is intellectual capital.

—WALTER WRISTON, FORMER CEO OF CITICORP

Higher education is in transition, and technology is a major force driving the change. Some colleges are expanding beyond their traditional buildings and campuses into cyberspace in order to reach out to students who want or need to study in nontraditional ways. Technology will not replace colleges, but it is already affecting how we learn. In the next decades, many new information technologies will emerge. As a result, students will experience new and exciting methods of teaching and learning.

As you begin your college experience, you will witness many of these changes. How you adapt to and learn about technology in college will affect how well you later adapt and learn in the workplace. Information technology is changing the nature of jobs and how workers do those jobs. It is projected that by 2015, 90 percent of all workers will be affected.

This unit touches on some interesting facts, applications, and opinions about technology and the influence it has on our lives. Starting with a comparison between imaginary classes—one at the University of Bologna in 1349 and a second taught via distance learning from a yacht off Vancouver Island in 2003—A. W. Bates and Gary Poole sketch some foreseeable challenges of new educational technology. Don Tapscott talks about the development, and some of the hazards, of the emerging social aspects of the Internet, focusing on Facebook and its creator Mark Zuckerberg. Leonard Pitts, Jr. comments on the changes brought about by new technologies by noting some things we have lost in the exchange, and the unit closes with some advice on writing effective e-mail.

The Challenge of Technology

A.W. Bates and Gary Poole

A. W. Bates is director of distance education and technology in the Department of Continuing Studies at the University of British Columbia in Vancouver. Gary Poole is director of the Centre for Teaching and Academic Growth at the University of British Columbia. This reading is from their book *Effective Teaching with Technology in Higher Education,* published in 2003.

Imagine the medieval city of Bologna in 1349. At the university, Professor Ricardus Angelicus is giving a lecture on the differences between the four epistles in the Christian Bible's New Testament, drawing especially on the work of St. Augustine and Thomas Aquinas. The lecture is entirely in Latin. He depends very heavily on the manuscripts collected by the library of the University of Bologna.

Indeed, the session is called a *lecture*, which stems from the Latin word for a "reading," because it is mainly based on readings in Latin from ancient handwritten manuscripts. The philosophical position underpinning the teaching methodology is scholasticism, "training the students to consider a text according to certain pre-established officially approved criteria which are painstakingly and painfully drilled into them" (Manguel 117).

The professor is moving on to the University of Paris at the end of the semester, then will return to his position as a senior administrator in the Vatican in Rome. Later he becomes Bishop of Chichester in England.

There are nine students in the class, and they come from many parts of Europe. They pay a fee directly to the professor. Most are younger sons of nobility or high-ranking clergy, although one or two may also be sons of wealthy merchants. Most are destined for careers in the church or law.

Students are given oral examinations by the professor. The examination contains mainly factual questions around interpretations of the Bible. There is a heavy emphasis on memorization and *rote* learning, as many of the manuscripts are unique or very rare. Also the Roman Catholic Church is anxious that religious texts are interpreted "correctly."

Now let's switch to a small yacht just off the coast of Vancouver Island in Canada in 2003. Roger Boshier, a professor at the University of British Columbia, is online to graduate students in the Masters of Educational Technology program being offered jointly with Tec de Monterrey in Mexico. He is discussing with his students in an online forum the impact of globalization and information technology on national cultures. Roger has been directed to an online article by one of the Australian students and is commenting on it. The session is in English but includes several students from Latin America. An instructor from Tec de Monterrey is offering a similar online discussion forum at the

110

same time in Spanish. Students who are bilingual often switch between the two forums.

The philosophical position underpinning the teaching methodology is *constructivism*, whereby students are encouraged to construct their own meaning through discussion and reflection.

Roger has to return to Vancouver the next day, as he also teaches several oncampus courses, although most of these also have an online component. He will be taking a *sabbatical* next year in New Zealand but plans to continue to teach the Masters in Educational Technology course while away.

He has twenty students in his seminar group, and they are from all over the world. Most are working professionals: teachers in secondary schools or instructors in universities and colleges. Most already have a graduate degree but are taking this program because of the rapid changes occurring in the field. . . .

Which of these two *scenarios* matches most closely your own learning experiences at your university or college? Which of these scenarios would most suit your comfort level (assuming you know Latin)? If Rip van Winkle awoke from his sleep of eight hundred years, would he feel out of place in your typical university or college class?

Our point is not that universities today are old-fashioned. Much has changed and more is changing. We are not suggesting either that newer is better. Does the "modern" scenario challenge the basic values and tenets of higher education? We don't think so. But the two scenarios do indicate the close interrelationship between technological development and the practice of teaching in universities.

We deliberately pitched our first scenario just before the invention of the Gutenberg press. The invention of the mechanical printing press was a product of changing times but further became a major influence on change in society. Information technology, and particularly the Internet, is a similar consequence and cause of major change in our society, including how we teach and learn.

We believe that technology has an important place in university and college teaching, but it needs to be used with care and discrimination. The question then is not, Should we use technology? The questions are: In what contexts and for what purposes is technology appropriate for learning and teaching? What do we need to do to ensure that when we use technology for learning and teaching purposes we use it effectively? . . .

Over the last ten years the Internet has become a major influence on a wide range of activities. It is now used for communications (e-mail, World Wide Web), banking, hotel and travel reservations, entertainment, news, and a host of other applications. The Internet is now an essential feature of work, leisure, and study for many people, and its influence is likely to grow as more and more people are able to access the technology on a global basis.

Its impact on education and training has been as great as on any other area. Web sites provide instant access to data from active volcanoes, Web cameras record events as they happen, and Web databases provide access to a multitude of academic resources. More online courses are becoming available.

Students need to learn how to use technology to seek, organize, analyze, and apply information appropriately. It will become increasingly difficult to accept someone as being fully educated if they do not know how to use the Internet to communicate with other professionals, if they do not know how to find Web sites that will provide relevant and reliable information within their field of study, or if they do not know how to develop their own multimedia reports for communicating their knowledge or research. Therefore, we cannot ignore technology in learning and teaching. The best way to help students understand the strengths—and weaknesses—of technology in their field of study is to use it in teaching.

One frequent criticism of the use of technology in teaching is that we are being driven by a technological *imperative*: We have to use technology because of a blind belief that it is good for us. If we don't agree to the use of technology, we will be considered out of date and may lose our credibility.

Those who challenge the technological imperative do so from a variety of perspectives. Some ask, *What is technology doing to our ways of thinking and understanding*? Those who ask this question usually answer that technology weakens our ability to think rationally or logically. Others go further and suggest that the pressure to use technology in education is a conspiracy by multinational companies and big business to sell technology and hook young people forever into being technology consumers.

Some supporters of the use of technology in teaching believe that there are important educational benefits in using technology but recognize the pressure, especially on senior management, to be fashionable and to have the latest "toys," and they lever that pressure to win support for their technology-based teaching initiatives.

Finally, many postsecondary teachers are aware that whereas technology ought to be able to help them in teaching students, their knowledge of technology is often less than that of their students, and in particular they are unsure of how best to use it to achieve their teaching goals.

Those who believe that technology can play a valuable role in teaching and learning, understand the "technological imperative" arguments. They accept that some of these arguments are valid, but believe that they are insufficient for a blanket denial of the use of technology. We recognize that there is a great deal of hyperbole and exaggeration about the benefits of technology in education. There are pressures from the commercial sector to use technologies for teaching that are based on profit, not educational benefits. And without major changes in the way we work, technology will be time-consuming and require an unreasonable amount of dedication to learn new skills.

Nevertheless, such arguments should not blind us to the genuine benefits technology can bring when used wisely. Pressures for change on the university and college from both within and outside require us to look afresh at how students learn and how teaching is organized and delivered if quality is to be maintained or even improved.

Work Cited

Manguel, Alberto. *A History of Reading*. New York: HarperCollins, 1996.

 ## Vocabulary

As you think about this essay, these definitions may be helpful to you:
1. **rote**   to learn "by rote" is to learn with the use of memory but little intelligence or understanding.
2. **constructivism**   a philosophy (or system of thinking) in which meaning is not inherent in a word or object but is attached to that word or object ("constructed") by the author or creator
3. **sabbatical**   short for "sabbatical year"; a leave of absence from regular teaching duties, often with pay, granted to professors usually every seventh year, for rest, travel, or research
4. **scenario**   a possible course of action, usually imagined or projected
5. **imperative**   necessary, not to be avoided

 ## Discussion Questions

1. Compare the two scenarios that these authors use to open their essay. What are the major points of difference? Of similarity?
2. How do Bates and Poole feel about the use of up-to-date technology in college teaching? Do you agree?
3. What benefits do Bates and Poole identify for the use of technology in the classroom?

 ## Suggestions for Your Journal

It may not be possible for you to imagine yourself back in the University of Bologna in 1349, but try to imagine what it was like to attend school before the advent of the personal computer. If you are 18 or so, talk first with someone old enough to have attended school before, say, 1970. Would you have preferred his or her classroom environment to the one you have now, or do you prefer school in the 21st century?

Have you decided on a future career? For the purpose of your journal, select one and discuss some of the ways that, in your view, college should prepare you for the technological demands of that profession.

A Generation Bathed in Bits

Don Tapscott

Canadian Don Tapscott is chairman of the nGenera Innovation Network and an adjunct professor of management at the Joseph L. Rotman School of Management at the University of Toronto. He has authored or coauthored thirteen books on the application of technology in business and society. His most recent book, entitled *Grown Up Digital— How the Net Generation Is Changing Your World* (from which this excerpt is taken) was released in 2009 and is based upon a research study of over 11,000 young people. It examines how the "net generation" is changing the world.

In January 2004, Mark Zuckerberg had a real-life version of a common nightmare. He was facing his first round of exams at Harvard and he hadn't studied or read anything the professor had assigned for a first-year art history course called Rome of Augustus. Zuckerberg hadn't even gone to class during the term. He was too busy creating a cool computer program called Facebook that would help students get to know one another and share information. Now, a few days before the exam, Zuckerberg was, in his words, "just completely screwed."

But he had an idea, straight out of twenty-first century computer science. He created a Web site and put pictures from the course on it, with a little discussion beside each picture. Maybe the other students could help out by filling in the blanks. Within 24 hours, Zuckerberg's classmates helped out all right, with notes so cogent that everyone, Zuckerberg included, passed the test with flying colors. And according to Zuckerberg, the professor didn't see it as cheating. Instead, he was "really pleased" to see the students collaborate in such a creative fashion.

After acing his art history test, Zuckerberg returned to his school project, Facebook, which has since become one of the most *ubiquitous* social networking sites in the world; on it, friends and acquaintances keep up with each other's news. Now, with more than 70 million active users and a market value estimated at a couple of billion dollars or more, Facebook is a great example of how this generation uses and revolutionizes technology. They want to be connected with friends and family all the time, and they use technology—from mobile phones to social networks—to do it. So when the TV is on, they don't sit and watch, as their parents did. TV is background *Muzak* for them, to which they listen while they check out information and talk to friends online or via text message. Their mobile phones aren't just useful communication devices, they are a vital connection to friends. And now that the "phones" are increasingly connected to the Internet, the Net Geners can stay connected with friends online wherever they go.

The Net Generation uses digital technology in a very different way than Boomers do. The Net Geners have developed different reflexes and behaviors which they use when they are on their mobile phones or are surfing the Internet. But the differences don't stop there.

This generation is revolutionizing the very nature of the Internet itself. Zuckerberg's Facebook is just one example of the popular social networking sites that are turning the Internet into a place to share and connect, a kind of cyber community center. Net Geners are transforming the Internet from a place where you mainly find information to a place where you share information, collaborate on projects of mutual interest, and create new ways to solve some of our most pressing problems.

One way that they are doing this is by creating content—in the form of their own blogs, or in combination with other people's content. In this way, the Net Generation is democratizing the creation of content, and this new paradigm of communication will have a revolutionary impact on everything it touches—from music and movies, to political life, business, and education.

They might just be the generation to activate that slogan that Boomers chanted in their youth—Power to the People. It can happen now because the Web 2.0 makes it easier for ordinary people to organize themselves, instead of having to do so under the control of hierarchical, often authoritarian, organizations. Instead of being just small cogs in a large and impersonal machine, they now may be finding the power to become autonomous entities unto themselves.

But this sunny story may have a dark cloud hanging over it, one that few Net Geners have yet seen. They are sharing intimate details about themselves, lavishly illustrated by pictures that might come back to haunt them once they are seeking public office, or a high-ranking job in a public corporation. This generation is giving up its privacy, not only because of the social networks, but because they are happily answering questions from the corporate world about their private lives. George Orwell, as it turns out, was only partly right when he wrote *1984*. It's not Big Brother who is watching you just yet; it is Little Brother—your friendly marketer. And this is only the beginning. We appear to be moving into a world in which you will be connected to everyone all the time wherever you go, from the little device in the palm of your hand. Will that finally signal the end of privacy?

Technology is influencing the way kids think and behave, but it's a two-way street—the way kids think and behave is influencing and shaping the Internet itself. In the twenty-first century, knowledge is flowing more freely than ever, thanks to the Internet, but the Internet's true potential was not realized until young people started using computers. Now they're helping to transform it into something new—Web 2.0, the living Web, the Hypernet, the active Web, the read-write Web. Call it what you like—this ain't your daddy's Internet. It's become a global, active, networked computer that allows everyone not only to contribute but to change the very nature of the beast.

Just as the Web was beginning to change into a platform to contribute and collaborate, Mark Zuckerberg entered Harvard University. A few weeks after passing his exam on Augustus in Rome, Zuckerberg launched Facebook from his college dorm. He moved to California that summer, intending to return to Harvard to complete his degree in computer science. Instead, he dropped out to become full-time CEO of Facebook, the archetypal social network for friends. It wasn't a public space like MySpace, where you can connect with 1,000 of your "best friends." Nor was it a chat room, where you were supposed to be interested in conversing with an anonymous person called Mooselips or Cyberchick.

This was a place where you could be yourself, a real person, and feel free to talk with your close friends or your wider circle of friends. You could show them pictures, tell jokes, make plans, and do many of the things that friends do together. Facebook allowed you to create an online community for friends. You could also shut out people you didn't know, or didn't want to have in your circle of friends. It's a community independent of time and space. You can contribute whenever you can, from wherever you are.

This rise of social networking sites could be the new grid for the Internet. It could have a significant impact on everything the Net Generation touches, from games to music to global civic action. The Net Geners are just starting to use the tremendous power of this digital tool. Yet this great new opportunity also raises a significant new challenge—for privacy, the right to be left alone. Facebook is beginning to grapple with this challenge, but I don't think the Net Geners fully understand the long-term consequences of sharing intimate information about themselves with the world. But in other respects, I believe that the young people who have grown up immersed in these very technologies that are presenting such a challenge are especially equipped to navigate this new terrain. There is strong evidence that as their mastery of the Internet evolves, they will be able to adjust and handle whatever comes along.

Vocabulary

As you think about this essay, these definitions may be helpful to you.

1. **ubiquitous**   existing or being everywhere at the same time; constantly encountered

2. **Muzak**   Sometimes called "elevator music," referring to instrumental arrangements of popular music designed for playing as background sound in shopping malls, telephone systems (while the caller is on hold), and other places where some gentle "white noise" can be welcome. Also frequently applied as a generic and often derogatory term for any form of Easy Listening music

3. **Boomers**   Short for "Baby Boomers," the generation of Americans born after World War II who reached maturity in the 1960s–70s and now are retiring from careers. In this essay they are contrasted with the Net Generation educated after the rise of the Internet.

Discussion Questions

1. In what sense is "the Net Generation . . . democratizing the creation of content"? To answer this, consider who used to control the content of public discussions before the development of the Internet.
2. In what way is "your friendly marketer" (a sarcastic phrase) like the Big Brother of George Orwell's *1984*? How much do marketing professionals know about you just by the ways you shop and order items on the Internet? Is there anything sinister (i.e., unfriendly) in their marketing techniques?
3. Author Tapscott claims that people in your generation "are sharing intimate details about themselves, lavishly illustrated by pictures that might come back to haunt them once they are seeking public office, or a high-ranking job in a public corporation." Is he right? What can you do to avoid this behavior?

 ## Suggestions for Your Journal

Tapscott sees the Net Generation as a possible force for "global civic action." Can you give examples that make this claim plausible? As a member of your cyber generation, you have greater access than any generation before you to publishing and publicizing your opinions for an audience that is literally worldwide. With very little difficulty or cost, you can establish yourself as a "blogger" and comment on just about anything you like—or don't like. (Libel is still not allowed!)

Losing Stuff Has Never Been So Sad

Leonard Pitts, Jr.

Leonard Pitts, Jr. is a columnist for the *Miami Herald*. He won the Pulitzer Prize for commentary in 2004. He is the author of *Becoming Dad: Black Men and the Journey to Fatherhood* (1999) and *Before I Forget* (2009), his first novel.

Our subject today: the end of the physical world.

Which is, yes, a tad hyperbolic, but it contains a nugget of truth. Bear with me.

Last week, I fell into a conversation with a fellow named Bud and shared something that has been rattling around my head for a while now: a sense that, as intellectual properties become ever more digitized, we are seeing the appearance of, well . . . "things." Physical artifacts that once were as much a part of every day as ketchup stains on your tie are now disappearing inside hard drives.

Bud, a musician, knew exactly what I meant. He used to play with a band. Now he has a band, if he so desires, inside his keyboard.

But it's not just live music. It's recorded music. I have a huge collection of CDs and vinyl albums that these days is used mainly for décor; when I want tunes, I turn to my iPod.

And it's photography. We used to have these things called snapshots, but no longer. Photos are digitized now.

And it's books, where you can instantly, cheaply download that novel or biography right to your reading device.

And it is, of course, newspapers. Enough said.

Nor is it only the artifacts themselves we lose. We also lose the factories that used to make them, the trucks that used to ship them, the vendors that used to sell them. I want to write a column about this, I told Bud, but I'm not sure how to frame it. If I lament the change, isn't that a bit like lamenting seasons and tides? Isn't it futile? Time marches, whether you lament it or not.

But I find I can't celebrate it, either. So I suppose I am here simply to bear witness for the world that now passes, a world where, when you bought or made something, you received for your effort some tangible physical evidence of what you did. Now you just get an electronic tone telling you the transfer is complete.

Which is, granted, easier and more convenient, and if you are twenty-something, you may wonder what's the fuss, because this is all you've ever known. If, however, you are old enough to remember the old world, you may be like me: constantly marveling at the wonders of the new, yet also left vaguely uneasy by the ease of it. Like you were cheating the universe or putting one over on God.

I think that's how my sister felt the other day when she called and asked me to tape a song and mail it to her. I told her she was showing her age. She asked what I meant. I told her to check her e-mail; the song was already there. Linda was amazed. Next time I'm in town, I'm to show her how I did that.

As it happens, I saw two movies over the weekend: *State of Play* and *The Soloist*, one about a fictional reporter who uncovers a scandal, the other about a real reporter who befriended a mentally ill homeless man. Both films send their heroes out to seek truth, scraping against the hard realities of the real world, shoe leather on concrete, cars rushing past, people right up in your face. And both feature loving, almost sensual shots of the physical product those efforts produce: newspapers.

Fittingly enough, I started work Monday and found the intraoffice message board full of farewell notes from colleagues caught in the last layoff.

"All my best to everyone . . ."
"Keep the faith . . ."
"I walk to the parking lot in tears . . ."

Farewell to co-workers. Farewell to a world that was.

Let me leave you with this: I saw a story in the paper a few days ago that said toymakers expect to have on store shelves "this Christmas" new devices that will allow users to move objects telekinetically, i.e., by concentrating on them. It made me smile for the rude awakening that awaits the twenty-somethings. The old world passes, the new world is born, but the "next" world lies ever in wait. Time marches. And soon enough it will be their turn to bear witness in wonder and in loss.

© THE MIAMI HERALD, 2009.

? | Discussion Questions

1. This brief essay was first published in newspapers which, according to author Pitts, are dying throughout the country. He blames their demise— and the disappearance of CDs, vinyl albums, snapshots, and books, on the public's increased dependence on digital storage and digital communication. Do you agree?

2. Part of the reason, Pitts suggests, to lament the loss of artifacts like the ones he mentions is that when no one buys CDs or vinyl albums, no one any longer has a job making CDs or vinyl albums. He is especially moved by this because of the "goodbye" notes of his friends and colleagues in the newspaper business. But virtually every advance in technology means the death of the older technology that is replaced—as well as the jobs lost from that older technology. As he puts it, "the 'next' world lies ever in wait." What should be done about this, if anything?

Suggestions for Your Journal

Many other social network sites have been developed since the advent of Facebook. Just a year ago (as we are writing in 2009), Twitter became popular and was particularly visible as a new force in politics: Suddenly users could comment almost immediately on the latest appearances by Barack Obama, John McCain, and many other political figures. No doubt other sites will be developed between the time this work is written and the time you read it.

Do you use MySpace, Facebook, Twitter, or any other social networking sites? How often? To do what? On a scale from 1 (low) to 10 (high), how useful would you say that these sites are for you? How reliable? How entertaining? How irritating?

E-mail Etiquette

Emailreplies.com

You probably send most of your e-mails to friends, but increasingly, business correspondence occurs on e-mail. The notes that you send to friends will be different from most of your business correspondence because when writing to someone you know, the relationship that you have with the intended reader governs much about the message: the tone, the jokes, the formality or style, and the like. Notes to businesses—or to your teachers, or to people you need to rely on and don't want to carelessly offend—will be direct and formal, rather than rambling or chatty. Even though you use e-mail as an informal means of communication most of the time, you need to remember to keep a somewhat more controlled style when writing to a business audience.

Here is an edited list of some of the major considerations to keep in mind when using e-mail for a formal purpose. We have adapted this list from one prepared by Emailreplies.com and available online. Here are the most important e-mail etiquette tips that you are likely to use in business correspondence done by e-mail.

1. Be concise and to the point. Do not make an e-mail longer than it needs to be. Remember that reading an e-mail is harder than reading printed communications and a long e-mail can be very discouraging to read.
2. Use proper spelling, grammar, and punctuation. This is important not only because improper spelling, grammar, and punctuation give a bad impression, it is also important for conveying the message properly. E-mails with no periods or commas are difficult to read and can sometimes even change the meaning of the text. If your program has a spell checking option, use it.
3. Make it personal. Not only should the e-mail be personally addressed, it should include customized content. For this reason auto replies are usually not very effective.
4. Answer swiftly. Try to reply within at least 24 hours, and preferably within the same working day. If the e-mail is complicated, just send an e-mail back saying that you have received it and that you will get back to them. This will put the correspondent's mind at rest and usually he or she will be very patient!
5. Do not attach unnecessary files. By sending large attachments you can annoy people and even bring down their e-mail system. Wherever possible try to

compress attachments and only send attachments when they are productive. Moreover, you need to have a good virus scanner in place because your readers will not be very happy if you send them documents full of viruses!

6. Use proper structure and layout. Reading from a screen is more difficult than reading from paper, so the structure and layout are very important for e-mail messages. Use short paragraphs and blank lines between each paragraph. When making points, number them or mark each point as separate to keep the overall relationship of ideas clear.

7. Do not overuse the high priority option. We all know the story of the boy who cried wolf. If you overuse the high priority option, it will lose its function when you really need it. Moreover, even if a mail has high priority, your message will come across as slightly aggressive if you flag it as "high priority".

8. Do not write in CAPITALS. IF YOU WRITE IN CAPITALS IT SEEMS AS IF YOU ARE SHOUTING. This can be highly annoying. For the same reason, avoid using URGENT and IMPORTANT.

9. Include the message thread. When you reply to an e-mail, it is a good practice to include the original e-mail in your reply—in other words click "Reply" instead of "New Mail". People who receive many messages may not remember the context of your reply. Leaving the thread might take a fraction longer in download time, but it will save the recipient much more time and frustration in looking for the related e-mail's in their inbox!

10. Read the e-mail before you send it. Many people don't bother to read their e-mail before they send it out, as can be seen from the many spelling and grammar mistakes contained in e-mails. Apart from this, reading your e-mail through the eyes of the recipient will help you send a more effective message and avoid misunderstandings and inappropriate comments.

11. Be careful using "Reply to All." Only use Reply to All if you really need your message to be seen by each person who received the original message.

12. Take care with abbreviations and emoticons. Avoid abbreviations such as BTW (by the way) and LOL (laugh out loud). The recipient might not be aware of the meanings of these abbreviations and, especially in business e-mails, these are generally not appropriate. The same goes for emoticons, such as the smiley :-). If you are not sure whether your recipient knows what it means, it is better not to use it.

13. Don't get fancy with formatting. Remember that when you use formatting in your e-mails, the sender might not be able to view it, or might see different fonts than you had intended. When using colors, use a color that is easy to read on the background.

14. Do not forward chain letters. It is a safe bet that almost all of them are hoaxes. Just delete the letters as soon as you receive them.

15. Do not copy a message or attachment belonging to another user without permission of the originator. If you do not ask permission first, you might be infringing on copyright laws.

16. Do not use e-mail to discuss confidential information. Sending an e-mail is like sending a postcard. If you don't want your e-mail to be displayed on a bulletin board, don't send it. Moreover, never make any libelous, sexist, or racially discriminating comments in e-mails, even if they are meant to be a joke.
17. Use a meaningful subject. In the "subject" line, try to use language that is meaningful to the recipient as well as yourself. This usually means being specific about the subject, not general or abstract.
18. Avoid long sentences.
19. Use the "cc:" field sparingly. Try not to use the cc: field unless all recipients know why they are receiving a copy of the message.

From www.emailreplies.com

Discussion Questions

1. Do you have any additional suggestions about proper etiquette on e-mail?
2. Most of these suggestions apply to your writing in any forum. Which ones can you safely ignore when writing to your friends (or BFFS)?

Suggestions for your Journal

Do you get much "junk" mail on your computer? Review the "spam" that makes its way into your inbox in a week, and analyze it into the kinds of communications represented. How much is merely a waste of time? Is some of it offensive? Some comes from your friends who think you will enjoy the same "humor" that they like. Some may be actually dangerous to your files or your identity. What can you do to be sure that you are not sending along unwelcome stuff to your correspondents?

Unit Summary

The readings in this unit have covered a wide variety of topics and ideas about technology and how it is changing our school, work, and personal lives.

■ Summary Questions

1. Compare the library in your high school or community with your college library. Which offers the better access to technology? Which is easier to use? What changes might you suggest for your college library?
2. How has technology influenced your role as a student? How is it different from past generations' experiences?
3. What skills described in this unit's readings can you learn while in college?

■ Suggested Writing Assignments

1. A major blackout in the northeastern United States showed how dependent Americans are on electricity for their technology. Write an essay in which you assess this dependency: Is it tolerable in a risky world?
2. Visualize the world 25 years from now and write an essay about how you think technology will have changed the college campus and its students' ways of learning.

■ Suggested Readings

Bauerlein, Mark. *The Dumbest Generation*. New York: Jeremy P. Tarcher/Penguin, 2008.
Nye, David. *Technology Matters: Questions to Live With*. Cambridge, MA: MIT Press, 2007.
Prensky, Mark. *On the Horizon*, NBC University Press, Vol. 9, No. 5, October 2001.

Unit 6

What Are My Rights and Responsibilities as a Student?

The freedom from work, from restraint, from accountability, wondrous in its inception, becomes banal and counterfeit. Without rules there is no way to say no, and worse, no way to say yes.

—THOMAS FARBER

In many ways, the modern university forms its own community. Like a small town, a university or a college often has its own residential areas, business centers, spaces designed for sports and other recreation, food services including "fast food" options and some that are fancier, centers of government, a hospital or health service center, a security office, and so on. The resemblance is not limited to physical settings, because comparable lines of authority and responsibility can be found in both civil governments (as in villages or towns) and university structures. Like cities, colleges and universities have the authority to establish their own laws—codes of acceptable behavior—and penalties for violating those codes. As well, the state and federal laws apply both to cities and to colleges located within a given state or nation. Each of us is familiar with such laws—those against violence, theft of property, indecent or threatening behavior, excessive noise or other activities that constitute a public nuisance, and the like.

Because many new college students are near or at the age when civil laws apply to them in a new way, they need to keep in mind that the older we are, the higher the level of responsibility for our actions the law is likely to expect of us. Some behavior that may be cute from a 2-year-old and merely annoying from a 10-year-old might well be illegal from someone 18 or older. Moreover, the cities and states we live in give us greater freedom when we reach 18 or 21, and with that freedom comes a higher degree of accountability. If you drove your parents' car illegally when you were 13, your parents were usually held responsible (though they may have, in turn, imposed their own regulations on you!), but if at 18 you drive illegally (under the influence of alcohol, for example, or faster than the speed limit allows), it is your own license that will be affected, and your own record that starts accumulating.

Other laws relate specifically to the people who make up the university community. These are generally developed, implemented, and enforced within the university itself. Such laws authorized by a university community usually include the expectation that students, faculty, and staff members will obey and respect the civil laws of their city, state, and nation, but they go further as well. Because a university has special characteristics, its code of prohibited behavior will take its special characteristics into account. We begin Unit 6 with an essay about the special characteristics that make a university unique, "On Academic Freedom" by Halverson and Carter. With that essay to establish the context, the remaining essays in this unit take up the question of your rights and responsibilities as a student member of your college community. Minnick considers one of the ethical dimensions of your role as a student. Like many ethical questions, these essays raise issues that are perennially debatable, for which you may find only provisional answers. C. L. Lindsay discusses how some specific legislation affects you as a student. Researchers from the Carey School of Business at Arizona State use some basic principles of their discipline to analyze the effects of cheating in an academic context. All these topics are important in a university setting, where the search for truth is constant and the searchers are continually hopeful of better, clearer, wiser answers to such age-old questions as "What is the best way to proceed?" and "How can we make a stronger community?" Finally, Menager and Paulos offer twelve guidelines for avoiding plagiarism.

On Academic Freedom

William H. Halverson and James R. Carter

William H. Halverson is associate dean emeritus of University College at The Ohio State University. After completing academic studies focused on philosophy, Halverson authored well-known textbooks for college philosophy classes. More recently, he has translated several books from Norwegian into English. James R. Carter, also a philosopher by education, is assistant dean of the College of Arts and Sciences at the University of Louisville. In the following essay, Halverson and Carter define the notion of academic freedom, which is at the heart of a university as established and perpetuated in Western cultures.

People create institutions to serve a variety of purposes that they regard as important. They establish hospitals in order to care for the sick, retail stores to sell goods to consumers, banks to manage transactions involving the exchange of money, radio and TV stations to provide various sorts of program materials to the public, and so on. An institution is a means to an end, a way of doing something that society has decided needs to be done.

The Purpose of a University

What, then, is the purpose for which society has created universities? Why do people spend millions of dollars to build buildings—libraries, laboratories, classrooms, and the like—and additional millions to enable people like us (students, teachers) to occupy those buildings? What is a university for? What is its mission?

Try this: *the unique mission of a university is the discovery, preservation, and dissemination of truth.*

The discovery of truth: that is the heart and soul of the university. You must not think of professors and students as, respectively, those who already know the truth and those who do not. Professors have an edge on students by virtue of having been at the business of learning a bit longer than most students—but they would be the first to tell you, if they are candid, that even after many years of diligent study, their knowledge of the truth is limited, fragmentary, and mixed with error.

Our Common Ignorance

The professor's problem is the problem of human beings generally: we can rarely be certain that what we have learned, what we believe, is the *truth*. For many thousands of years, scholars believed that the earth was flat, and that it was stationary in the center of the universe, and that the sun, the planets, and the stars revolved around it. These beliefs, we now know with a high degree of certainty, were in error. We may be inclined to laugh at those silly people of yesterday who held such childish views. But let us not laugh too loudly, for it is highly likely that among the beliefs you and I hold today are some that will appear as foolish to future generations as the flat-earth theory does to us. Truth and error do not wear labels that enable us easily to distinguish between them.

Our situation, then, may be described as follows. We (that is, all people) hold many opinions, some of which are probably true and some of which are probably false. In addition, there are many matters about which we are totally ignorant, and about which we therefore have no opinions at all. Our task, if we wish to know the truth, is to rid ourselves so far as possible of both ignorance (no opinions) and error (false opinions), to exchange ignorance and error for the truth.

Seeking the Truth

How does one go about this? How does one attempt to determine the truth or falsity of any assertion? Clearly, one must look to the evidence that appears to be relevant to the truth or falsity of that assertion. *Paradoxically, the surest way to establish the truth of an assertion is to try to disprove it.* If there is some evidence in support of an assertion, and if nobody can find any evidence against it after making a reasonable effort to do so, then there is at least some reason to believe that the assertion may be true. Until, of course, some contrary evidence turns up, in which case one has to start all over again.

Thus we arrive at the following *axiom*: one who desires to know the truth concerning any matter must be persuaded by the evidence, and by the evidence alone. Anything or anybody who attempts to compel a conclusion based on anything other than the evidence is to that extent an enemy of truth.

Academic Freedom

Academic freedom is the opportunity to hold opinions based on the best evidence one has and to speak those opinions without fear of reprisal. Academic freedom means free and open discussion, a liberty to read what you want, to debate any issue, to defend new views and reinterpret or criticize old ones in an open forum.

Academic freedom can exist only when two conditions are met. First, it can exist only in a community of open and intelligent individuals who recognize that in principle every legitimate question deserves an answer, and that the legitimacy of question and answer cannot merely be assumed but must be shown capable of withstanding criticism. Second, academic freedom requires that this community make truth its common purpose, and free and open discussion the means to it. Unless both conditions are met, any freedom that there is will be purely accidental, and not very secure.

It is therefore an essential part of this idea to promote and provide for the intellectual development of every member of the academic community. In this community, it is not only those who have already cultivated a high degree of intellectual understanding who have a place. There must also be room for those who are just beginning their intellectual development. Students in each new generation must be allowed their skepticism; they must have time to examine and criticize even the most fundamental, most widely held views. But they in turn must be open to criticism and direction from their teachers and peers.

How does this notion of academic freedom affect your life? The university's need to maintain academic freedom means that *your* freedom to inquire is essential. You cannot be free if there is prejudice in the academic community. The idea of academic freedom requires that the individuals in the university actively help one another through the basic intellectual tactic of challenge and response. In his essay *On Liberty*, John Stuart Mill reminds us of this, and of the unique mission of an academic community, when he writes, "Complete liberty of contradicting and disproving our opinion, is the very condition which justifies us in assuming its truth. . . ."

Enemies of Academic Freedom

Anyone or anything that tends to inhibit free inquiry and discussion concerning any matter, or that attempts to compel a conclusion based on anything other than the relevant evidence, is by definition an enemy of academic freedom. And there are, unfortunately, many such enemies.

Some of these enemies are purely internal, within the individual. They can be rooted out only by great effort on the part of that individual.

One of these is *fear*. The most comfortable opinions to hold are those that we have held the longest, and so we fear the discomfort of abandoning long-held opinions. The most comfortable opinions to hold are those that are widely held by those whose esteem we crave, and so we fear to adopt opinions that we know will be unpopular. A sage once said, "I never learned anything of importance without feeling a sense of loss because of the old and familiar but mistaken view that had to be abandoned." But we are human, and we fear such loss—even though it be for the sake of truth.

Sheer laziness is an enemy of academic freedom. It is easier, it takes less effort, simply to adopt a view that one has heard expressed by someone else than to study the evidence and draw one's own conclusion. But the easy way, unfortunately, is not the best way, for it gives us no basis for distinguishing between opinions that are true and those that are false.

Undue respect for tradition is yet another internal enemy of academic freedom. Indeed, the opinions of one's forebears deserve considerable respect, for they represent the accumulated wisdom of many generations. Still we must not be bound by them, and we must be willing to abandon them if the weight of the available evidence suggests that they are mistaken. For we, too, will pass on a fund of accumulated wisdom to the next generation, and those who receive it have a right to expect of us that it will contain relatively more truth and less error than that with which we began.

Perhaps the more obvious enemies of academic freedom are the external enemies. Every one of us is capable of being such an enemy and probably has in fact acted as one at one time or another. If in the course of a discussion one shouts down a would-be participant instead of allowing him or her to speak, one is playing the enemy. The same is true if one heckles, and so prevents from being heard, a speaker who holds views with which one disagrees. An instructor who uses the threat of a bad grade to compel agreement (or the *appearance* of agreement) with his or her own views is violating the academic freedom of students.

The administrator who denies promotion or *tenure* or a salary increase to an instructor because the instructor advocates views with which the administrator disagrees is violating the academic freedom of that instructor. A citizen who demands the ouster of a faculty member on the grounds that he or she holds views that are "dangerous" or "unorthodox" is asking (usually without realizing it) that academic freedom be abolished.

We repeat: anyone or anything that tends to inhibit free inquiry and discussion concerning any matter, or attempts to compel a conclusion based on anything other than the relevant evidence, is by definition an enemy of academic freedom. That academic freedom has so many enemies, both internal and external, underscores the important fact that the pathway to truth is not an easy one to find or to follow.

Academic freedom, then, is by no means a cloak for nonsense. It does not confer approval upon ideas that are *demonstrably* false, unsupported by evidence, or just downright silly. To the contrary: academic freedom makes it more likely that in due course such ideas will be shown up for what they are, and that views that are supported by the evidence—that is, truth—will prevail. In an institution whose business is the discovery, preservation, and *dissemination* of truth, academic freedom is the *sine qua non*—the "without which nothing," the essential condition in the absence of which it would cease to be a university.

James Carter and William Halverson, "On Academic Freedom," reprinted by permission of the author.

 ## Vocabulary

As you think about this essay, these definitions may be helpful to you:
1. **paradoxically**   in a manner seemingly contradictory to common sense and yet perhaps true
2. **axiom**   a fundamental notion or idea that is assumed to be true
3. **tenure**   used within universities, this term denotes an earned privilege of assured continued employment following a long period—usually seven years—of probation during which a faculty member is evaluated on teaching ability, research productivity, and community service
4. **demonstrably**   capable of being proved, either logically or by reference to the real world
5. **dissemination**   dispersal; thus, universities are said here to exist for spreading the truth (by teaching and publishing, for example), not hiding it

Discussion Questions

1. Identify and explain the paradox in the statement "The surest way to establish the truth of an assertion is to try to disprove it."
2. What, according to Halverson and Carter, are the two necessary conditions without which academic freedom cannot exist?
3. Halverson and Carter argue that "one who desires to know the truth concerning any matter must be persuaded by the evidence, and by the evidence alone." What else are people persuaded by?
4. What, according to Halverson and Carter, are the enemies of academic freedom?
5. How, according to Halverson and Carter, should we regard the opinions we have received from people we respect?

Suggestions for Your Journal

Fear, laziness, and undue respect for tradition—have you ever struggled with these internal enemies of academic freedom? Write a journal entry in which you select one of these and advise a younger friend how to deal with them successfully.

Academic freedom seems to be in conflict with the idea of majority rule. Do you agree? Why or why not?

How does the university differ from other institutions that seem to be, or ought to be, concerned about the truth—churches, for example, or the federal government?

Ideas as Property

Thomas L. Minnick

Thomas L. Minnick, an English teacher who admits to having graded more than 25,000 English composition papers, has served as an expert witness and researcher on issues relating to intellectual property and plagiarism in cases tried in New York, Ohio, and California. In this essay he emphasizes the positive value of ideas and other intellectual creations as property and draws attention to the fact that as property, under the law, ideas can be stolen or mistreated with serious consequences for the thief.

The idea of "property"—that is, something owned by one person or group and therefore *not* owned by anyone else—is among the oldest, most widespread notions that humans share. Even cultures that believe that all things are owned jointly and equally by all members of the society (usually a tribe or clan) also believe that no single individual can claim ownership of those things. For example, because they believe that the land belongs to all, they also regard any individual who claims to own a part of it as violating the property rights of the group. The notions of "thieves" and "theft" depend on the idea of property, since stealing is defined as the act of taking something that does not belong to the thief. The ownership of property is also one of our most important ideas: many of our laws are based on the principle that three rights guaranteed to individuals living in a society are the right to life, the right to liberty, and the right to own property. Thomas Jefferson, writing the Declaration of Independence, paraphrased this already well-established principle when he identified "life, liberty, and the pursuit of happiness" as three *inalienable* rights of Americans.

We take for granted certain categories of property and, along with them, certain kinds of theft or other violations of property rights. For example, if you (or you and your local lending agency together) own a car, then a person who steals your car, drives it carelessly until the fuel is almost gone, then wrecks it, is unquestionably a thief, because he or she has taken your property without your permission and deprived you of it. Even if the car is returned to you no worse for wear, your rights have been violated, and no reasonable person would disagree that a theft has occurred. The same is true if someone takes your watch, your backpack, your pet, or your jacket identifying your favorite sports team. Furthermore, if someone takes your credit card and buys a substantial amount of merchandise in your name, even if the physical merchandise was never yours (and wouldn't fit you anyway), those items have been stolen from you since your property—in this example, your credit line and the dollars from it that will go to pay the bills—has been taken without your knowledge or approval.

Sometimes it may be less clear that *your ideas are your property*, but that is exactly what they are, and the courts recognize them as such. A specialization in legal studies is the field of intellectual property law, which is based on the premise that an idea belongs to the person who created it, and therefore that any profit, financial or otherwise, derived from that idea also belongs to the originator. The theft of ideas takes many forms. Suppose you design and *patent* an important new drug for the treatment of arthritis and, learning of your research, others market that drug under a different name. Unless you and they have entered into a prior agreement about distributing your drug and sharing the profits, their action violates your rights to your intellectual property. Or again, suppose you write a song, both words and music, and someone else, hearing it, decides the words are effective but that the music is not—then adapts your words to new music of their own. Given adequate evidence to establish your claim of prior ownership, you should be able to show that your intellectual property rights have been violated, and you should further be able to claim a monetary award for damages due to the violation of those rights.

Universities, whose defining reason to exist includes the development and teaching of ideas,[*] have a special stake in the principle that an idea belongs to the person who first conceived it. The integrity of a university depends on a strong belief in this principle, and so universities defend this principle in all they do. For what would a degree from your college or university be worth if students could be caught cheating and nevertheless receive credit for the courses where that offense took place? Undergraduates writing English compositions or research papers for courses in psychology or history, graduate students preparing their master's or doctoral theses, faculty members engaged in leading-edge research—all these participants in the university have a stake in preserving the principle of a creator's right to his or her ideas as property. If they misrepresent themselves as originating ideas that do not belong to them, they are violating the intellectual property rights of others. If they themselves are victims of plagiarists (people who copy their ideas, word-for-word or in paraphrases), then they are deprived of meaningful ownership of what they have created. Even if a particular idea is not worth much money on the open market, the theft of that idea means that the true originator may not receive the *intangible* credit or respect that that idea has earned. So it is essential to the credibility and integrity of a university, and therefore of the degrees that it confers, that it provide the best defense it can for the intellectual property of the members of its community. People who create new ideas should be respected for doing so, and people who claim as theirs those ideas that truly belong to others should be condemned.

Unfortunately, it is part of the nature of ideas that we find it harder to prove ownership of a new idea than, say, of a microwave oven. When someone has stolen your microwave oven, two statements are true: first, you no longer have your microwave, and second, someone else probably does. Ideas are not like that: it is in the nature of ideas that I can tell you my idea, and then you and I both

---

[*]See the essay "On Academic Freedom" by William H. Halverson and James R. Carter earlier in this unit—ED.

will have it. If I tell you my answer to the third question on our final examination in American history, I will know that answer and so will you. For that matter, I could tell my answer to everyone in our class and we all could produce the same answer on request. And so on: I could tell everyone at my college, or everyone in my state, or everyone in our country, or in the world—and yet I would still have the idea in the same way that I did before, while everyone else also now has it. Moreover, if someone steals your microwave oven, you will probably be able to identify it by brand, size, model number, and condition. If you have had the foresight to mark it as yours—by engraving it with your social security number, for example—then identifying it as your stolen property will be substantially easier. But it is very difficult to mark an idea as yours. Usually the proof of ownership for intellectual property takes the form of a patent or copyright, although it is possible to document prior ownership of an idea in other ways as well.

How can a university protect ideas from thieves? The first step is to make clear to every member of the university that ideas are a kind of property, and that the protection of those ideas really does matter to the well-being of the university. A second step is to teach students at all levels the conventions for acknowledging when they adopt or develop the ideas of someone else. The third is to deal seriously with instances of the theft of ideas, which in an academic setting commonly takes one of two forms—cheating (that is, copying someone else's answers during an examination) and *plagiarism*, the unacknowledged dependence on someone else's ideas in writing, usually in out-of-class assignments. That you are reading this essay is part of your university's effort to make clear that it values and protects ideas as property.

The second step, training in common academic procedures for acknowledging sources, involves learning the accepted forms for footnotes, bibliographies, and citations to other authors in the text of your work. If you have had to write a research paper as a composition exercise in high school or previous college work, then you have probably learned one of the many conventional systems available for acknowledging sources you have used and identifying the specific ideas and language from others that you cite in your own work.[1] What matters is that your reader should be able to tell what ideas are your own original work and what ideas you have adopted or adapted from others. If you quote a section of someone else's writing verbatim, you must enclose the quoted material within quotation marks *and* tell your reader where the original statement appeared. If you rely on someone else's ideas, even if you do not quote them word for word, then a footnote identifying your source and indicating the extent of your indebtedness is appropriate.

---

[1] Perhaps the most widely used guide for authors using footnotes and bibliographies is "Turabian"—which is the shorthand way that writers refer to Kate L. Turabian, Wayne C. Booth, Gregory G. Colomb, and Joseph M. Williams, *A Manual for Writers of Term Papers, Theses, and Dissertations*, 7th ed. (Chicago: The University of Chicago Press, 2007). Other well-regarded guides of this sort include *MLA Handbook for Writers of Research Papers*, 7th ed. (New York: Modern Language Association, 2009); *The Chicago Manual of Style*, 15th ed. (Chicago: The University of Chicago Press, 2003); and *Publication Manual*, 6th ed. (Washington, D.C.: American Psychological Association, 2009). Your instructor can help you decide among them.

The third step a college or university must take to ensure that ideas are credited to their true creators—namely, dealing seriously with instances of the theft of ideas—will be evident in the ways that instructors and the systems of the university react when a case of cheating or plagiarism is suspected. If an instructor suspects that a student has cheated on a test or copied someone else's essay, the easiest action to take will always be no action at all. But would such a lack of action be the right way to proceed? If cheating or plagiarism mean so little that they can be ignored, then the instructor is contributing to the institution's loss of integrity and the weakening of the degree—of *your* degree. Indeed, by such inaction an instructor would become an accessory to the theft. The right way to proceed is to put the investigation of the facts of the alleged case into the authority of a separate group of people—often called the Honor Board or the Committee on Academic Misconduct. By hearing many cases of this kind, such a group becomes familiar with the kinds of questions that should be pursued, the kinds of evidence that can be gathered, and the appropriate resolution of the incident. Since effective teachers make a commitment to put forth their own best efforts for their students, those teachers may feel a degree of betrayal when a student knowingly tries to misrepresent someone else's work as his or her own. Therefore, it is usually wiser for a neutral party or group to investigate and *adjudicate* a case of suspected misconduct.

Some schools automatically suspend a student who has been found in violation of the rules on cheating or plagiarizing. Such a suspension may be in effect for a term or several terms, and the student will not be permitted to re-enroll until that assigned time period has passed. Other schools dismiss a student permanently for violating the rules of proper academic conduct. The consequences of academic misconduct can be devastating: law schools, medical schools, and the other professional programs available to you may be permanently closed if your record contains a notation about academic misconduct. You need to know what your college considers to be academic misconduct, and you need to know what the penalties for committing such misconduct can be. At many colleges and universities, students are bound by an "honor code" that requires them to notify instructors of any cheating they may be aware of. In such places, the failure to notify an official about suspected misconduct also qualifies as a violation and is grounds for disciplinary action.

Know the relevant policies at your institution, but do not let the seriousness of those policies paralyze you when you start to write an essay or a research paper for one of your classes. Some students ask, with justification, "How can I be sure that my ideas are original? Surely someone else has had almost every idea before me at some time or another. How can I be safe from misconduct accusations?" When you are told to be original, your teacher does not expect that every idea in your essay will be unique in the history of human thought. But a teacher does have the right to expect that *when you knowingly depend* on the thinking of someone else, you will acknowledge that in the conventional way (using quotation marks, footnotes, and a bibliography). You can express your own original turn of thought by seeing an idea in a new light, or combining ideas that you have not read before in the same combination, or by modifying the acknowledged ideas of someone else with critical commentary or new emphasis, and so on. And just to be sure, if you really have any doubts about the originality of your work, talk to your instructor about them before you turn the work in for a grade.[2]

[2]I am pleased to record my gratitude to my colleagues Professor Sara Garnes and Dean Virginia Gordon for their conversations with me about the topic of this essay.

Vocabulary

As you think about this essay, these definitions may be helpful to you:
1. **inalienable**   incapable of being surrendered or transferred
2. **patent**   a license securing for an inventor the exclusive right to make, use, or sell an invention for a term of years
3. **intangible**   not capable of being precisely identified; abstract
4. **plagiarism**   stealing or passing off the ideas or words of another as one's own
5. **adjudicate**   to act as judge

Discussion Questions

1. What is the historical basis for ownership of property?
2. How does the author define ideas as property? How do ideas and material property differ?
3. Why is the concept of ideas as property so important in a university setting?
4. What steps can be taken by a university to ensure ideas as property are protected, according to the author?
5. What can happen to a student who is found to have cheated or plagiarized?

Suggestions for Your Journal

Find out and write down in your own words your college's policies and procedures for deciding cases of alleged academic misconduct. This exercise is important so that you know what those policies and procedures are: They identify your responsibilities and your rights. Then comment on whether, in your judgment, those policies are justified and those procedures are fair.

You and the Family Educational Rights and Privacy Act

C. L. Lindsay III

C. L. Lindsay III is the founder and executive director of the Coalition for Student & Academic Rights (CO-STAR). A graduate of Denison University, he completed his law degree at the University of Michigan. This information about the Family Rights and Privacy Act is taken from his book, *The College Student's Guide to the Law* (2005).

Although most of us think of educational records in terms of grades and transcripts, your college has a wealth of other data at their fingertips. Some of it is mundane—payment schedules, housing forms, and so forth. But student files do contain some sensitive materials. And even seemingly benign information needs to be guarded carefully. Identity thieves don't need much—a social security number, for example—to make off with your persona.

There is a federal statute in place that guarantees students a certain level of privacy in such matters. The Family Educational Rights and Privacy Act (FERPA), sometimes called the Buckley Amendment, is the law that governs student records. It gives students the right to inspect and review their records, contest and amend inaccurate records, and control the disclosure of information about them. We'll look at each of these areas in turn and explain the exceptions and caveats that accompany them.

Educational Records Defined

FERPA doesn't protect every piece of paper the school has; it only applies to "educational records" as defined in the act. The rule of thumb: If it personally identifies a specific student, then it's an educational record. This includes transcripts, financial aid records, class schedules, letters of recommendation, and most other things that have a student's name attached to them. The records don't have to be printed on paper. E-mail, electronic records, and even audio recordings count. And they don't have to include the student's actual name. Any mark that identifies the student is good enough. The most common offending collegiate example is the practice of "anonymously" posting grades, where professors list final grades by social security number and tack them to a wall. Since the lists identify the students, they fall under FERPA's purview.

Exempted Records

A few types of records are specifically exempted from FERPA protection. Most significant is directory information. This is "phone book" type of data—name, address, home and local telephone numbers, dates of attendance, major extra-curricular activities, and date and place of birth. For student athletes the concept of directory info is a bit expanded. Height, weight, and performance statistics are considered part of their listing. Schools are allowed to disclose all of this information to anyone they please.

Campus law enforcement records are also exempted from the act. So if your name is included in an incident report or some other type of enforcement related record, it's public. Actual police records are always publicly available, so if your campus security is a commissioned force (or if you get arrested on campus by real cops), the records aren't private.

FERPA also excludes records that are kept in the sole possession of the maker for personal use. For example, if one of your professors commits some comments to paper so that she can grade you later, those notes wouldn't be covered by FERPA. You have no right to inspect or amend them. However, this is only true if she's the only one who ever sees them. If they're ever included in any permanent file or given to any other person, they become *bona fide* educational records and FERPA applies.

Treatment records kept by a campus doctor, counselor, psychiatrist, or any other recognized professional aren't covered by FERPA either. This may seem like a big loophole, but health-related records are covered by the Privacy Rule under the Health Insurance Portability and Accountability Act of 1996 (HIPAA). Much like FERPA, HIPAA guarantees patients the right to inspect and amend their medical records and limits their disclosure.

Finally, information the school gathers about former students isn't covered. So any records created by the school after you graduate fall outside FERPA coverage. "Why would the college keep records about me after I've left?" you might ask. Well, the day after you graduate your school's focus will shift immediately from educating you to trying to squeeze donations out of you. They'll gather all sorts of information to help them gauge how much money you have and how much they can get you to fork over. Even though these files would make for some interesting reading, you have no right to access or amend them. And the school can disclose the information without your consent.

Which Schools and Students?

Like *Title IX*, FERPA applies to all schools that receive any kind of federal aid, so pretty much every school in the country, private or public, must live by FERPA's rules. FERPA rights only vest in students who have actually enrolled in a school. If you've applied to a college but never actually got in or attended, you have no FERPA rights regarding the school's info. And FERPA rights terminate at death. If a student or former student dies, the school can do whatever they please with the remaining records.

Your Right to Inspect and Amend under FERPA

You have the right to inspect all of your educational records—with two exceptions. First, your parents' financial records are off-limits. The forms they've filled out for financial aid and other payment purposes are their business, not yours. Second, you don't have the right to view any confidential letters of recommendation. You've probably already run into this once or twice in your academic career. Recommendation forms usually have a confidentiality statement on them. They say something along the lines of "I openly and freely waive my right to view this recommendation" and have a space for your signature. If you sign on that line, you've waived your FERPA rights.

The Process

Aside from that, you have the right to review and inspect to your heart's content. The process is simple enough. All you have to do is go to your college's student records office or the student affairs office and ask to see your files. There's no specific requirement that the request be made in writing, but if you are serious about getting your hands on your records, it makes sense to submit your request in a letter.

The school then has forty-five days to accommodate you. They can give you either the originals or copies. If there are documents in your file that name other students, the information about them must be *redacted* before the files are given over to you (they have FERPA rights, too).

Inaccurate Records

If something's amiss, you can request that the record be amended to more accurately reflect the truth. Again, you don't have to do this in writing, but you probably should. At this point, the school may just cave and let you amend the file. But if they refuse, you also have a right to a hearing in front of an impartial board. If you prevail at the hearing, then the school has to make the change. If you lose, you still get to add your own statement to the file contesting the contents.

This amendment process is only meant to remedy clerical errors—not the substance that underlies the records themselves. For example, if you got an A in one of your classes but your transcript says you got a B+, then you'd be able to contest under FERPA. On the other hand, if you were awarded a B+, but you think you really deserved an A, you're out of luck—at least as far as your FERPA rights go. You'd have to take that issue up with your professor.

The School's Prohibition on Disclosure

FERPA prohibits any disclosure of your educational records without your written permission. They can't give any identifiable information to your roommates, prospective employers, other schools, the press, or anyone else without your okay. Of course, there are a number of exceptions.

University Employees

The FERPA prohibitions don't apply to disclosure within the campus's professional community. School employees can share student-specific information for educational purposes without prior consent. Without this exception, each professor would have to ask your permission before they reported your final grade to the registrar, your financial aid adviser would have to get consent to discuss your case with a colleague, and so on.

Your Parents

Most parents and legal guardians can access their kids' records. The test is one of legal dependency. If your parents claim you as a dependent on their tax return, then they have the same rights as you. Parental FERPA rights don't replace student rights. They exist in addition to them. So even if you're a legal dependent, you still have all of your FERPA rights. But so do your parents. This means that, just like you, they can inspect and review all of your educational records and consent to their disclosure. So just forget any fantasies about keeping your grades or other school business a secret from Mom and Dad. If push comes to shove, they probably have a right to see your transcript.

Health or Safety Emergencies

If there's a health or safety emergency, FERPA allows colleges and universities to disclose information that's necessary to protect the student in question or others. Personally I can't imagine how this would come up: "There's a flood coming, and the only way to stop it is to release your official transcript." But there it is.

Disciplinary Proceedings

If a student is accused of a violent crime or nonforcible sex offense (date rape and the like), the results of the on-campus disciplinary hearing may be disclosed under certain circumstances. First, the school is allowed to disclose the final results of the hearing, whether guilty or innocent, to the alleged victim. Second, if the student is found guilty, then the school can disclose the name of the student, the violation committed, and the sanction imposed by the school. All other records created in disciplinary hearings are educational records and are given full FERPA protection.

Drug and Alcohol Violations

If a student under the age of twenty-one has violated any drug- or alcohol-related law, the school may notify the legal guardians or parents of the offending student. This exception applies regardless of the dependent status described above.

Subpoenas

If the school is served with a lawful *subpoena* or court order, then they may disclose protected records without the student's permission. Normally, if a university is served with such a subpoena, they'll notify the student before the records are produced. And the court will almost always notify the target of the investigation that a subpoena has been issued. This gives the students a chance to seek an injunctive court order of their own if they wish.

The USA Patriot Act and Student Records

While we're talking about the disclosure of student records, it makes sense to touch on the recently passed antiterrorism laws. As I'm sure you know, the USA PATRIOT ("Uniting and Strengthening America by Providing Appropriate Tools Required to Intercept and Obstruct Terrorism") Act of 2001 was passed by Congress shortly after the September 11 attacks. It amended fifteen federal statutes in an attempt to give law enforcement agencies expanded resources to investigate terrorism.

Although the PATRIOT Act's purpose may have been to "unite and strengthen" America, its effect on civil liberties has been quite the opposite. Many basic constitutional rights were seriously compromised by these laws. Student privacy is no exception. The PATRIOT Act gives the government two new ways to get at your records. And, what's worse, it allows them to invade your privacy without any notice to you at all.

First, FERPA was one of the affected statutes. The PATRIOT Act amendments allow the government access to student records through ex parté court orders (ones that are issued without notice to the adverse party) in connection with the investigation or prosecution of terrorism crimes. Second, the act expanded the government's investigative powers under a law called the Foreign Intelligence Surveillance Act (FISA). Under FISA, government agencies involved in an authorized investigation can get a court order to obtain tangible evidence—including private student records—from colleges and universities. The law mandates that the disclosure be kept a secret.

From THE COLLEGE STUDENTS'S GUIDE TO THE LAW. Copyright 2005 by C.L. Lindsay III. Reprinted by permission of Taylor Trade Publishing and Rowan & Littlefield Publishing Group.

 Vocabulary

As you think about this essay, these definitions may be helpful to you:
1. **bona fide**   Literally, "in good faith"; without fraud or deceit.
2. **Title IX**   One of the 1972 amendments to the federal Civil Rights Act of 1964. Title IX was the first law prohibiting discrimination on the basis of sex in educational programs. Its most widely known results relate to athletics, since based on Title IX, college and universities needed to provide equity of opportunity for both men and women to athletic teams.
3. **vest**   As a verb, this word primarily means to place designated authority, property, or rights in the control of a person of group. For example, after you work for some organizations for a defined period of time, you may be said to be "vested in the retirement program," which means you have earned the right and expectation to certain property or income.

4. **redacted**   "Redact" is a verb meaning to edit or revise.
5. **subpoena**   A court order requiring the person(s) named in it to appear in court.

 ## Discussion Questions

1. The provisions of FERPA apply to college students. How are these rights different from the rights of students at lower-level institutions, such as high schools? Put another way, how does FERPA make a difference in your life, now that you are a college student?
2. As you understand FERPA, is it a good law?
3. C. L. Lindsay III, the author of this essay, believes that "although the PATRIOT Act's purpose may have been to 'unite and strengthen' America, its effect on civil liberties has been quite the opposite. Many basic constitutional rights were seriously compromised by these laws." From what you know about the changes in your FERPA rights brought about by the USA PATRIOT Act, is Lindsay correct? If so, how does that matter to you?

 ## Suggestions for Your Journal

Your FERPA rights are only one part of the changes that surround most new college students. Assuming that you are a traditional-age college student (that is, someone who has just finished high school at about the age of 18), what other changes are occurring in your world—especially your life as related to the law?

If you are not a traditional-age college student as defined in question 1, or if you are an international student, FERPA may still affect you but will probably do so in a somewhat different way. For example, many international students are supported by funding managed by their home governments, so they may have to consider obligations to someone other than their parents. How does FERPA matter to you if you are a nontraditional-age or international student?

College Cheating Is Bad for Business

W. P. Carey College of Business

The W. P. Carey School of Business is headquartered at the Tempe campus of Arizona State University. The Carey School, one of the largest business schools in the United States with 190 faculty, 1,500 graduate students and more than 5,600 undergraduates, is internationally recognized for its leadership in business education and is highly regarded for its renowned faculty and their research productivity. This essay from the school's website tells about a study conducted by two members of the business faculty.

In an age where a new cheating/corruption scandal is front-page news nearly every day—think Enron, Barry Bonds, Eliot Spitzer, and Marion Jones for starters, it is perhaps not surprising that dishonesty is a problem on most college campuses.

Academic dishonesty, which runs the gamut from plagiarizing to purchasing papers and theses, sharing answers on assignments, taking another's exam, and failing to do work for a team project, is, unfortunately, part of the college experience for many students today. Researchers at Pennsylvania State University, Rutgers University and Washington State University surveyed 5,331 graduate students at 32 universities in 2006. Of these, 56 percent of the graduate business students and 47 percent of the non-business graduate students admitted to cheating one or more times in the past year.

These numbers are an ominous sign for the academic and business communities.

"It's not just a matter of cheating on a test and getting ahead; there are all kinds of systemic implications that result from academic dishonesty," says Marianne Jennings, professor of legal and ethical studies at the W. P. Carey School of Business.

The legitimacy of college diplomas and the colleges that grant them may be at stake, says Jennings, who, along with W. P. Carey economics professor Stephen Happel, examines the reasons behind rising academic dishonesty in a just published paper. If two students—one a cheater and one an honest student—can gain the same degree, they ask, does that degree really convey an honest representation of academic accomplishment?

In addition, an abundance of cheating on college campuses threatens to demean the integrity of universities as a whole. "If a school becomes known as a place where you can cheat and get away with it and get a degree without working very hard, eventually that is the kind of students the school will attract," says Robert Mittelstaedt, dean of the W. P. Carey School, who has taken an active role in trying to reduce academic dishonesty within the business school.

College cheating also works its way into the business marketplace. "Students don't just say OK I cheated in school, but now I'm in the workplace and it ends here. They are forming bad habits that carry over into the market," says Jennings.

Employers eager to hire graduates with prestigious degrees and excellent grades may be in for an unpleasant surprise when their new hires don't live up to expectations, which can be especially damaging for business schools because support from the business community is crucial. If employers too often find the schools' students to be less-than-stellar employees, they may look elsewhere when hiring. "If an ASU student cheats his or her way through school and goes out into the workplace and is then found out, that comes back and reflects poorly on us," explains W. P. Carey Associate Dean Kay Faris.

The Cheating Market

How best to approach cheating in an academic research setting is tricky. Professors who shine a spotlight on the controversial issue when other schools are not openly talking about it are not usually rewarded. But Jennings and Happel argue that publicizing the academic dishonesty problem is the first step toward combating it. Their unique approach is to examine the cheating phenomenon through a microeconomic lens.

"What we tried to do is approach cheating the way economists approach any basic problem. There is a demand for something and a supply for something and a price that results," explains Happel. This method helps to strip the issue of its emotional baggage, and allows the researchers to delve into the problem as they would any other. It also has the added benefit of helping students see the relevance of their actions beyond the confines of the classroom. "When students realize that this rampant cheating ultimately leaves us no way of measuring merit—which is the basis of all economic, free-market systems—then it makes perfect sense to them," Jennings says.

Jennings and Happel propose that a student market exists for academic dishonesty and a faculty market for honesty. Though the two markets work against each other, in both cases, supply and demand combine to result in an equilibrium price in the market. "If a student goes to a Web site to get a term paper, he has to pay money for it. Or if he is cheating through a buddy, he may be paying in kind—'If you help me out with this paper, you can borrow my car this weekend,'" Happel explains.

From the faculty perspective, the "price" of increasing the supply of academic honesty includes the time and energy spent pursuing a cheating incident—which can be significant, and often includes legal battles. In addition, say Jennings and Happel, many professors cite a lack of administrative support when fighting these cases as a deterrent to being more diligent about curbing cheating. As a result, the supply curve for cheating remains in students' favor.

Deterring Dishonesty

But the balance in this equation may be starting to shift—at least within the W. P. Carey School. Since Jennings and Happel first wrote about this topic a few years ago, the school has increased efforts to deter academic dishonesty. Cheating is now discussed frequently with students, starting during orientation week, and continuing throughout the year.

"I'm not sure the dean ever speaks with a group of students without mentioning it," says Faris, adding that this attitude "infiltrates to all of us who have connections with students, making the issue at the forefront of everyone's minds."

Dean Mittelstaedt has also upped the administration's support for faculty seeking to prosecute cheaters, and offers reminders to professors at the beginning of each semester about the importance of going after academic dishonesty. And the school has backed up these actions with stricter sanctions for students who are caught engaging in cheating.

Dean Mittelstaedt shares the tale of one student who was recently barred from graduating. The student, who was on track to complete his degree with honors in three and one-half years, created a fictitious e-mail account made to look like that of a faculty member. Using that e-mail address, he falsified a note to the Honors College saying that he had successfully completed the honors thesis, when in fact, he hadn't done the work. "In this case, the sanction we took was that the student didn't graduate at all," explains Mittelstaedt. "It was a very sad situation, but to maintain the reputation of our institution we have to have standards. In addition, we have an obligation as educators to help students recognize when they are in an ethical quandary, and teach them to do the right thing in those situations."

A Hard Problem

While stricter measures have helped, it is clear that cheating will be nearly impossible to stamp out completely. Whether the blame is placed on a culture that rewards success at all costs, driving students to dishonesty in order to get ahead; or to the introduction of a cheater's paradise of technology such as cell phones, text messaging and the Internet; or to the perceived lack of penalty for cheating, students will likely continue to engage in this behavior for some time to come. And they are quite skilled at it.

"Part of what makes this issue so difficult is that you rarely see the same cheating problem a second or third time. Something new and innovative always pops up. No two cases are the same," notes Faris. Jennings and Happel also cite the economic argument that things persist in the marketplace for a reason. The thinking on cheating—and it's the same thinking you see executives using—is, "I am rewarded for this behavior, so why would I not do it? It is basic economics," explains Jennings.

"The fact that people are not rising up in arms throughout society and screaming about this issue means something is going on that isn't all bad," adds Happel. Perhaps it's the division-of-labor arrangement that many cheaters rely upon. "If I'm good at English and you're good at math, the idea is you help me out and I'll help you out," he notes. Yet even though such "teamwork" skills are valuable in the marketplace, their existence in a university setting stretches the boundaries of acceptability—something students don't always recognize.

Raising the Cost of Cheating

So while the root causes and the reasons for cheating persist, should we expect the market rewards for cheating to change at some point and tip the scales toward greater honesty? Here again, the supply and demand argument comes into play. "If we really shift the supply curve back and reduce the number of suppliers to students in the cheating market—pass laws, and eliminate these Internet sites which provide thesis papers, for instance—this raises the price of cheating among students so that it is much more difficult and time-consuming to find someone to cheat from that won't turn them in, then you can certainly cut back on cheating," explains Happel. "That is just common sense in a demand-and-supply framework."

Happel admits, however, that this is not the likely outcome. What is more feasible is bringing the "costs" of enforcement down so academic dishonesty becomes a less attractive option for students. "If you change those costs, and if you also introduce the element of self-enforcement among students, then the risk and cost for students increase so much that they say never mind to cheating," Jennings says.

Jennings reports that last semester, for the first time in years, she did not have a cheating scandal among her students. And overall within the business school, the number of cases that are serious enough to land at Dean Mittelstaedt's door remains small. Among approximately 7,000 graduate students, the dean reports dealing with about six to eight cases within the last year. "I think we are successfully changing the culture," he says.

Bottom Line

Cheating is a problem among many college students: In a recent study, 56 percent of graduate students admitted to cheating one or more times in the past year. Engaging in academic dishonesty has systemic implications beyond the classroom—it hurts fellow students by skewing the grading system, threatens the integrity and reputation of the university, and can damage businesses that hire graduates who don't have the skills they are expected to have.

Analyzing academic dishonesty through a microeconomic lens helps illuminate what drives students to cheat, and shows how the demand, supply and price of the cheating "market" function. By reducing the "cost" of enforcement and raising the "price" of cheating, and by discussing cheating openly among students and faculty, the W. P. Carey School has made strides in reducing cheating among its students.

First published September 24, 2008, in Knowledge@W. P. Carey, a free email newsletter and web site published by the W. P. Carey School of Business. http://knowledge.wpcarey/asu.edu.

Vocabulary

As you think about this essay, these definitions may be useful to you:
1. **plagiarizing**   Representing someone else's work as your own, usually in the form of copying word for word or idea for idea.
2. **microeconomics**   A branch of economics that studies how households, firms and some states make decisions to allocate limited resources, typically in markets where goods or services are being bought and sold. Competition and supply and demand are important forces within this study.

Discussion Questions

1. The authors of the study say that using their technique (that is, applying some basic laws of economics to the study of academic cheating) "helps to strip the issue of its emotional baggage." What do they mean by the "emotional baggage" of the issue of cheating? Many people would argue that the "emotional baggage" is the heart of the issue, and that treating the subject of cheating without the emotions it raises leaves out a lot. What are the advantages and disadvantages of the authors' unemotional (that is, scientific) approach?
2. The method of this research is based in business theory which here is applied to a business school setting. Does the value of the study apply to areas other than cheating in business?

Suggestions for Your Journal

Is cheating a personal issue for you? Has anyone ever cheated in school by using your work and representing it as their own? If so, how did that make you feel? What was your reaction to the incident? Did you report the cheating? Why, or why not? Have you tried to protect yourself from being used in this way again?

Avoiding Plagiarism

Rosemarie Menager and Lyn Paulos

Rosemarie Menager is a psychology professor at Foothill College. She is an expert on student success in online learning. Lyn Paulos is a technology lab technician at Santa Barbara City College where she manages an adaptive technology learning lab. This essay was taken from their booklet called *Quick Coach Guide to Avoiding Plagiarism*.

What do you want from college? There are many answers to this question, and certainly one of them is to succeed in your coursework. Probably the last thing you would want is to fail a class for cheating or *plagiarizing* by mistake. If you are unfamiliar with the practices and rules of incorporating work from other sources, then you will find the twelve guidelines below useful.

Doing Your Own Work, Using Your Own Words

College gives you the opportunity to be exposed to new ideas, to formulate ideas of your own, and to develop the skills necessary to communicate your ideas. Strengthening your writing skills requires hard work and practice, but you learn thinking and communicating skills that will benefit both your studies in college and your career.

Expressing a thought in your own words may seem overwhelming. The difficulty may stem from not understanding the language, not understanding the research material, or lacking confidence in expressing ideas and concepts. Don't be discouraged by the thought that your paper may not sound as professional as you would like. By creating and practicing your own personal style, you improve your ability to state ideas clearly and support your arguments, as well as increase your vocabulary.

These skills are not built by using another researcher' or student's words or by paying a service to write a paper for your class. Attempting to cheat on your paper cheats you the most because you are depriving yourself of the thinking, learning and writing practice that benefits every aspect of your education and beyond.

Cheating also creates the risk of humiliation and punishment. Most professors are so familiar with the work in their field that they can spot a fake quickly. New plagiarism detection methods are also making it easier for professors to catch cheaters electronically. Finally, all institutions punish students who plagiarize. Doing honest work is the way to avoid the negative consequences of cheating.

Allowing Enough Time

Often, students caught plagiarizing claim that they didn't have time to do the work. This excuse rarely works. Allow sufficient time to do all the steps necessary in an assignment. The best way is to plan for each part: selecting the topic, doing the research, then writing and refining your ideas. Minimizing the time it will take to do the work, or procrastinating because you feel that you do better work when you are anxious, more often than not leads to trouble.

The most productive strategy is to begin the assignment as soon as it is given and try to complete it early. This allows you to adjust the schedule if you encounter any research difficulties, provides time for questions or clarification, and offsets other events that can interfere or cut into study time. If you are unsure about how to plot out your time for each step, ask your instructor to help you plan your schedule.

Keeping Track of Sources

As you look through books, articles, online sources, and other materials, you will be able to identify which content is relevant to your paper. The sources from which you decide to take notes are the ones for which you will need to keep careful records.

Create a master list of all your sources that contains detailed *bibliographic* information for each item. (You need to record the author, the title of the source, its publisher, the date, and page number.) As you conduct your research, you will likely add or delete sources from this list, but keeping it current and complete will make your work much easier when it comes time to format your list of Works Cited or References. This list of references enables your readers to locate the exact content you discuss in your paper—as well as assists you in finding it again.

Taking Notes

Some students find they take better and more easily referenced notes if they make photocopies of relevant pages from their sources. If you decide to use this method for print sources such as articles and books, photocopy the copyright page and make a copy of the relevant table of contents pages for each source. Make sure the page numbers or other identifiers are visible on each page. For electronic sources, such as websites, databases, CDs, or even blogs, print out both the home or copyright page and the relevant content pages, making sure that identifiers such as page numbers—and (for online sources) the URL and access date—are visible.

If you take notes instead on note cards or in computer files, then make sure to keep a detailed record of where each note came from and take down the information carefully and accurately.

Next, scrutinize your resources, thinking about the ideas expressed, noting and recording the relevant points, and adding to the notes your reactions, questions, and thoughts. If you find a particular phrase that you want to quote, then high-light it to separate it from the regular notes.

Clarifying Who Is Speaking

As you write the first draft of your paper, make sure you express your thoughts and ideas in your own voice. Use the thoughts or words of others only to support your thoughts, not to make your point for you. Your writing should make clear at all times who is speaking.

Decide from your notes whether you need to quote, summarize, or paraphrase the source. Then make sure to introduce the guest voice (the source) and explain why the source's information is relevant to your topic.

Crediting the Source

When you draft your paper, if you are stating another person's thought, make the source or origin of that thought clear. Identify the source of any and all borrowed content in your paper. Your readers need to know where to find the original source if they want to explore the idea further.

The academic departments of virtually every college and university recommend that their students use a particular style guide. The guides issued by the Modern Language Association (MLA) and the American Psychological Association (APA), as well as the University Chicago's *Manual of Style* (CMS), are the most common. Each features a method to identify your source by inserting a brief *parenthetical* citation where the source's content appears and then creating a list with the complete source information placed at the end of the paper. Follow whichever style your instructor specifies.

Citing Sources Correctly

A **citation**—a statement of the source of an idea, a conclusion, or a specific collection of information—of another person's work is the highest form of respect that a serious writer can make. It is also the single best way to avoid accusations of plagiarism and cheating. Properly citing sources involves acknowledging them both in the body of your work (when and where your writing borrows from a given source) and in a list of all the sources at the end of your paper.

Check with your instructor or writing center for the proper format style of your writing project. Citation styles differ by subject or discipline, and many overlap in the areas of study and writing for which they were originally intended. For English and the other humanities, the MLA style is typically used. Psychology, Sociology, Business, Economics, and similar disciplines typically follow APA. More specialized style guides exist for other disciplines, including the Council of Science Editors (CSE) style, which is used in scientific writing.

Quoting

Quotations should be used only to emphasize your point, which you have already stated in your own words. A good quotation from an original source can underscore a theme and introduce thoughts or direction, but quotations should be relevant, necessary, accurate, and limited.

Using too many direct quotations (more than ten percent) is a sign both that you have not developed your own idea enough and that you are relying on others to make your point for you. Over-quoting is also an opportunity for plagiarism to creep in. If you are using several sources, then limit how much those sources contribute, and give a correct citation and credit every time you use them.

Paraphrasing

The practice of taking another writer's sentence and then looking up words and replacing them with synonyms is a common way for students to think they are paraphrasing from a source. Merely changing some of another writer's words, or reversing the order of the clauses in the sentences is still copying. This is another way you can inadvertently plagiarize. Use paraphrase to state in your own words what another writer believes or argues.

Avoiding Patchwriting

Patchwriting consists of mixing several references together and arranging paraphrases and quotations to constitute much of a paper. In essence, the student has assembled others' works—with a bit of embroidery here and there—but with very little original thought or expression. Work that has been simply patched together is very likely to contain plagiarism.

To avoid patchwriting, develop a position and bring in sources only as needed to support your viewpoint or argument. Read the material several times to make sure you understand what the source is saying. Then put it aside and think about it. Analyze the readings and what they mean, and then try to organize the main points. Create an outline of what you want to say and go back and pull in the supporting information from the sources. Good writers think of the reader as listening to what is being said; this process will help you create and organize your own original work and find your own voice in your writing.

Summarizing

Most word processors have an automatic summarize function that can take 50 pages and turn them into ten. The problem with this feature is that it condenses material by selecting key sentences. Therefore, a summarized version is still in the exact words of the original source, only shorter and does not necessarily make the same point as the original. The auto-summary feature is intended for writers to summarize their own work, not the work of others. If a paper uses any portion of an auto-summary generated from another writer's work, then it is plagiarism.

If you wish to summarize another writer's work, then describe briefly in your own words the writer's idea, identifying who that writer is and providing a citation of the work, and state how it relates to your own ideas.

Avoiding Using Other Students' Papers and Paper Mills

Don't cross the line from looking at someone else's paper to presenting it as original work. A paper written by another student can be an example of how to do the assignment. Reworking or rewriting that person's paper for submission is plagiarism.

Similarly, buying papers from paper mils, or paying for someone else to write a paper, is obviously dishonest and is a clear example of plagiarizing. Databases of written papers are often kept by colleges and by plagiarism detection services, so instructors who question the authenticity of a student's paper can easily verify its source.

Academic integrity and the validity of a college degree are vitally important to institutions of higher learning and so they create codes and policies governing instances of dishonesty. Don't gamble with your academic future. Taking a risk with the expectation that you won't get caught can result in consequences much worse than a warning or a simple fail on an assignment. If you aren't prepared, it's better to get a poor grade on one assignment than to fail in a class (or worse) because you panicked and plagiarized.

Vocabulary

plagiarism   using someone else's work and passing it off as one's own. The term comes from the Latin word **plagiarius,** which means *kidnapper*. It also has another root word in Greek, **plagios,** which means *crooked or treacherous.* (Reader's Digest Great Encyclopedic Dictionary 1031)
bibliographic   referring to a list of works written by an author
parenthetical   an explanatory word, phrase or sentence inserted in a passage from which it is set off by punctuation

Discussion Questions

1. What are your college's or university's policies about plagiarism? Where are the policies officially written? What is the official procedure for a student who is caught cheating or plagiarizing on your campus?
2. Do you ever have difficulty in writing a paper "in your own style"? What do you think the authors mean by this phrase?

3. Have you ever been late in writing a paper? How did you feel? Do you think this situation could encourage plagiarism as the authors suggest?
4. What is the best way to take notes when writing a paper? How do you use your "notes" when you want to use an idea or cite a source?
5. What is the most difficult aspect of crediting a source? Which style guide does your college recommend? Is this the same style you have used in the past? Have you ever used an online citation generator to help you use the correct format?
6. The authors describe what they call "patchwriting." Have you ever caught yourself using many sources in this way? Did you ever think of the reader as listening to what you are saying? Is this a good technique? Why?

 ## Suggestions for Your Journal

The authors think that many students plagiarize because they are not aware of the rules governing it. Before reading this essay were you fully aware of the many ways that plagiarism can be possible? Have you ever been close to plagiarizing without knowing it? Which of the authors' twelve tips for avoiding plagiarism impressed you the most? Why? How can you use their advice in the future?

Unit Summary

The essays in this unit focus on ethical values, especially those that relate to institutions of higher education. Halverson, Carter, and Minnick discuss aspects of intellectual honesty as they relate to academic study, and Lindsay explains some important legal issues relating to college students. Personnel of the Carey School argue that a business analysis of cheating has helped reduce it in their classes. Finally, Menager and Paulos offer twelve guidelines for avoiding plagiarism.

■ Summary Questions

1. Do you agree with the essentially intellectual picture of the university that the authors in this unit share? What are some alternative views of the purpose of a university or college education? Can your alternatives fit compatibly with the views these authors offer?
2. An important qualification in most ethical theories is the belief that "ought implies can"—that is, that we cannot be expected to measure up to impossible standards. In the essays in this unit, does any of the authors ask you to do what you cannot reasonably be expected to do?
3. What university courses might you take to further explore the kinds of moral and ethical issues discussed in these essays?

■ Suggested Writing Assignments

1. Write a short essay connecting your ethical beliefs to those given in one of the essays in this unit. Show how your beliefs significantly differ or coincide with those expressed here.
2. The authors in this unit agree that acts of intellectual dishonesty, like cheating on tests and plagiarizing, are not acceptable at a university. Write a short essay identifying some other forms of behavior that are inappropriate at a university. Suggest a plan for limiting such inappropriate activities.
3. Might you expect your sense of values or virtues to change as you complete an undergraduate degree? Why? How?

■ Suggested Readings

Darwall, Stephen. *The Second-Person Standpoint: Morality, Respect and Accountability*. Cambridge, MA: Harvard University Press, 2006.

Kamm, F.M. *Intricate Ethics: Rights, Responsibilities, and Permissible Harm*. Oxford University Press, 2006.

Unit 7

What Is Diversity and Why Is It Important?

We reason deeply when we forcibly feel.

—MARY WOLLSTONECRAFT

Just about anyone interested in American higher education can start an argument these days by bringing up the topic of "political correctness." The phrase is highly specific to our time and became important largely because of changes in the way that educators think about how to design a college curriculum.

Before 1980, the question of what to include in a well-designed college program of studies would have had different answers from different scholars, but most of them would have differed only in matters of degree. The questions people asked were "How much science should be required? How many courses of European, English, or American literature should be expected? Should Faulkner receive as much emphasis as Melville?" More recently, debates on the appropriate content of a required curriculum in general studies have grown louder, more political, and nastier. The questions people now tend to raise include "Why have you omitted literature by women and people of color? How can you prefer courses about the European cultural tradition when students will increasingly need to deal with Asian, African, and Hispanic cultures in their daily lives in the 21st century? Will the courses you propose to require prepare students to improve the world, or just to describe it?" The "gentleman's agreement" (to use a phrase that some would argue expresses the problem) about what to include in a college degree program and how to talk about it is no longer in effect.

Detachment from political considerations used to be thought of, among scholars, as an ideal to be cultivated by educated people. Now many regard such detachment as an illusion and say that every author, teacher, and speaker should begin by identifying his or her

157

political assumptions. So let us say up front that without abandoning the rich history of Western thought, we value diversity and believe that the free expression of diverse points of view is essential to the well-being of a university.

We do not regard that as a predominantly political point of view, though it certainly is a notion with political consequences. On this principle, for example, we oppose all intellectual straitjackets—such as those the Nazis imposed on German universities in the period from their rise to power until the end of World War II, a time when faculty members and students alike suffered imprisonment and death for expressing ideas that were politically incorrect according to the ruling powers of the time. Further, we believe that argument and dissent need to proceed within a civilized framework— that there are reasonable constraints on behavior that all members of a community need to observe and respect. But the essential nature of a university cannot long survive in the presence of restraints on thinking and expressing ideas.

We value diversity of opinions and cultures because the free exchange of ideas is the surest way to expose bad thinking and to find the good. The essay on academic freedom by Halverson and Carter in Unit 6 provides the rationale for this belief.

We also value diversity on the fundamental ground of our shared nature as human beings: We all want to be treated fairly, and we all object to unearned punishments and rewards. So Unit 7 continues with essays in which many individuals speak about why the fact that they are different from the majority—in race, religion, gender, looks, sexual preference—should not disqualify them from the respect accorded to us all in a civilized environment, especially in a free democratic nation. In these essays, authors talk about the ways that thoughtless or premeditated comments or other forms of behavior have affected them and made them feel like outsiders. This feeling of alienation is often the motivation that opens the dialogue among diverse groups, a dialogue that is most evident on our campuses perhaps because no other class of institutions is better suited for carrying on just such a dialogue.

Defining dialogue is not an easy task. The sort of dialogue we mean is not merely a conversation. Rather, we intend this term in the way that thinkers such as the 19th-century Catholic philosopher John Henry, Cardinal Newman, and the early 20th-century Jewish teacher Martin Buber have meant it: one person speaking to another, heart to heart, and listening. Universities and colleges offer unequaled opportunities for students to meet others who are different from themselves and to enter into dialogue with them. The goal of dialogue is understanding and connecting with another person, and the result of dialogue is often to understand oneself better through understanding someone else. International students, students from different religions and cultures, students who share your goals in education but may differ from you in almost every other way—these are people worth seeking out for what they can teach you about themselves and about yourself. Dialogue is the means by which we discover and evaluate truth, and diversity is the starting point for dialogue. Anthor Tom Brown offers some specific advice on how to develop this dialogue.

Among the most powerful statements of the reasons that America—and especially American universities—needs to keep this dialogue alive will be found in the speech "I Have a Dream," which Reverend Martin Luther King Jr. delivered a few years before his assassination. His vision of a society free at last from judgments based narrowly on the accidents of birth joins in perpetuity such other classic statements of the need for freedom of expression as "Areopagitica," the poet John Milton's defense of a free press, and "On Liberty," philosopher John Stuart Mill's reasoned explanation of the essential character of a free society. We include some personal statements from individuals who have direct experience of different kinds with "being different." To close the unit, Ingram and Parks comment on racial developments since 1963, when King delivered that famous speech.

From Diversity to Inclusivity

Thomas Brown

Thomas Brown served as an educator in academic and student affairs for 27 years, most recently as the Dean of Advising Services/Special Programs at Saint Mary's College of California. He has served as a consultant to more than 350 colleges and universities and has published and spoken extensively related to creating inclusive campus communities. Additionally, he has held numerous leadership positions in the National Academic Advising Association (NACADA).

> *E Pluribus Unum. (Out of many, one.)*
>
> —THE MOTTO ON THE GREAT SEAL OF THE UNITED STATES

Diversity is a reality of the human experience; the question is what we do with the diversity we encounter in our lives. The issue today seems to be less about diversity and more about creating inclusive communities from diverse individuals and groups.

College is a place, a time, and a series of unlimited opportunities to learn more about the world and about yourself, as you continue to author the story of your life. The American college or university campus is one of the few places on earth where people from so many different experiences, backgrounds, and beliefs come together for a common purpose. (In this essay America is used to refer to the United States, although North and South America include other nations and peoples—from Canada, to Mexico, to the tip of South America.)

American college students played a major role in the civil rights struggle, women's and gay rights movements, and the environmental movements. They have also led campaigns to secure fair wages for overseas workers who produce their school's team uniforms, caps, and hoodies.

Men and women whose countries, ethnic, or tribal groups are at war with each other sit together as classmates on American campuses. Shiite and Sunni factions may battle each other in the Middle East, but Muslim Student Associations bring these students together at Yale, the University of Texas, and the University of Southern California. India and Pakistan have moved to the brink of war in recent years, but joint Indian-Pakistani student organizations flourish at the University of North Texas, Babson College, and McGill University, and they jointly celebrate South Asian culture at UCLA. Students enter college as strangers and depart as friends for life, having forged bonds that cross national, racial, ethnic, and other lines that divide people one against the other.

Allan Johnson, a University of Michigan Professor and author of *Privilege, Power, and Difference*, observed that college is where many people have their first true experiences with people unlike themselves (2006). Most students come to college from communities and schools where everyone looks pretty much alike. For example, of white students who entered four-year colleges in 2006, 75 percent came from high schools that were mostly or completely white, while nearly 90 percent grew up in neighborhoods that were completely or mostly white (Higher Education Research Institute, 2008). Asian and Latino students were more likely to come from mixed race schools and neighborhoods; however, most African American/Black students continue to grow up and attend schools in communities that are predominantly composed of people who share their race and ethnicity.

As a first-year student, you will encounter a wide range of people. Many will have beliefs, values, and backgrounds vastly different from your own, your family's, or the friends you have grown up with. Through your interactions with educators and your fellow students, inside and outside the classroom, you will examine more closely and understand more deeply what society makes of difference, or "diversity," and what it means in your own life. As a learner, you will be seeking to develop attitudes, skills, and behaviors to be personally and professionally effective in an increasingly diverse country and interconnected global community. This will require you to be open to the world as it is rather than as you think (or have been told) it should be. Being an individual and a member of a campus community also requires you to develop understanding of others and their perspectives—even, and most especially, when you may disagree with them. Appreciating diversity is not about agreement. It is about making an effort to recognize that your worldview may be different from someone else's and to consider the possibility that you might both be right—or wrong.

What Is Diversity?

Cultural diversity has always been part of the history of this land, even before there was a United States. Before the arrival of European colonizers, enslaved Africans, or subsequent immigrant waves from around the world, Native American/First Nations People were from different tribal groups; they spoke different languages and embraced different values and belief systems. Hopefully, as you come to appreciate diversity, you will strive to understand others based on the qualities they possess rather than based on myths, bias, and stereotypes that you have absorbed from living in the world, or that others have passed on to you—much like a virus.

Dr. Beverly Tatum, a psychologist and Spelman College President, observed that there are seven kinds of diversity that are most relevant to life in the U.S.: Race/ethnicity, Gender, Sexual orientation, Age, Socio-economic status,

Ability/disability, and Religion. She added that for each kind of diversity, there is a distinct form of intolerance, oppression, or an ism:

Race/ethnicity	Racism/ethnocentrism
Gender	Sexism
Sexual orientation	Homo-negativism/homophobia
Age	Ageism
Socio-economic status	Classism
Ability/disability	Ableism
Religion	Religious intolerance (e.g., anti-Moslem, anti-semitic, anti-atheism)

In addition to these more familiar forms of discrimination and intolerance, people are judged, valued, or devalued based on what they look like, their body size, or their lifestyle choices regarding clothes, music, and/or the way they wear their hair. College student athletes often find themselves the target of negative stereotypes depending on the sports they play, while members of fraternities and sororities are often the targets of unfair generalizations.

Researchers have found that every inch of height is worth nearly $800 more in annual salary. Accordingly, a person six feet tall could earn $5500 more per year more than a person who is five feet five inches tall (Gladwell, 2005). Over a lifetime, that's hundreds of thousands of dollars in additional income for the "unearned privilege" of having been born taller than someone else, someone who might be just as smart, or just as hard working, but who happens to have been born with different genes.

Diversity is not an issue or problem in itself. The "problem" emerges because we live in a world that "encourages people to use differences to include or exclude, reward or punish, credit or discredit, elevate, or oppress, value or devalue, leave alone or harass" (Johnson, 2006, pg 16).

Dr. King's "I Have a Dream" speech expressed the hope for a day when people would be "judged on the content of their character." However, the best evidence tells us that day has yet to fully dawn in America. If you think that difference doesn't matter or that discrimination no longer exists, just imagine what would happen if you announced to your family and friends that you were gay or lesbian. What would be the reaction if you told your Jewish parents that you were becoming a Christian, or your Christian parents that you were converting to Islam? How would your life be different if you were of another race, or if your socio-economic status changed for the worse? Progress has been made, but there is more to be achieved before we can claim victory over inequality, intolerance, and discrimination in American life.

Why Does Diversity Matter?

As the U.S. and world become more closely connected, it will be increasingly important for you to interact effectively with people from backgrounds and experiences that are very different from your own. Thus, it is somewhat surprising that nearly half of students entering college in 2006 did not feel it was important to improve their understanding of other countries and cultures, and less than one-third planned to participate in study abroad programs.

Learning opportunities are increased in classroom settings where there are people from a variety of backgrounds who can share their perspectives and experiences on various issues. Discussions of challenges for people with disabilities, women's rights, or gay and lesbian rights are enriched and deepened when people living these experiences bring them into the classroom and into co-curricular settings.

A critical element in learning from those who are different from you is to listen to what they are saying, especially when it relates to their feelings of being "the other" in some area of their lives. What often happens in discussions of race, gender, or other complex issues is that we don't want to hear others talk about their pain because it makes us feel uncomfortable. Yet it is precisely when we experience discomfort that we may be on the verge of new learning which occurs when we listen well to others. Men hear women's stories of being afraid, marginalized, or put down, and they take it personally. Whites listen to discussions of race and racism and take it as an accusation of moral failure. Heterosexuals often accuse gays and lesbians of seeking "special rights," when all they are seeking is equal rights. We can't move to unity from diversity—from *Pluribus* to the *Unum*, many to one—unless we are willing to talk about issues, problems, and our experiences. If we can't talk and listen to each other, we will never be able to move forward—as a class, a campus, a community, as a nation, or a global community.

Professor Johnson is on the mark when he says,

> "The words are not about me because they name something much larger than me, something I didn't invent or create but that was passed on to me as a legacy because I was born in this nation. If I am going to be part of the solution to that difficult legacy, I must step back from my defensive position. . . . Then I can understand what it has to do with me and, most important, what I can do about it" (pg 11).

What is needed is a civil environment wherein you are willing to listen to your fellow learners, respect one another's experiences and perspectives, as you engage in the common quest for learning about the worlds in which you will live your life. You certainly did not create the "pollution of the isms," but you have the opportunity, indeed the responsibility, to try to clean up the dirty air as part of your efforts to create a better future for us all.

Martha Vasquez, winner of the 2009 Diversity Matters essay contest at the University of Hawai'i at Manoa observed,

> "Embracing diversity enables people who have been placed in the category of 'other' to affirm their dignity, recover from exclusion and claim representation.

We believe that dignity, inclusion and full representation are the foundations of a just society; therefore, we strive to recognize and support all people regardless of their gender, age, race, disability status, sexual orientation or socioeconomic background."

Engaging with Diversity: Stretching Your Comfort Zone

Many students of color come to college and have the experience of being in the minority for the first time, or being "the only one" in their classes, their residence halls, or elsewhere on campus. Asian, Black, and Hispanic/Latino students are frequently asked why they sit together in the cafeteria. How often are white students asked the same question? Multi-cultural students function in diverse environments, as they prepare themselves for lives of work and leadership where they will frequently be the "only one." A significant challenge is providing opportunities for majority-group students to become engaged in diverse settings and to consider their role in creating inclusive communities wherein all students feel welcomed, valued, and empowered to do their best work.

Students entering college often expect that they will have opportunities to interact with people from different backgrounds, but research finds this is usually not the case. International students who come to the U.S. from other nations often report that they had few opportunities to interact with Americans in social settings. At the same time, many students from different nations establish lifelong relationships with students from around the world as the result of their having met on the "neutral ground" of the US campus, where their status as "strangers in a strange land" becomes a shared commonality.

In his book, *Making the Most of College*, Harvard professor Richard Light asked a wide variety of college students about learning experiences that affected them profoundly. He was surprised to discover that four out of five chose a situation that had happened outside the classroom.

People who expand or stretch their comfort zones to include more people and experiences, often report more complete, rewarding, and successful lives—during college and beyond. Instead of withdrawing to the safety of what is familiar when they experience discomfort, they force themselves to move forward, through awkwardness and anxiety until such feelings subside. The result is new learning, growth, and the capacity to manage new situations more effectively.

Here are some suggestions for stretching your comfort zone:

- Learn a language (or two!) other than your own. Learning to speak another language gives you the experience that is experienced by many people whose first language is not English and/or who are experiencing a new culture. Speaking another language will also be a career asset, especially Arabic, Mandarin, or Spanish.
- Reach out to international students. The world turns to the U.S. for higher education and more than 600,000 students from abroad currently study in the U.S. Unfortunately, too few international students have opportunities to

meet and know US students and people. Explore opportunities to become a language partner for students seeking to improve their language skills; join the international club and attend events, and invite international students to participate in social and cultural events with which you are involved.

· Take classes about cultures other than your own to expand your knowledge and increase your cultural competence.

· Participate in service learning, volunteer work, community service, and other programs that will enable you to become more engaged with diverse individuals and groups.

· Invite friends outside your identity group(s) to come with you to events and activities. This will not only allow them to make personal and social connections, it may also enable them consider their own feelings of "being in the minority."

· Challenge racist, sexist, and homo-negative comments and jokes that demean others. Racism and other forms of discrimination may persevere in part because people who anticipate feeling upset and who believe that they will take action when faced with an act of intolerance may actually respond with indifference (Kawakami, Dunn, Karmali, & Davido, 2009).

As Dr. King wrote in his 1963 *Letter from a Birmingham Jail*, "We will have to repent in this generation not merely for the hateful words and actions of the bad people, but for the appalling silence of the good people."

In addition to trying to learn more about people and groups different from your own, try to examine the roots of your own attitudes, biases, and stereotypes. Where did they come from? Malcolm Gladwell (2005) observes that we often form snap judgments—"blinks"—about people, usually without thinking. Once we have formed these unconscious judgments, or "stereotypes," they usually won't change unless we take the time to examine and *consciously* consider their accuracy. This is what it truly means to be a student and a scholar.

Your Personal Role in Creating an Inclusive Campus Community

As a member of a campus community, you have the responsibility to contribute to creating an environment wherein all people feel safe to be themselves. Whenever you are about to make a comment or take an action, imagine what would happen if you asked yourself a simple question: Is what I am about to say or do going to bring me closer to this person or is it going to drive us further apart? The choice is yours and you should consider whether you will choose community over chaos as you seek to create the *Unum* from the *Pluribus* that is at the heart of the American Dream.

You may never have another opportunity to be fully engaged in a community as diverse as your campus—that is until you enter the workplace. You will likely then discover that much of what you have learned in college is transferable and extremely useful to the rest of your life.

References

Gladwell, M. *Blink: The Power of Thinking Without Thinking*. New York: Bay Bay Books, 2005.

Johnson, Allan G. *Privilege, Power, and Difference*. New York: McGraw-Hill. 2006.

Kawakami, K., E. Dunn, F. Karmali, and J.F. Dovido. "Mispredicting Affective and Behavioral Responses to Racism." *Science,* 9 January 2009: Vol. 323, no. 5911, 276–278.

Tatum, Beverly Daniel. *Why are all the Black Kids sitting together in the cafeteria?* New York: Basic Books, 1999.

Higher Education Research Institute. *The American Freshman: National Norms Fall 2008*.

Used by permission from Thomas Brown.

 ## Discussion Questions

1. Brown points to the fact that "As the U.S. and world become more closely connected, it will be increasingly important for you to interact effectively with people from backgrounds and experiences that are very different from your own." Most professionals in education, government, business and many other fields agree with him, and they add that during the 21st century in the United States, no single race will be able to claim that it is "the majority" while all others are "minorities." Some cities and some universities are already at this point demographically. What is the proportional mixture in your hometown? At your university?

2. Brown also argues that interactions with people who are different from us can cause personal discomfort, but adds "Yet it is precisely when we experience discomfort that we may be on the verge of new learning which occurs when we listen well to others." Is Brown correct on this point? Have you ever found yourself in a position where discomfort with your surroundings led to new learning? How did you deal with that discomfort?

 ## Suggestions for Your Journal

Carefully review the "suggestions for stretching your comfort zone" that author Brown lists near the close of this essay. Make a good faith effort to put two or three of these into practice and record your experience doing so. What made you uncomfortable? What step(s) did you take to try to change? What was the outcome of your actions? Are there some suggestions you would not be willing to try? Are there additional suggestions that you can add to Brown's list?

I Have a Dream

Martin Luther King Jr.

On August 28, 1963, Dr. Martin Luther King Jr. the preeminent civil rights leader in America during the 1950s and 1960s, delivered this speech as the keynote address of the March on Washington for Civil Rights. His widow, Coretta Scott King, said of that occasion: "At that moment, it seemed as if the kingdom of God appeared. But it lasted for only a moment." This speech is one of the enduring documents of 20th-century American history.

I am happy to join with you today in what will go down in history as the greatest demonstration for freedom in the history of our nation.

Five score years ago, a great American, in whose symbolic shadow we stand today, signed the *Emancipation Proclamation*. This momentous decree came as a great beacon light of hope to millions of Negro slaves who had been seared in the flames of withering injustice. It came as a joyous daybreak to end the long night of their captivity.

But one hundred years later, the Negro still is not free; one hundred years later, the life of the Negro is still sadly crippled by the manacles of segregation and the chains of discrimination; one hundred years later, the Negro lives on a lonely island of poverty in the midst of a vast ocean of material prosperity; one hundred years later, the Negro is still *languished* in the corners of American society and finds himself an exile in his own land.

So we've come here today to dramatize a shameful condition. In a sense we've come to our nation's capital to cash a check. When the architects of our republic wrote the magnificent words of the Constitution and the Declaration of Independence, they were signing a *promissory note* to which every American was to fall heir. This note was a promise that all men, yes, black men as well as white men, would be guaranteed the *unalienable* rights of life, liberty, and the pursuit of happiness.

It is obvious today that America has defaulted on this promissory note insofar as her citizens of color are concerned. Instead of honoring this sacred obligation, America has given the Negro people a bad check, a check which has come back marked "insufficient funds." But we refuse to believe that the bank of justice is bankrupt. We refuse to believe that there are insufficient funds in the great vaults of opportunity of this nation. And so we've come to cash this check, a check that will give us upon demand the riches of freedom and the security of justice.

We have also come to this hallowed spot to remind America of the fierce urgency of now. This is no time to engage in the luxury of cooling off or to take the tranquilizing drug of gradualism. Now is the time to make real the promises of democracy; now is the time to rise from the dark and desolate valley of segregation to the sunlit path of racial justice; now is the time to lift our nation from the quicksands of racial injustice to the solid rock of brotherhood; now is the time to make justice a reality for all of God's children. It would be fatal for the nation to overlook the urgency of the moment. This sweltering summer of the Negro's legitimate discontent will not pass until there is an invigorating autumn of freedom and equality.

Nineteen sixty-three is not an end, but a beginning. And those who hope that the Negro needed to blow off steam and will now be content, will have a rude awakening if the nation returns to business as usual.

There will be neither rest nor tranquillity in America until the Negro is granted his citizenship rights. The whirlwinds of revolt will continue to shake the foundations of our nation until the bright day of justice emerges.

But there is something that I must say to my people who stand on the warm threshold which leads into the palace of justice. In the process of gaining our rightful place we must not be guilty of wrongful deeds.

Let us not seek to satisfy our thirst for freedom by drinking from the cup of bitterness and hatred. We must forever conduct our struggle on the high plane of dignity and discipline. We must not allow our creative protest to degenerate into physical violence. Again and again we must rise to the majestic heights of meeting physical force with soul force.

The marvelous new militancy which has engulfed the Negro community must not lead us to a distrust of all white people, for many of our white brothers, as evidenced by their presence here today, have come to realize that their destiny is tied up with our destiny, and they have come to realize that their freedom is inextricably bound to our freedom. We cannot walk alone.

And as we walk, we must make the pledge that we shall always march ahead. We cannot turn back. There are those who are asking the devotees of civil rights, "When will you be satisfied?" We can never be satisfied as long as the Negro is the victim of the unspeakable horrors of police brutality.

We can never be satisfied as long as our bodies, heavy with the fatigue of travel, cannot gain lodging in the motels of the highways and the hotels of the cities. We cannot be satisfied as long as the Negro's basic mobility is from a smaller ghetto to a larger one.

We can never be satisfied as long as our children are stripped of their selfhood and robbed of their dignity by signs stating "for whites only." We cannot be satisfied as long as a Negro in Mississippi cannot vote and a Negro in New York believes he has nothing for which to vote. No, we are not satisfied, and we will not be satisfied until justice rolls down like waters and righteousness like a mighty stream.

I am not unmindful that some of you have come here out of excessive trials and tribulation. Some of you have come fresh from narrow jail cells. Some of you have come from areas where your quest for freedom left you battered by the storms of persecution and staggered by the winds of police brutality. You have been the veterans of creative suffering. Continue to work with the faith that unearned suffering is redemptive.

Go back to Mississippi; go back to Alabama; go back to South Carolina; go back to Georgia; go back to Louisiana; go back to the slums and ghettos of the northern cities, knowing that somehow this situation can and will be changed. Let us not wallow in the valley of despair.

I say to you today, my friends, that even though we must face the difficulties of today and tomorrow, I still have a dream. It is a dream deeply rooted in the American dream. I have a dream that one day this nation will rise up, live out the true meaning of its creed—we hold these truths to be self-evident, that all men are created equal.

I have a dream that one day on the red hills of Georgia, sons of former slaves and sons of former slave-owners will be able to sit down together at the table of brotherhood.

I have a dream that one day, even the state of Mississippi, a state sweltering with the heat of injustice, sweltering with the heat of oppression, will be transformed into an oasis of freedom and justice.

I have a dream my four little children will one day live in a nation where they will be not be judged by the color of their skin but by the content of their character. I have a dream today!

I have a dream that one day, down in Alabama, with its vicious racists, with its governor having his lips dripping with the words of interposition and nullification, that one day, right there in Alabama, little black boys and black girls will be able to join hands with little white boys and white girls as sisters and brothers. I have a dream today!

I have a dream that one day every valley shall be exalted, every hill and mountain shall be made low, the rough places shall be made plain, and the crooked places will be made straight, and the glory of the Lord will be revealed and all flesh shall see it together.

This is our hope. This is the faith that I go back to the South with.

With this faith we will be able to hew out of the mountain of despair a stone of hope. With this faith we will be able to transform the jangling discords of our nation into a beautiful symphony of brotherhood.

With this faith we will be able to work together, to pray together, to struggle together, to go to jail together, to stand up for freedom together, knowing that we will be free one day. This will be the day when all of God's children will be able to sing with new meaning—"my country 'tis of thee; sweet land of liberty; of thee I sing; land where my father died, land of the pilgrim's pride; from every mountainside, let freedom ring"—and if America is to be a great nation, this must become true.

So let freedom ring from the prodigious hilltops of New Hampshire.
Let freedom ring from the mighty mountains of New York.
Let freedom ring from the heightening Alleghenies of Pennsylvania.
Let freedom ring from the snow-capped Rockies of Colorado.
Let freedom ring from the curvaceous slopes of California.
But not only that.
Let freedom ring from Stone Mountain of Georgia.
Let freedom ring from Lookout Mountain of Tennessee.
Let freedom ring from every hill and molehill of Mississippi.
From every mountainside, let freedom ring.

And when we allow freedom to ring, when we let it ring from every village and every hamlet, from every state and every city, we will be able to speed up that day when all of God's children—black men and white men, Jews and Gentiles, Protestants and Catholics—will be able to join hands and sing in the words of the old Negro spiritual, "Free at last, free at last; thank God Almighty, we are free at last."

 ## Vocabulary

As you think about this essay, these definitions may be helpful to you:

1. **Emancipation Proclamation**   issued by President Abraham Lincoln in 1862 freeing all slaves in all territory still at war with the Union
2. **languished**   suffering neglect
3. **promissory note**   a pledge to pay a debt; an "I.O.U."
4. **unalienable**   incapable of being surrendered or transferred

 ## Discussion Questions

1. What does King mean by the phrase "the tranquilizing drug of gradualism"?
2. King argues that physical force must be countered by "soul force." What does he mean?
3. Using the language of his own time, King speaks of "the Negro." Today's authors would probably not use this word. Why?
4. Discuss the ways in which repetition of key words and phrases plays a part in making this an effective speech.
5. As a Christian minister, King drew heavily on the language of the Bible, which was natural to him. What effect does including such language ("we will not be satisfied until justice rolls down like waters and righteousness like a mighty stream," "every valley shall be exalted, every hill and mountain shall be made low") add to this speech?

 ## Suggestions for Your Journal

Write about the social or political cause for which you would be willing to demonstrate in a public way. In your comments, describe how you came to feel as strongly as you do about this cause.

Martin Luther King Jr. is closely related intellectually and historically to another great social leader, India's Mahatma Gandhi. Both were known for a form of, in King's words, "militant nonviolence." King expressed his admiration for Gandhi by arguing: "We must forever conduct our struggle on the high plane of dignity and discipline. We must not allow our creative protest to degenerate into physical violence." Write an entry in which you agree or disagree with King's statement.

How Discrimination Works and Why It Matters: Five Personal Statements

Edward A. Delgado-Romero is a psychologist at the University of Florida Counseling Center in Gainesville. Donna M. Talbot coordinates the student affairs graduate programs in the Department of Counselor Education and Counseling Psychology at Western Michigan University, Kalamazoo, Joy E. Weeber was a graduate student in a doctoral program in psychology at North Carolina State at Raleigh. Lisa J. Brandyberry is a senior psychologist and director of adult outpatient and emergency services at Piedmont Behavioral Health Care in Albemarie, North Carolina, and Skylar Covich was a senior at St. Mary's College of Moraga, California.

Discussion Questions and Suggestions for Your Journal for these essays appear on pages 180–181.

The Face of Racism

EDWARD A. DELGADO-ROMERO

When thinking of racism, people might imagine the vision of a hooded Ku Klux Klan member lighting a cross, a "skinhead" wearing swastikas, or an angry lynch mob. However, when I think of racism, one image is clear. I learned about racism in the face of my father. I learned hatred, prejudice, and contempt, and, most important, I learned how to turn that racism inward. After many years of self-reflection and healing, I have just begun to understand how deeply racism has affected my attitudes toward others and toward myself. I have begun to understand that racism works on two fronts. One is the overt and obvious racism of the Klan member. The other is the covert and subtle racism that the victim of overt racism begins to internalize, the racism my father taught me.

My father came to this country seeking to escape the personal demons that had haunted him throughout his life. He saw the United States and New York City as a new opportunity, a new beginning. Part of that beginning was rejecting all the things that he had been. My father sought to reinvent himself as an American. In those days, being an American meant being White (some people might argue that this is still true). My father felt he *was* White, because part of his family was descended from Spaniards. Somehow my father thought being Spanish (and

171

therefore European) was better and of higher status than being a South American or a Colombian, and it was certainly better than being *Indio* or native. Our ancestral records show that the Delgado family was a virtuous family with a long tradition in Spain. However, the only records that remain of my ancestors who were native (South) Americans are a few photographs and some of their physical features that were passed along through "blood."

The United States of America taught my father to hate anyone who was not White. Richard Pryor once observed that the first English word that an immigrant is taught is "nigger." Always a quick learner, my father learned to hate "niggers," "gooks," "spics," "wetbacks," and any other "damn immigrants." However, my father soon found out that he was not excluded from the hatred. After days filled with jokes about "green cards" and "drug dealing," my father would return home to his wife and children, full of pent-up rage. We lived in fear of his anger and his explosiveness. My father tried to transform himself yet felt ambivalent about losing his security. Therefore, we were not allowed to speak Spanish to my father, and my mother was not allowed to learn English. By attempting to separate his children from their culture while denying his wife the chance to acculturate, my father replicated his divided psyche. My mother was forced to be the keeper of the culture and language, which she did with incredible bravery and pride. It was through the courage of my mother that I was eventually able to reconnect with my Latino heritage.

My father's drive to be accepted and to be acceptable knew no bounds. I remember one time as a child, we were driving a long distance to go to a restaurant (which was unusual for us). We sat and ate fried chicken and blueberry pie as my father anxiously waited for the owner of the restaurant to come over and acknowledge him. The owner finally did come over, and I remember how proud my father was to meet "a great American." It was only when I was older that I realized that this man was Georgia politician Lester Maddox. Maddox was one of the fiercest opponents of integration during the civil rights era. He was made infamous by keeping a bucket of ax handles by the door of his restaurant as a reminder of the violence that he had threatened to use against any Black person who would try to integrate his home or business. It shocks me to realize how racism had blinded my father to the fact that his fate as an immigrant and a minority group member in the United States was tied to the fate of other minorities.

As hard as he tried to fit in, my father never really succeeded. Often his physical features, his accent, or his clothes would give him away as being different. My father would react violently when confronted with his failure to become one hundred percent American. For example, during an interview for a promotion, the interviewer asked my father about the "good pot" grown in Colombia. At the time my father laughed it off. However, when he returned home he exploded in rage. These explosions became a daily event. My brother, sister, and I were a captive audience. We had no choice but to listen as he would berate us for being worthless. The angrier he became, the more pressure my father would put on us to "be American." We were wildly successful at being American, which only made my father angrier. As I became a teenager, my father became increasingly competitive with and abusive toward me. The fact that I physically resembled him only made things worse. He saw in me things he could never achieve: I spoke English without an accent, was headed toward college, and I dated Caucasian women exclusively.

I learned racism from my father, and just as he had done, I turned it inward. I came to hate the fact that I was Latino, that my parents spoke with an accent, that my skin, although light for a Latino, was darker than it should be. I wanted to be a White Anglo-American, and for many years, I actually thought I was. During my high school and college years I was in deep denial that I was Latino. I believed that America was a "color blind" society that rewarded people solely on the basis of hard work. I remember my Caucasian high school guidance counselor steering me away from minority scholarships for college and telling me "Ed, you want to get in on your own merit." At the time I believed her, and my "own merit" led to my status as a "token" at a predominantly Caucasian college, thousands of dollars in student loans, and 4 more years of denial.

I remember being deeply embarrassed by Latino music, food, customs, and history. My mother would often talk about her home country with pride and fondness. I used to get angry with her because she was being so "un-American." One time, in an attempt to share her culture with me, my mother gave me an expensive recording of Colombian music. I actually had the nerve to give it back to her because I was ashamed of everything Latino. I was particularly ashamed of my Spanish surname because of the way that my peers could mispronounce it in demeaning ways. I became so used to being called names that often I would participate in using ethnic slurs against myself and other minorities. I remember vividly a Latino varsity football player who was proud that his nickname was "Spic." Having a racial slur as a nickname was a badge of honor; it meant he was accepted. As an enthusiastic participant in the ethnic name-calling, I could continue to deny that I was different. The height of my own denial was when I told a Mexican joke to a priest, who was Mexican. The priest laughed, more out of shock than humor. The joke was, quite literally, on both of us. He confronted me, and pointed out that he was Mexican. As I stood in awkward silence, having offended someone I cared about, something began to awaken within me.

I began to realize that I was an impostor and that there was another side of me that I was denying. Although I felt intimidated and uncomfortable around people of color, there was a depth of connection that was missing in most of my relationships. I struggled to make sense of what I was feeling. My longing for connection with other minorities was first manifested in college through my participation in a fraternity. When I joined the fraternity, the membership was almost exclusively White. However, as I was able to influence member selection, the membership became increasingly diverse. I began to surround myself with other people who could understand what it felt like to be of two worlds and never fully at peace in either one. These were my first steps toward healing the racism that I felt inside.

My cultural explorations coincided with the divorce of my parents. My father eventually left our home and emotionally and financially disowned his family. This split helped me to continue the self-exploration and reclamation of my heritage that had begun in college. I learned about my ancestors, their names, and their lives. I learned my full name and the proper way to pronounce it. I was able to become friends with Latino men and Latina women. I asked my mother to give me back the recording of Colombian music I had refused to take from her and asked her to teach me about her culture. My mother saved up her money and took me on a trip to Colombia. I wish that I could say that I found my "home" in Colombia. I wish that I could say that I reconnected with my ancestors on some deep level. However, in Colombia I felt every bit the foreigner that I was. What I gained from my trip to Colombia was an understanding and appreciation for the enormous sacrifice that my mother had made for her children. In Colombia I realized that I was neither fully Colombian nor fully American. I had to find a way to make sense of my divided identity.

Many of my colleagues in psychology say that therapists enter the profession motivated in part by a need to deal with their own issues. As much as I used to argue that I was the exception to the rule, obviously I was not. In an effort to somehow identify, understand, and deal with my issues, I was drawn to graduate study in counseling psychology. I was offered a lucrative fellowship at a major university. However, only one professor (who later became my adviser and mentor) was honest enough to tell me that it was a minority fellowship. Many of the faculty and students saw the minority fellowship as a way for me to cheat the system because they did not think I was "really" a minority. One student explained his belief that I was not a real minority because I did not speak "broken English." The pressure to fit in and deny that I was different was enormous. I was faced with a choice that reminded me of dealing with my father: stay quiet and accept the status quo of the University and the program (basically "pass" as Caucasian) or assert myself and challenge a culturally oppressive system. I wish I could say that I chose to try to change the system simply because it was the moral or just thing to do. However, I think I chose to fight the system because I was tired of being quiet. Multicultural psychology became my passion and the focus of my career. I have my doubts as to how much I was able to change a deeply entrenched racist, sexist, and homophobic system, but I have no doubt that I underwent tremendous personal and professional growth.

As I progressed through my graduate training and into internship, I found that I surrounded myself with other people who could understand what it was like to face overt and covert racism. I formed a supportive network of friends and colleagues of all colors. At first I felt some animosity toward Caucasian people, but a Caucasian friend once pointed out that all people would benefit from being liberated from racism. I found that the term *liberation* captured the essence of what I was searching for: liberation from hatred and racism and, personally, a liberation from the past. I realized that liberation meant letting go of the intense anger and resentment I felt toward my father. My anger toward my father was like wearing a shrinking suit of armor: Although the anger could make me feel powerful and protected, the anger was not letting me grow and, in fact, was starting to choke me. However, I was concerned that, stripped of my armor, I would lose my motivation to fight racism. I was surprised to find that by liberating myself from my father's legacy, I was able to find peace and that from this peace I could generate more energy and motivation to face racism than I had imagined possible.

As I grow older and consider having my own children, I find myself looking in the mirror to see if I can see my father's face. There have been times when I have been both shocked and disappointed to hear his voice angrily coming out of my mouth or have seen my face contorted with his rage. I was surprised to find out that liberation did not mean I could change the facts of my past or get rid of any influence from my father. However, I gained something even more valuable: I learned that because of my experiences, I can understand why some one would be racist. I can understand what it is like to be both a perpetrator and a victim of racism. I have also come to understand that the answer to fighting racism begins with a moral inventory, a fearless look at oneself. I have come to the conclusion that I can never afford myself the luxury of asking the question "Am I racist?" Rather, I need to continually ask myself, "How racist am I?" As I struggle to deal with the reality of racism in my personal and professional life, I will continue to check my mirror and look for the face of racism.

Personal Narrative of an Asian American's Experience with Racism

DONNA M. TALBOT

Growing up in New England during the '60s and '70s had its benefits and difficulties. Although the northeast region of the country had larger pockets of people of color and immigrants than most other parts of the United States, the stiffness and arrogance of old money and elitist educational institutions created some inevitable friction among people with greatly diverse cultural backgrounds. It is in this environment (less than 5 miles from a large Air Force base) that I began my identity development, although unknowingly, as a person of color—as an Asian American.

My parents are both naturalized citizens; they were thankful to be in the United States, the land of opportunity and upward mobility. My father is French Canadian and Huron Indian and my mother is 100 percent Japanese. Although my two brothers and I were clearly raised with Japanese values and culture, my mother, our primary caretaker, insisted that we should grow up to be "good American citizens." This was driven by her pride in being a U.S. citizen and her fear of racist acts against us. What she didn't realize was that, despite her wishes, she couldn't help but raise good Japanese American citizens. . . .

Many of my most vivid memories of what I believe to be acts of racism, sexism, and oppression took place in "American institutions," such as schools, social organizations (Moose and Elks Clubs), and church. This fact has largely influenced my decision to become an educator, student affairs practitioner, and counselor; unfortunately, I think these experiences have also influenced my decision to move away from Christianity and to explore other forms of spirituality. In my professional roles, I address my agenda openly—to advocate for oppressed and marginalized populations so that they may not have to be subjected to the same negative experiences that I was.

My first overt experience of racism and recognition that I was "different" took place in school around the third grade. I remember waiting with my classmates in the hallway to go into social studies class. As I was standing there, several boys started to circle me while chanting that their fathers, uncles, and other male relatives had bombed my people. Then, they proceeded to pull up the corners of their eyes with their fingers, so they appeared slanted, and made funny noises like "ching," "chang," and so forth. For me this was extremely confusing because we had all grown up in the same neighborhood; but as I cried in the bathroom and looked in the mirror, it was the first time I cognitively realized that my eyes were different from theirs. Probably the most embarrassing part of this experience for me was that the teacher just stood in the doorway and laughed at the boys taunting me; he never tried to stop them or indicate that they were wrong. From that time on, through most of grade school, I hated myself and my mother for looking and being different.

A few years later, I learned how to be angry toward bias and ignorance. My older brother wanted to play baseball with his friends during the summer. To do that, my parents had to join the local Moose Club so that he could play in their leagues. Because my family would have been classified as "working class poor," this was a major commitment of which my parents were very proud. My father went to the club, completed the paperwork, and paid the application and membership fee. Everything seemed fine for about 2 weeks until we received a call from the membership person at the Moose Club; he explained to my father that the Moose, and other similar clubs, had a policy that prohibited interracial members from joining. The only apology he made was for not catching it sooner!

It wasn't until high school that I started to realize that there were benefits to being different—although I still resented being Asian. Teachers remembered me because I looked so different from my classmates, and the boys liked my long, black, straight hair and clear, olive complexion. Even colleges were interested and pursued this "high achieving" minority student. Although I was encouraged (actually, I was tracked) to take honors math and science courses, I had a strong interest in the social sciences and education. Most people were surprised, even shocked, when I turned down large scholarships from institutions with well-known engineering and computer science programs to go to a small liberal arts college. This marked the second most significant racist, or "classist," event in my educational experience. Early in my senior year, I was the first person in my local public high school ever to be accepted (early decision) to a very prestigious, liberal arts college—Amherst College. Soon, after the word was out that this had happened, I was summoned to the vice principal's office. Being the arrogant young "scholar" I thought I was, I assumed that the vice principal was calling me to give me "strokes" for my accomplishment. Several minutes into the discussion, a dark haze started to crowd my mind as I realized that this was an entirely different conversation than I had anticipated. Very confused and angry, I finally asked the vice principal what, exactly, she was trying to say to me. Her words rang loudly, almost deafeningly, in my ears, "Frankly, Donna, we're not sure you come from the *right kind of family* to be the first to represent our high school at Amherst College." At that point, I remember standing up and announcing that this meeting was over; however, as I was walking out, I suggested that this was a conversation she needed to have with my father. Although there were several other minor attempts to block my efforts to attend Amherst College, they were unsuccessful. I don't think I ever mentioned these incidents to my parents because I didn't want them ever to feel the humiliation that I had. Needless to say, the vice principal never called to have that conversation with my father.

College was an amazing experience for me—every day was a challenge to grow (personally and academically). Toward the end of my sophomore year, I was suspended, with many other Amherst students, for participating in demonstrations and a lock-out of the administration building. During that time, we had an African American dean who believed that the damage from slavery was over and that it was time to eliminate the programs and services that were created in the '60s to assist African American students. Naturally, we just labeled him an "Uncle Tom" and protested these decisions as well as demanded that the college divest its stocks in South Africa. My parents, especially my mother, were very angry with me; they were embarrassed that I would show such blatant disrespect for "authorities" and that I could jeopardize my education. During one of the many scoldings I received for this inappropriate behavior, my mother asked why I always had to be the one to stand up and challenge things, even the issues that didn't apply to me. My response to her was that I had to object twice as loud and twice as often because she wouldn't; either she was going to ride in the boat of change or she would be left behind on the shores of oppression and discontent. This response startled her and, though I didn't know until years later, pushed her into thinking about the role of "activism" and her own multicultural journey.

My faculty adviser at Amherst was a Returned Peace Corps Volunteer (RCPV Micronesia). As well as turning me on to liberation theology through Freire's (1970) *Pedagogy of the Oppressed*,[1] he also taught me about the "toughest job I ever loved." Three weeks after graduation, despite my parents' hope that I would go to law school, I was on a plane to Ghana, West Africa. Before [I left] for the Peace Corps, friends and family would ask me what I thought about moving to an "uncivilized" country. I thought I knew what they meant, though I had no answers. After several months in my small village in Ghana, my host country friends and colleagues finally felt comfortable enough to ask me what it was like to live in an "uncivilized" country—they were referring to the United States. It suddenly became clear to me that oftentimes we speak the same language, use the same words, and we assume that we all mean the same thing. When my family and friends in the United States used the term "uncivilized" to describe Ghana, they were making comments about the less industrialized nature of the country; when my Ghanaian friends and colleagues called the United States uncivilized, they were referring to the need to lock our doors and to never walk alone at night for fear of

---

[1]P. Freire, *Pedagogy of the Oppressed* (New York: Continuum, 1970).

our personal safety. This taught me to resist assuming that I understand another person's experience well enough to casually ascribe meaning to his or her words.

When I entered the Peace Corps, I had lofty goals; these idealistic plans soon took a backseat to survival, literally and figuratively. It struck me as humorous, at some point in my service, that I felt less like an outsider here (in Ghana) than I did in my own home country. On one of my many travels across the country, I was stranded on the road without food or shelter as nighttime approached. A young Ghanaian man saw me standing by the road and realized my situation. He invited me home to his village where his family gave me a place to sleep, shared what little food they had, and fetched me drinking and bathing water from a well nearly a mile away. When I was leaving in the morning, I asked if I could give them something for their troubles. They refused my offer, indicating that they did what anyone would do. With this comment, I became extremely embarrassed and uncomfortable as I imagined how this young "Black man" would be treated in the United States if he were stranded by the road. Stimulated by this incident and many other experiences, my time in Ghana was a time of deep introspection and what I now refer to as my "rebirth." Though returning to the States was more traumatic and painful than moving to Ghana, I knew that I had to return because there was work to do here in the United States. . . .

What Could I Know of Racism?

Joy E. Weeber

What could I know of racism, being a middle-class, college-educated White woman? What could I know of the pain of being rendered invisible because of a single characteristic? What could I know of having the complexity of myself, a Dutch American from a large extended family living around the world, reduced to that feature which marks me as "different" from the dominant culture? What could I know of being denied entrance to public facilities or required to sit in segregated places because of that characteristic? What could I know of being forced to use a back service entrance, like a second-class citizen? What could I know about being told that if I "work hard enough" I could make it, although getting in the front door for an interview seems an impossibility? What could I know about having to endure painful procedures to make my appearance more acceptable? What could I know of being charged a higher price for services because of the way I look? What could I know about not being able to ride a bus with dignity? What could I know of having a hard time finding a place to live because of housing discrimination or being unable to visit in the homes of my classmates? What could I know of growing up in a society that never portrays my people with positive images in the media, except for those exceptional, inspirational heroes who have more than made it? What could I know of being viewed as less intelligent simply because of the way I look? What could I know of being educated in a segregated school setting, not expected to amount to much and denied opportunities because of it? What could I know of being thought of as less than acceptable because of the way that I speak? What could I know of having to work twice as hard as others just to prove I am as good as they are? What could I know of being viewed as a charity case, rather than one who possesses civil rights?

I can know the pain of all of these things because I am disabled. My disabled brothers and sisters and I experience such acts of discrimination on a daily basis, and the pain these encounters cause is the same pain that racism causes people of color. It is the pain caused by the unconscious beliefs of a society that assumes everyone is, or should be, "normal" (i.e., White and very able-bodied). It is the pain caused by the assumption that everyone should be capable of total independence and "pulling themselves up by their own bootstraps." It is a belief in the superiority of being nondisabled that assumes everyone who is disabled wishes they could be nondisabled—at any cost. In the disability community, we call this "ableism," a form of prejudice and bigotry that marks us as less than those who are nondisabled. In this narrative, I use language the disability community claims in naming its own lived experience. And although it may not be "politically correct," it is meant as a true reflection of how many of us view ourselves and our lives as members of the disability community.

Ableism causes pain because it convinces us that there is something fundamentally wrong with us, that we are not acceptable just as we are. After all, we are the ones who are "defective," with bodies, speech, hearing, vision and emotional or cognitive functioning to be fixed by doctors and therapists. Ableism also causes pain to nondisabled people who are unprepared to deal with their own vulnerability and mortality when accidents and aging require that they do so. I did not understand the pain these attitudes had caused me until I was 35, despite having lived with the effects of polio since I was an infant. Until then, I did not know that I had spent my entire life trying to prove how I had "overcome" my polio, which is no more possible than overcoming being female or African American! I did not understand that these ableist attitudes and acts devalued my body and denied an essential element of who I am.

I only began to understand all of this when I read an essay, "The Myth of the Perfect Body," by Roberta Galler (1984),[1] who also had polio as a child. I felt as if I were reading my own diary! I was not an alien; I had a disability! I was the "supercrip" she wrote about, the defiant opposite of the pathetic cripple I had been made so deathly afraid of being. I had spent enormous amounts of my energy proving how "able" I was, to counter society's belief that I am "unable." I

[1]R. Galler, "The Myth of the Perfect Body," in C. Vance (ed.), *Pleasure and Danger: Exploring Female Sexuality* (Boston: Routledge and Kegan Paul, 1984), pp. 165–172.

thought I had "passed" as normal in my nondisabled world (despite my crutches and braces), because I was often "complimented" by strangers and friends who "did not think of me as handicapped." Only when I read this woman's words did I begin to understand how my life had been shaped by living with a disability, even though my family and I had not been able to acknowledge that it existed! Only then did I begin to understand how my sense of self had been constructed by how my body had been touched, treated, and talked about by those who had been my "caregivers." Only then did I begin to understand how my life had been lived as an outsider, struggling unconsciously for acceptance.

Throughout my childhood, I had successfully resisted sincerely religious strangers' urgings for me to get "healed," people who thought of me as sick and infirm. Although these encounters left me feeling violated and nauseated, I knew I was fine and intact the way I was! Why did they think I was sick? I lived in a tight-knit community that accepted me as a whole person; they did not see me as sick. Not once had I been stopped from living life fully by anyone's low expectations, fear, or lack of imagination in how to change the world to meet my needs. I had been allowed to participate on my terms and discover my own physical limitations. My parents understood the stigma that society places on people with disabilities and were determined to nurture a sense of self that could deflect such negativity.

And yet, at the age of 10, I was marked as "other" by a diagnosis of scoliosis, found to be "defective" with a curving spine and weak leg muscles, and in need of "corrective" surgery. Thus began my searing journey into a medical world that would teach me well what it really means to be disabled in this society! It was a world that taught me I was invisible, a defective body part to be talked about as if not connected to a lonely, hurting child. It was a world that taught me I had to be tough to survive, cut off from the emotional support of my family for all but 2 hour visits a week. It was a world that taught me that it was okay for others to inflict pain on me—if their goal was to make me more "normal." This world taught me that what I felt or wanted had nothing to do with what happened to my body, that it was okay to publicly strip children and parade their defects in front of strangers. The result of seven surgeries and innumerable scars was a girl who was numb, disconnected from both body and soul. I was fragmented and lost to a family who had no clue of my inner devastation. The emotional isolation of the hospital followed me home, as I heard in my family's lack of understanding that something was "wrong" with how I responded to life—emotionally, psychologically, spiritually, and politically!

My response to the horror of those years was to make myself outdo everyone, need help from no one, and take care of everyone else's needs. I was constantly proving I was the "exception," not one of those dependent cripples society cannot tolerate. Never mind that I spent my entire adult life struggling with devastating bouts of exhaustion-induced depression—although others only ever saw my bright, cheerful self. Never mind that I was alone, unable to sustain any vital romantic relationships, ever untouchable and independent. I became the angry one who spoke out against social injustice and felt the sexism in our community and family. I was the one who felt the arrogance and violence of racism. I was the one who felt the fragmentation of only seeking spiritual and physical sustenance, while psychological and emotional needs went unacknowledged. Being alone in the hospital, and the thought of seeking the company of those who might share them, never crossed my mind.

At no time did I connect my different ways of perceiving and responding to the world with my experience of living with a disability. I couldn't. There was no disabled person in my world to help me understand that my empathy for those who suffered from injustice or were devalued because of race was rooted in my own experience of being devalued because of my disability. In the 7 years since my first encounter with a disabled person who understood, I have never felt alone. I have come to know the healing of belonging, of being understood without a word in a community of people who validate my feelings. I did not know how fragmented I was, and I needed other disabled people to teach me to love myself wholly! I had needed them to teach me how to embrace that part of myself that society so devalues. I needed them to show me the commonalities between our experiences of ableism and others' experiences of racism. I needed them to give words to the feelings I had never had reflected back to my self in my nondisabled world.

Most of us with disabilities learn to survive alone and silently in our nondisabled families and worlds, never knowing a disability community exists. I was the only disabled person in my family, my community, schools, and my adult social world. As a child, I had learned an aversion to the company of other disabled people because they were associated with being "defective" and stigmatized, and I was neither of those! My only experiences with other disabled people had been in situations in which nondisabled professionals "medicalized" our lives, defining us negatively. I even had my own turn at working in such settings, "helping" others in sheltered workshops and group homes, although always quitting for emotional reasons I only now understand. I had never been in an environment in which disabled people defined themselves in their own terms and celebrated their uniqueness. And now, in the written words and in the company of disabled people, I have found brothers and sisters who are teaching me that there are powerful ways of dealing with the pain of being "other." They are helping me find the words to express what I have always "known" in my body, but had no language to express.

James Baldwin (1972) wrote that "to be liberated from the stigma of blackness by embracing it, is to cease, forever, one's interior argument and collaboration with the authors of one's degradation (p. 190)."[2] It has been my experience that learning to embrace my whole self, disability and all, was not a task I could do alone. I needed the support and guidance of others who not only had lived my experience but also had ceased their internal collaboration with the negative voices of society. It is the same process that bell hooks (1989) speaks of in *Talking Back: Thinking Feminist, Thinking Black*,[3] as the need to "decolonialize" one's mind by rooting out all that does not honor one's own experience. I have found that in

[2]J. Baldwin, *No Name in the Street* (New York: Doubleday, 1972).
[3]b. hooks, *Talking Back: Thinking Feminist, Thinking Black* (Boston, Mass.: South End Press, 1989).

addition to decolonializing my mind, I have also needed to decolonialize my body. I have had to cease my interior argument with society's negative messages that I am not as good as everybody else by no longer pushing my body beyond its limits. As I have learned to listen to my body's limits, honoring them as a source of wisdom and strength, I have experienced the healing and liberation of the embrace, and I have begun to thrive.

A most profound way that I have begun to thrive is that I no longer require that I spend most of my energy walking to get around—I have begun to use a scooter for mobility. What an act of liberation—and resistance—this has been! I felt like a bird let out of a cage, the first time I used one! I could go and go and not be exhausted! I was able to fully participate in the conference I was attending, rather that just be dully present. To choose to use a scooter, when I can still walk, flies in the face of all the "wisdom" of those without disabilities. We are taught that to walk, no matter how distorted or exhausting it is, is far more virtuous than using a chair—because it is closer to "normal." Never mind that my galumphing polio-gait twists my muscles into iron-like sinew that only the hardiest of masseuses can "unknot." Never mind that my shoulders and hands, never meant for walking, have their future usefulness limited by 40 years of misuse on crutches. To choose to use a scooter also places me squarely in that stigmatized group of "pitiful unfortunates" who are "confined" to their chairs. It removes me from the ranks of "overcomers," such as Franklin Delano Roosevelt, Wilma Rudolph, or Helen Keller, whom society mistakenly believes actually "got over" their disabilities. My using a scooter is an act that scares my family. They are afraid that somehow giving up walking will make me give up—period! It makes them think that I am losing ground, becoming dependent on the scooter, when they and society need me to act as if I am strong and virile. Only now that I am embracing my limitations do I know how I spent much life-energy protecting my family from them. I rarely slowed them down or burdened them with feelings they could not understand. Only now can I celebrate my unavoidable need for interdependence in a society that oppresses everyone with its unattainable standard of independence!

Traditionally, families are taught by professionals that their child's disability is an individual functional problem that can only be remedied by individualized medical interventions. And so it remains the focus of many families to adapt their child to a society that needs them to be "normal. "The larger social and cultural oppression that some of those interventions represent is only now being raised by those of us former disabled children who question the extreme and painful measures taken to "fix" us, measures that went beyond what may have been truly needed to ensure our full, unique development. In my scooter, I am choosing now to live by other values—the values of the disability community that require society to adapt to our needs rather than vice versa.

In using my scooter, I experience the full range of the disability experience, including those aspects I avoided when I thought I was "passing" as normal. In my scooter, I experience being denied access to places walking people enter without a thought, because they are inaccessible. In my scooter, I am eligible to use service entrances near stinking dumpsters and seating at public events that is seg-regated from my walking companions. Seated in my scooter, I am even more invis-ible to those who could never look the walking-me in the eye—an averted gaze not even required to obliterate my presence. In my scooter, I cannot visit some friends' homes because of stairs or use their bathrooms because of narrow doors. The very cost of my scooter includes a sizable "crip tax"—as the sum of its component parts is far less costly than its hefty price tag in the inflated (and captive) medical equipment market. In my scooter, I don't have full assurance that I will even be able to get on public transportation, much less treated with dignity when I do. In my scooter I feel the insult of those telethon hosts who want to paint my life as pathetic, not livable, unless I am cured. In my scooter, I know that I am viewed as far less able, needing public assistance rather than ramps and power doors to get into job interviews. Although my speech was not affected by polio, my scooter provides further reason to dismiss me, as society dismisses my brothers and sisters who use voice synthesizers to communicate their artistic vision of the world. In my scooter, I am inextricably and unavoidably a member of the disability commu-nity, with all the pain and privileges associated with that membership.

I am proud to have found my way home to the disability community. I am now able to "hang out on the porch" and hear stories from the elders of how their visions of equal justice for all took shape, how legislation acknowledging our civil rights was passed. And although it is true that we continue to struggle to define our own lives and live it on our own terms, we have also begun to create a culture that brings us together and celebrates our unique ways of being in the world. I am moved when I hear poetry that speaks my truth and read books that truly reflect my life experiences. I am healed when I see unflinchingly honest performances dealing with the reality and pain caused by ableism. I now know that I have indeed experienced the pain of ableism and I know why I felt the pain of racism when I had words for neither. I now also know the liberating power of embracing my disability and of celebrating who I am because of it.

Pain and Perseverance:
Perspectives from an Ally

LISA J. BRANDYBERRY

I grew up as "poor, White, trash" in the middle of the Midwest. The city I lived in was an industrial one—mostly union workers—and always smelled like french fries or rubber. It was mostly White, but there were a fair number of African Americans and Latinos living in various monoracial communities throughout the city. From beginning to end, the schools I went to were integrated, so there is no time I can remember that I didn't know any Black (the term I grew up with) people.

During grade school one of my best friends was Garth, a Black child in my class. We hung around a lot together during lunch hours. I don't remember being upset about the fact that when he and I played together none of my White friends would join us. Some other Black children would come over and join us from time to time. I couldn't have both his friendship and the other White kids' friendships simultaneously.

I felt good around Garth and many of the other Black children. I felt all right around most of the other White children. I was one of few working-class Whites in that particular school. I never had the right clothes because my family shopped at Kmart and hoped for blue-light specials while we were there. My mother gave me haircuts; unfortunately, it wasn't her talent. I was often too loud in my laughter, too crude in my language.

I was also fat, an automatic object of ridicule and harassment for other children. Between being too poor and too fat, there was a lot about me to pick on and many reasons to ostracize me. But, I was never totally rejected. Somehow, something in me was enough to compensate for my "failings," so I always had friends. But with most, if not all, of my White friends, I always knew I was inferior. After the sixth grade, Garth and I were shuffled to different schools, and I didn't think I'd ever see him again.

By my senior year in high school, I had become painfully aware of what made me "inferior" to my classmates. As do many people struggling with internalized oppression, I worked hard to compensate for my failings because I had grown to believe that there was something wrong with me. I worked hard at my classes and did very well; I was always smiling, always willing to do more for others, to laugh at myself when the ridicule would come my way.

My senior year the city closed down one of the other high schools, and the students were bused to different schools. Garth ended up at mine. I saw him one day walking down the hall near my locker, and I started laughing and walking toward him, remembering how good it had felt to have him for a friend. Initially, I thought he didn't recognize me, but he did. He was uncomfortable; he didn't want to be found talking to me. I tried for a few more minutes to talk with him, to find out about what had happened to him. Then I gave up, maybe too soon. After so many years of rejection from others, I was pretty aware of what it felt like to be with someone who didn't want to be with me. We ended with a "see you around" after about 2 minutes of awkwardness. That's the last time I ever spoke to him.

Being a White female, I had learned that my weight was a primary reason for rejection from others, especially males. When Garth seemed not to want to be seen with me, I assumed it was for that reason. I was too fat, too ugly. Who knows? Maybe that was part of it. But now, looking back, I believe it was probably more about race than weight. He had spent the previous 5 years in a predominantly Black school. Who knows how White people had treated him, a Black male adolescent, during those years?

My college life intensified my feelings of being an outsider. I received a scholarship to a small, private liberal arts college where the majority of the students were wealthy and White. There were a few of us paying for school through scholarships, jobs, and loans. There were even fewer Black students on campus, but they were there. All the pain I felt growing up being poor and fat was multiplied at this college, but it was there that I got angry about it. Angry about the privileges of wealthy people who seemed to believe that it was normal to have more than enough money to go to Europe on vacations, to shop for new clothes every weekend, to have cars at their disposal, to have plenty of leisure time because they weren't trying to fit in a job on top of classes and studying.

I tried reaching out to some of the few Black students on campus and became close with one woman, Doris. I cannot begin to imagine what it was like for a young Black woman from Chicago to have to survive in that small Iowa town. After we had struck up a friendship, she started pushing me to go to Black dance clubs in a nearby city. I initially refused—I didn't even go to White dance clubs. But, eventually, I agreed to go. She took charge of what I was going to wear because I couldn't dress like those "White folks," who dressed down to go out. This was time to go all out with jewelry, makeup, and hairstyles. I remember being very nervous on the long drive to the city, scared about being the only White person in the club. I was too embarrassed by this to tell my friend.

Through this experience I got my first taste of being a racial minority. Although this was unpleasant, it was vital in my development. I felt what it was like to have people be angry that I had merely walked into their place, to feel cautious about what I said and how I said it, to feel like a complete outsider, to imagine that everyone in the room must hate me because of my skin color. I am thankful that Doris didn't allow me to disappear into a corner. She pushed me out on the dance floor and pulled me around introducing me to people she knew. By the end of the night I had had a great time, and we went back together several times during the next year.

Graduate school pushed me more than any other experience to really examine myself. I was fortunate to end up in a program that emphasized diversity issues. There were many times it was painful and frightening, because I was challenged to look beyond my "liberal" attitudes to honestly examine myself. I had to go deeper than focusing on all the positive experiences I had had with people of color. I had to examine all the negative messages I had absorbed and determine how much they were still affecting me. I had to learn to see myself as part of the White race, whether I liked it or not.

My family, church, and the media were major influences on me. I went to a church that was entirely White and remember watching how any Black families that would come to visit would have it made clear to them that they weren't welcome. They were treated much like I was when I went to the Black dance club, except they didn't end up having fun and meeting nice people. The stares and whispers didn't end; the shared laughter never started.

I was affected by hearing my brothers talk about "niggers," or more often about "Black bitches." I remember my parents not allowing one of my brothers to go play basketball at a certain court because it wasn't safe around "those" people. I remember my father pointing out what we thought was a garishly painted house and saying "colored" people have no taste. I also remember him making it clear that he didn't want me ever to bring home a Black man. As much as I want to believe I never accepted these attitudes, I know they influenced me and what I believed. I came to believe that "they" were different from "us."

The process of acknowledging what was meant by "us," of owning my own racial heritage, included owning all the history that goes with being White. During this process, the only part of that history I could see was its shame: slavery and genocide of Africans, American Indians, Asians, and Mexicans. There didn't seem to be any horror that wasn't committed in the name of the "manifest destiny" and superiority of European Whites. My reaction was to feel an incredible amount of guilt and shame; I didn't want to be White, didn't want to belong to this group, didn't want to be part of this "us."

Even more painful than that was having to examine how I had benefited from racism. I had to question how I could hold so much anger toward those who were wealthy (or male) because they didn't recognize their privileges but had never acknowledged the privileges I enjoyed from my skin color. It had never crossed my mind that there was a way in which I was privileged. I didn't come from money, I wasn't born beautiful, my family life had been far from perfect, and I had struggled to get where I was.

It wasn't easy to look at the probability that I had struggled less than if I were a person of color. That maybe my White skin had allowed me access to the upper-level college preparatory classes despite being working class, which, in turn, probably increased my test scores, which opened doors to receive academic scholarships and, basically, gave me the opportunity to achieve a level beyond where I was born. I'd like to think that I earned everything I have, but I can no longer tell myself that. I earned some of it, and some of it was very likely given to me because of being White. I have grown to recognize the privileges I receive every day for being White.

It was during this time of feeling overwhelmed with guilt and shame about my race that I worked for a year as the only White person in an all-African American agency. It was not a job I had applied for or wanted; it was a job I was requested (and eventually forced) to accept. I didn't want the job because I was afraid the staff would hate me. I remember talking with my boss about my fears. He was an African American man with whom I'd worked before and who had requested my placement in the position. He never denied that hostility was possible, but he never let me off the hook regarding my responsibility. He made it clear that it was my place to deal with any prejudice directed at me and that he would support me in that process, but that it was something I would have to face. He also reminded me that it was something minorities face on a daily basis. Again, in having to walk through my fear, I enjoyed a wonderful experience. There was only one person who made it clear she didn't want me there, and even she taught me a valuable lesson. She taught me how subtle sabotage can be. I would miss meetings because I never received the memorandum informing me of them. I wouldn't receive phone messages. I'd receive paperwork late or not at all, and I could *feel* her dislike emanating from her. It was through this experience that I learned to be very hesitant to question the experiences of persons of color who feel they are being discriminated against but can't name anything grossly inappropriate.

My professional life has moved me farther in my journey to overcome racism. A large part of that has come from my close work and friendship with an African American lesbian, Jan. We connected immediately when I came to interview and quickly became friends. We have done numerous programs together focusing in general on oppression issues and, often, specifically on race. We have had to struggle together with issues of race more so than any other issue. What has saved our relationship is our willingness to talk about race, to put our "raggedy selves" on the table.

Many of these struggles have come from my desire not to have race separate us and Jan's desire to keep part of her personal space monoracial; that is, sometimes she just wants to hang with the Black folks. Intellectually, I understand this. I sometimes don't want men around because there is a comfort in groups of women that doesn't exist with men present. It has nothing to do with disliking men; it's simply a different vibe that exists. But on a personal level, it continues to hurt. I struggle with feeling rejected, separated because of my skin color, not seen as the person who is Jan's friend but as a representative of the White race. She knows this because we've talked about it at length. She struggles with it as well because she knows it hurts me, but she wants to have her needs met too.

I now understand why I sometimes feel closer to, and more connected with, some people of color than with many White people. My understanding came through viewing oppression as encompassing all the different groups experiencing it. Having been born into a working-class family, I share many cultural dynamics with people of color also born into this economic sphere. It is often difficult for me, and apparently others, to figure out how to separate race from class. My sensitivity to how I've experienced oppression personally, through class, body size, and gender issues, has allowed me to have some sense of perspective on the pain of racism. Finally, my willingness to admit to and name privileges that I experience because of my race seems to afford me some credibility with people of color . . .

My conclusion, sadly, is that most people of color simply don't expect much from White people. They don't expect us to be open, to have thought about these issues, to have thought about ourselves (rather than them) in terms of these issues, to be working against racism inside and outside of the therapy room. I believe it is my responsibility, as a member of the majority group, to fight racism. As I benefit and derive increased societal rewards from racism's existence, perhaps my voice may reach other White ears that refuse to listen to the voices of people of color. I believe this as passionately as I believe that men must speak to other men about sexism, that heterosexuals must speak to members of their own group about homophobia, and so on.

Those of us committed to being allies must be willing to persevere in this struggle. People of color do not have the option of ignoring racism and its effects; therefore, we must not ignore it either. We must choose to persevere in the face of rejection, criticism, and suspicion from members of majority and minority groups. Not everyone wants Whites to be involved in this struggle, and I understand this lack of trust. But racism is the problem of the racists, not those who are oppressed by it. As a part of the problem group, I must be involved in eliminating the problem itself.

Some say that no one willingly gives up power, and while members of majority groups refuse to see any benefit to themselves for changing the system (personal and institutional), progress will be slow and painful. But when majority group members can see that *their* lives will improve, *their* accomplishments will be seen as more completely due to merit rather than privilege, that the quality of life will improve for all of us, then, perhaps, change will be possible.

A College Senior Speaks about Diversity: The Disability Perspective

SKYLAR COVICH

I was born blind and went to regular public schools from kindergarten through high school. I had special aides and teachers who helped me learn to adapt; I learned how to read Braille, use a computer, and travel with a cane, among many other skills. When the time came to apply to colleges, my parents and I eventually decided that a small private school would be best for me. Large schools like UC Berkeley and Michigan State University have many blind students who are successful and enjoy the environment of a huge, urban campus. However, I felt that I would enjoy the small class sizes and tighter community of a place like Saint Mary's College, not only because of my blindness, but also because of my general personality. I have never regretted the decision to go to Saint Mary's; it has been a life-changing place that has shaped the man that I have become.

During my time at Saint Mary's College, I can honestly say that I have experienced no discrimination as a blind student. There have, however, been times when people have done things that are insensitive, such as leaving the table in the middle of a conversation without telling me, resulting in my saying something to another person that doesn't make any sense. On the other hand, sometimes blind people do this to each other. There may have also been social situations that, as I think back, did not go very well because people felt awkward about my blindness. However, I have been able to minimize these incidents by helping people understand me when they first get to know me. I answer any questions that they may have, and even bring up other topics that I think they might want to know about.

I have made many friends among the students that I went to school with at Saint Mary's. While most students make their best friends in the dorm, I found doing that somewhat difficult, although I did become good friends with some people in the residence halls. I was more successful at meeting people in the cafeteria (where other students would help me get food if a cafeteria worker wasn't available), through classes, and through extracurricular activities. I expected to make a lot of student friends, but what surprised me most is how much I was able to make friends with professors. While I had often heard of professors being very distant and insensitive to people with disabilities, I did not find this to be the case at all at Saint Mary's. I did not have even one bad professor; I developed close relationships with the majority of professors, and even with some professors that I did not have classes with. I also enjoyed getting to know the Christian Brothers, who run Saint Mary's College. I was always able to talk to professors about my needs, and we worked together with the personnel at the Academic Skills Center to help me succeed.

Professors were always available outside of class, not only for office hours but also on other occasions, and I often feel more at ease among professors than among many students. One professor encouraged me to develop a strong interest in Catholic theology, and religious studies became my minor; this professor convinced me to go to Rome for a January term class with him, which increased my social confidence even more because the students on that trip were very helpful as I went around the city with them. Another professor invited me to join his group which took trips to the San Francisco Symphony. I was even invited to serve as a student representative on two academic faculty committees. However, I was also a leader in student groups. In high school, I was active in music and skiing, but decided to give up these activities and focus on new things in college. At various periods during my undergraduate life, I was a member of the debate team, President of the Democrats club, a student senator, and a newspaper reporter, among other positions. Because it was easiest for me to make friends with people through these structured activities, it is possible that my blindness actually inspired me to be so active. Most blind students I know at a variety of different colleges are also strong leaders. However, the situation is different for every blind student. I think that my leadership and my interest in developing relationships with professors are mainly due to my academic and motivated personality.

For many blind people, meeting with other blind people is very important. During many summers throughout my childhood, I went to camps for blind people, and after high school I attended a 2-month skills training program for blind young adults. I was usually the only blind person at my school, however. During my first year at Saint Mary's there was a blind student with whom I became friends. We were both on the debate team. After her graduation, a blind professor came to the school, who happens to be a professor in my major, politics. We were able to help each other with some issues that we had in common, especially about technology. I am also in phone and e-mail contact with several blindness organizations. However, I have no problem with the fact that most of my friends are sighted.

My situation as a disabled person has made me more empathetic for other issues about diversity. I have tried to become friends with people from a variety of different backgrounds and cultures and to understand the issues important to them. My career goal is to become a college professor, and I have been accepted into the Ph.D. program in political science at UC Santa Barbara. As an academic,

I am particularly interested in studying and promoting political and religious diversity on college campuses.

College students should never be afraid to talk to people who are different from them in any way. While some blind and other disabled people have a different attitude, I think it is best to ask whatever questions you may have, although it is important to make sure to be open-minded. It is also a good idea to be involved in extracurricular activities, and if you see a student, especially a disabled student, who has potential to be a good person in your group, don't hesitate to invite them.

Reprinted by permission of Skylar Covich.

Discussion Questions

1. What do these 5 personal statements have in common?
2. Each of these essays considers diversity from a different kind of concern. Are they equally important concerns? If you had to rank them, how would you select the one that truly matters? If you find you cannot rank them in importance, why not?
3. Do these authors raise issues of political correctness? Or is that too narrow a way of viewing their experiences?
4. What other groups—minority or majority—might put forward similar experiences and draw similar conclusions from them?
5. Federal, state, and local laws now identify specific groups of people as "protected classes." These usually include groups defined by characteristics shared in common such as religion, race, gender, physical disability, and Vietnam-era veteran status. Should these be legally "protected" classes? Explain.

Suggestions for Your Journal

Most of us identify with many different groups. Thus a single individual college student might consider herself a member of all the following: her family, her church, her nationality, her race, her athletic team, her first-year class, her sorority, her armed forces unit, and many more. What groups do you identify with? How have you come to develop that many-faceted sense of identity? Rank those groups in order, from the ones you feel most closely tied to, to the ones that seem most distant to your feelings.

Have you ever felt that others discriminated against you as a member of some group? Write about that feeling and how you dealt with it. Is there a lesson in your personal experience for future action?

A university is a specialized kind of institution. In a journal entry or essay, write about the ways in which the specific character of a university does or should have implications for issues of discrimination.

Affirmative Action and Multiculturalism

David Bruce Ingram and Jennifer A. Parks

David Bruce Ingram and Jennifer A. Parks are professors of philosophy at Loyola University in Chicago. They specialize in ethics and have coauthored several books and articles.

I still get misty-eyed when I read Martin Luther King Jr.'s famous "I Have a Dream" speech, which he delivered in front of the Lincoln Memorial on August 28, 1963, at the height of the Civil Rights Movement. Here's King, dreaming about the day when people in America "will not be judged by the color of their skin but by the content of their character"; when "the jangling discords of our nation will be transformed into a beautiful symphony of brotherhood"; when "black men and white men, Jews and Gentiles, Catholics and Protestants, will be able to join hands and to sing in the words of the old Negro spiritual, 'Free at last, free at last; thank God Almighty, we are free at last.'"

We've come a long way since King delivered those mighty words. We've outlawed segregation and legal discrimination and our society has made tremendous strides in racial healing. But I wonder whether we have gone far enough in eradicating racial injustice and bringing about equal opportunity for all. Blacks as a whole lag far behind whites economically (the typical black family has one-tenth of the assets of a typical white family); they continue to be underrepresented in legislatures and on corporate boards; they have a lower life expectancy and suffer a higher rate of infant mortality; and they continue to face discrimination at all levels of life, from police profiling to discrimination in securing loans and real estate "red-lining."

In Census 2000, the U.S. Government tried to take a nose count of all Americans, including asking each of us to identify what race and ethnicity we belong to. Persons were asked if they are Hispanic or not, and then they were invited to pick one or more (up to six) racial categories that best described them. What was remarkable about this approach was that it recognized that racial identification is not an all-or-nothing affair—none of us, in fact, is racially pure when it comes right down to it. Furthermore, it *tacitly* recognized that race itself is largely a matter of personal preference.

Not so long ago Americans thought that race was an all-or-nothing affair—something fixed in nature, having to do with the blood you inherited from your parents. For example, among whites it was assumed that if you inherited even a drop of "black" blood from, say a great-great-grandparent, then you were totally black. Modern genetics has totally refuted this biological notion of race. A person's racial features express his genetic make-up, which in turn is the product of recombining the genes he inherited from his parents. Depending on how his genes are recombined, persons may or may not look very much like their parents. Genetically speaking, persons who look racially alike are as different as, or more different from, each other than persons who don't look racially alike.

If race doesn't exist in any biological sense, should people still think of themselves racially? Perhaps in an ideal society they wouldn't. Racial distinctions are a modern invention. Prior to the European conquest of the New World, people divided themselves mainly on the basis of religion and culture. Religious and cultural conversion on the part of the heathen/barbarian was almost always possible. The only differences that were regarded as natural were differences between the sexes and, to a far lesser extent, differences between nobles and commoners.

So you see, we didn't always divide the world along racial lines. Racial distinctions were invented to justify the enslavement of Africans and Native Americans by Europeans. Perhaps in an ideal world, differences in skin pigmentation would matter about as much as differences in eye pigmentation.

We often think of cultural differences as forming the basis for ethnic identifications and biological differences as forming the basis for racial identifications. Reality is more complicated than this. Members of the same ethnic group often share overlapping physical features; and members of the same racial group often share overlapping cultural traits. This isn't surprising, since both physical and cultural traits are passed down from generation to generation, the former through genes, the latter through *socialization.*

If race and ethnicity are so closely linked together, then it seems that what applies to one ought to apply to the other. For instance, if we think that an ideal world would be a world without racial distinctions, then it seems that we should also think that an ideal world would be a world without ethnic differences. In fact, if you consider some of the changes that would have to happen in order for racial thinking to disappear, such as complete residential and occupational integration of all races—it becomes clear that these changes would have deep cultural repercussions as well. For many aspects of ethnic culture are also cultivated in relatively tight-knit and geographically bonded racial communities.

This takes us to a very hard question. Is complete racial and ethnic integration a desirable ideal to strive for? We think that racial integration is desirable for fighting racism. However, even after the elimination of legal segregation we see that many blacks prefer to live in black communities because they feel more welcome there. Even after all traces of racism are gone, some blacks may still prefer to live among blacks for cultural reasons. For example, although certain aspects of the African American spiritual tradition can be (and have been) transported into all cultures, the black church as the bedrock of a distinctive black identity can't be. Some blacks might still prefer to live in predominantly black communities in order to preserve this identity.

The problem of integration suggests two ways of fighting discrimination against religious, ethnic, and racial groups:

· anti-racism
· multiculturalism

Anti-racism targets racial segregation, and so promotes the aim of racial integration at all levels of life. It reminds us of our common humanity, and the universal rights we share with all others. Its ideal is that of a raceless society, where physical differences between people are as insignificant as differences in eye color.

Multiculturalism, by contrast, targets cultural domination—or the attempt by a dominant culture to eradicate, assimilate, or otherwise integrate subordinate cultures to the point where they no longer exist as distinct and independent. As a positive agenda, multiculturalism encourages us to respect all cultures as equals. Unlike anti-racism, it sees positive value in preserving and promoting differences, even if this requires granting special exemptions and privileges to minority cultures that are endangered.

So where does affirmative action fit into all this? Affirmative action initially meant actively recruiting qualified minorities—mainly blacks. Good faith recruitment policies didn't work very well, so the government asked businesses to set deadlines for hiring a certain number of blacks. This didn't work very well either, so the government started imposing quotas—a set number or percentage of jobs—that had to be filled by blacks. Along the way, women and other minorities were added to the list of protected classes. Courts have since ruled that the use of affirmative action quotas in college admissions is unconstitutional and that their use in government contracting is highly suspect.

Affirmative action now effectively protects most of the American population. In 1996 the Clinton administration expanded the list of affirmative action beneficiaries of federal contracts to include small businesses owned by women, the disabled, and the socially disadvantaged, in addition to those owned by blacks, Latinos, Indians, Asians, Eskimos, and Native Hawaiians.

In order for affirmative action to be an effective tool for leveling the playing field it must be administered in a way that is sensitive to individual differences in comparative disadvantage. This will be difficult to do, although not entirely impossible. For example, being a woman today is much less of a disadvantage than it was thirty years ago (in fact, women have made the greatest strides in educational and economic advancement of any group and now comprise a solid majority of all students attending institutions of higher education). Being a Native American resident of an impoverished reservation, by contrast, is still (at least in most cases) a very serious disadvantage.

Does affirmative action elevate the less qualified over the better qualified? Yes, if you think that the only relevant qualifications for measuring future job performance are things like where you went to school, what grades you got, and how well you performed on standardized tests. Surely these qualifications matter. The question is, how much?

Pronounced differences in test scores and grades may sometimes predict different levels of job performance. In some cases, grades and test scores might be irrelevant—you don't need to be a literary genius or mathematics whiz to be a good electrician. Other kinds of qualifications—such as speech, appearance, friendliness, and so on—are more subjective, and therefore more prone to racial biases. Experience is an important qualification but it, too, can sometimes mask true ability. And let's not forget that some qualifications are not at all related to future performance. Princeton University admits 40 percent of all admissions applicants whose parents were former students of the university in comparison to just 15 percent of the regular applicant pool. Last but not least, race itself might be a relevant qualification when filling a high-profile post in a Black Studies Program at a university; for typically, such positions involve role modeling and mentoring as well as teaching and research.

Affirmative action is indeed a strategy for "leveling the playing field," but unlike past forms of racial discrimination, it doesn't try to accomplish this by dragging one segment of the population down to the level of oppressed populations. Rather, its aim is positive: to compensate for the continuing effects of sexual and racial discrimination. In other words, its aim is to elevate the oppressed populations to the current, privileged status enjoyed by all the rest.

 ## Vocabulary

As you think about this essay, these definitions may be helpful to you:
1. **tacitly**   expressed silently or understood without the use of words
2. **socialization**   the process of becoming part of a group and fitting in with that group's culture and values

? Discussion Questions

1. Ingram and Parks ask what they consider to be "a very hard question"—namely, "Is complete racial and ethnic integration a desirable ideal to strive for?" How do they answer that question? How would you answer it?
2. In your experience, is it true, as Ingram and Parks assert, that "experience is an important qualification but it . . . can sometimes mask true ability"? Give some examples to support your response.
3. Ingram and Parks comment parenthetically that "being a woman today is much less of a disadvantage than it was thirty years ago. In fact, women have made the greatest strides in educational and economic advancement of any group and now comprise a solid majority of all students attending institutions

of higher education." Assuming that this claim is true, identify some reasons that such a considerable change should have happened.

 ## Suggestions for Your Journal

It is difficult for students just entering their college years to imagine what was true of students at the same age 20 or 30 years ago. Interview someone who is at least 20 years older than you are and a college graduate. Summarize their sense of how the world has changed in the intervening years.

Ingram and Parks suggest that there have been improvements related to many of the social problems they talk about and that Dr. Martin Luther King Jr. addressed in his famous 1963 speech, "I Have a Dream." Is there still a need, in your view, for affirmative action programs? How do they affect you personally? How would discontinuing affirmative action affect you?

Unit Summary

The essays in this unit discuss some of the conditions necessary to ensure that the pursuit of truth, identified in Unit 6 as the defining characteristic of a university, can be carried out by all participants in the university community without interference. Some observers believe that university faculty and students are just trying to be "politically correct" when they acknowledge and try to protect diversity. However, the essays in this unit are not grounded in the relatively recent notion of "political correctness." Instead, these essays address contemporary topics of concern within the framework of a vision of all individuals exercising their freedom to express ideas—a freedom that is essential to, and therefore precious within, the university.

■ Summary Questions

1. Were you surprised by any of the conclusions that these writers defended? How do they differ from your own current, or previous, beliefs?
2. Can you give examples of finding value in diversity—examples that have made a difference in the way you think or behave?
3. Many people would comment that visions of the future like that presented by Martin Luther King Jr. are attractive and useful as a goal but too idealistic to be realized in a complex society. Do you agree? How might we go about preparing the kind of world that King envisioned in his dream?

■ Suggested Writing Assignments

1. Do you tend to make judgments about any group of people (for example, a nationality group, a fraternity or sorority, or a religious group) based on membership in that group? If so, write a short essay explaining why you do this. Are there any times when *group* characteristics appropriately outweigh individual character?
2. Have you ever been the object of bigotry? If so, write an essay describing how you were singled out and suggest a plan for responding to such behavior.
3. Whose job is it to ensure that, within a university, people are judged only on the basis of their ability? Write an essay identifying those who need to act on this matter and specify the most important steps they should take.

■ Suggested Readings

Bucher, Richard. *Diversity Consciousness: Opening Your Minds to People, Cultures and Opportunities*, 3rd ed. Upper Saddle River, NJ: Prentice-Hall, 2009.

Tatum, Beverly Daniel. *Why Are All the Black Kids Sitting Together in the Cafeteria?* New York: Basic Books, 2003.

Wood, Peter. *Diversity: The Invention of a Concept.* New York: Encounter Books, 2004.

Unit 8

What Should I Know About Careers?

Our road to success is currently under construction.

—Anonymous

According to many students, one of the main purposes of acquiring a college degree is to prepare for a career. And yet this process remains a mystery to many students. The concepts of work, job, and career, although often used interchangeably, are very different. Work can be defined as an activity that accomplishes a task. Career is a lifelong process that usually includes many jobs. Work in our culture is often synonymous with one's identity. Even small children are asked what they "want to do" when they grow up. By the time students enter college, many have some idea of general areas of study they might want to explore or pursue. How work is valued by the individual shapes the perceptions of and attitudes about the meaning of a career as the exploration and planning process is engaged.

Many studies suggest that there has been an increase in careerism among college students over the last several decades. This trend has been documented in surveys of entering first-year students who indicated that "becoming an authority in my field" and "being well off financially" were of greater importance to them than other non-work-related goals. Students' choices of major have also changed. Majors, such as the health professions and computer science, have attracted increasing numbers of students.

Students entering college in the 21st century face a bewildering array of issues concerning their choice of career. Economic shifts, societal and environmental concerns, and the increased complexities of business because of new technologies create a volatile job market. Career-planning professionals encourage students to assess their personal strengths and limitations and base their choices on this knowledge rather than rely on external forces over which they have little control.

199

The readings in this unit represent a wide array of opinions and attitudes toward work and related issues. Nicholas Lore provides some specific ways to determine if a career fits you. Donald Asher discusses some relationships between your major and a career that may surprise you. Mark Ballard writes about searching for a job and provides some practical insights into how to prepare throughout the college years for the day after graduation. David Horne offers some tips on how internships during college can enhance your job search. Arthur Rosenberg discusses the importance of adapting to change, especially in today's job market.

All these thought-provoking ideas about work will offer a sense of how important identifying one's work values and purpose is. The college years are a time to explore, gather information, test alternatives, and finally make the first of many career decisions. Although most students approach this process from a very practical perspective, the readings in this unit should also help you think about your personal definition of work and how it will influence your ultimate career decisions.

A Career that Fits You

Nicholas A. Lore

Nicholas Lore is the originator of the field of career coaching; the founder of Rockport Institute, an international career counseling network; and the author of the *Wall Street Journal* bestseller *The Pathfinder.*

Why is it that some people absolutely love their work, while for others a day at the job is pure torture? How come some people are still energized at the end of a long day, while many others look like they need a long vacation? It's mostly a matter of how well people's careers fit who they are. So let's begin to take a closer look at you.

You are a unique, one-of-a-kind individual, not exactly like anyone else. To have a career that gives you the highest possible level of success as well as satisfaction and enjoyment, you need to design it yourself, piece by piece, so it fits *you* perfectly.

That's why it makes no sense to choose a career only because it's "hot"—or "cool"—or because Uncle Louie said the pay was great or because some people you know are going to do it. The first principle of choosing a fitting career is to focus your attention on yourself and figure out what comes naturally to you, so you can pick work that fits you instead of trying to squeeze into a job that doesn't.

What makes a career fit? Knowing the answer could have a huge impact on the quality of your entire life. The answer is so simple, that it is hard for most people to understand. *What makes a career fit is that it fits you naturally.* It uses your natural inborn talents fully. It fits your personality. You find the subject matter interesting and the work personally meaningful. The position fulfills your goals. Your work environment nurtures and rewards your best efforts. You enjoy what you do, and it stays interesting and challenging as the years roll by.

Jamming yourself into a career that is not a great fit is like swimming upstream. At first you may think of it as a challenge, something to conquer. But after a while, constantly fighting the current makes you feel drained. It becomes a struggle; then resignation and boredom set in. Plus, if you watch the trees along the bank, you notice you are not getting very far very fast. That's what work is like for many people, including plenty of extremely smart people who went to the best schools.

Sometimes they get tired of the struggle and find an eddy in their career's river. An eddy is little place in a river that's out of the main current. In the working world it is a job where you can relax, a peaceful little spot where not much is happening and not much is expected of you. Eddies are terrific if you are kayaking upstream and want to take a break. But spending your life that way gets dull. You never get anywhere. The scenery never changes.

Now, imagine that you are back swimming in the river again. But this time you are swimming in the same direction as the current. Every stroke takes you a good, satisfying distance downstream. You are moving quickly, getting somewhere. Putting in a big effort is not a struggle but a powerful move in the direction you want to move. You know your efforts are paying off. Like swimming downstream, a career that fits you naturally is much more satisfying and fun.

Every species except human beings spends every day doing what comes naturally. They know what fits and what doesn't. You don't have to train a duck to paddle. Drop him in a pond, and he instantly begins his perfect occupation. Drop a chicken in that same pond and listen to the frantic squawks of protest. Drop a human being into the pond and five years later you can still hear him muttering as he paddles around: "Why is this so difficult? Maybe I should take more courses in pondology. Maybe I should move to a different pond."

We humans are so smart and adaptable that we can do many different things with reasonable competence. Our fabulous ability for complex reasoning has a downside: we can talk ourselves into things instead of paying attention to the subtle signs that the careers we are considering might not fit us that well.

The Elements of a Perfect, Natural Fit

Natural Talents and Innate Abilities

Everyone is born with a unique group of talents that are as individual as a fingerprint. These talents give each person a special ability to do certain kinds of tasks easily and happily, yet also make other tasks seem like pure torture. Can you imagine your favorite stand-up comedian working as an accountant? Talents are completely different from acquired knowledge, skills, and interests. Your interests can change. You can learn new skills and knowledge. Your natural, inherited talents remain with you for your entire life. They are the hand you have been dealt by Mother Nature. You can't change them. You can, however, learn to play brilliantly the hand you have been dealt to your best advantage. This is the foundation of choosing a career that fits you like a custom-made suit.

The Work Matches Your Personality Traits and Temperament

Imagine a teacher who would rather spend time alone, a surgeon who hates the sight of blood, a shy salesperson. You want a career that gives you a chance to be yourself, that fits your personality, that makes you feel at home. Many people are engaged in careers that require them to suppress themselves while at the job. An elegant fit between you and your work supports your self-expression. Telltale signs that a career doesn't fit your personality include needing to assume a different personality at work or a suspicion that the people you work with may be aliens from another planet.

Rewards Fit Your Values

Like the biscuit you give the dog, rewards are the motivators that help keep you happily performing your tricks at work. Some rewards mean more to you than others. That is because they are linked with your values. If recognition for doing something well is important to you, then it may also be a necessary reward to motivate you to keep performing well. Doing without adequate recognition will slowly erode your well-being on the job as will the lack of reward for any other important value.

You Fulfill Your Goals

To have something to shoot for is an important part of the joy of working. A custom-designed career supports you to fulfill your life goals and gives you a sense of challenge on the job.

Your Work Is Interesting and Meaningful

People engaged in something they care about are proud of what they do and feel they are making a contribution. Their work fascinates them. They may need to go to work to pay the bills, but that is not what gets them out of bed in the morning.

You Find the Workplace Environment Compatible

Each person flourishes in some work environments and finds others stressful or otherwise inappropriate. "Environment" includes geographical area, company style, and corporate personality, as well as the physicality and mood of the work setting and your relationships with others including your supervisor, fellow employees, and clients or customers.

Obviously, you are not just your interests or personality or any other single factor. You are made up of many different elements. The trick to choosing a career that fits you is to find a way to express all of your unique self, with nothing important left out.... I have seen many thousands of people who shaped their lives, often far beyond what they thought was possible, once they discovered the degree of power they had to create a new and extraordinary future for themselves.... We have the power to invent our own individual futures, create a vision of the kind of life we most want to live, and then find a way, against all odds, to make it happen.

 Discussion Questions

1. Lore uses the word "career" in a very general sense. Besides a "job," what other factors are involved in one's career (e.g., work tasks, leisure time, education, life-style)? What does Lore mean when he says "What makes a career fit is that it fits you naturally"?
2. How does the author define "talent"? What is the difference between talent and skills, knowledge, and abilities? Why do you think he makes this distinction?
3. What are some of the telltale signs, according to Lore, that a career does not "fit"? What other signs can you name?

4. In what way can your values influence how your career "fits"? The author uses *recognition* to illustrate a work value. What other values might be important to you when considering if a particular career fits?

5. Why is a person's work environment so important in making a career satisfying and enjoyable. Describe some of the factors you might want in your preferred work environment.

 ## Suggestions for Your Journal

How would you describe your ideal job? How does this image match your current talents, knowledge, and skills? What will you need to do to prepare for this type of work? How does this compare to Lore's concept of "a career that fits you"?

The Relationship between College and Work

Donald Asher

Donald Asher is an internationally acclaimed author and speaker specializing in careers and higher education. He is the author of ten books and a contributor to many Internet career sites.

How did you pick your major? Because you loved the subject, or because you thought it would help you get a job after college, or to please your parents, or some combination of the above? We often go to college for the wrong reasons, and then compound the error when we try to launch a career afterwards. To put it plainly, those who go to school primarily in order to get a job are often poorly served by doing so. They are ill-served during the college experience itself and ill-prepared for the career marketplace afterwards.

Students may choose a major in order to have the career that they believe goes with that major. For example, they decide to become a chemical engineering major because they heard somewhere that chemical engineering majors are the highest paid upon graduation from college or university. Or they take pre-med classes because they think it will increase their chances of getting into medical school. Or they pursue accounting or nursing because they think they want to be accountants or nurses.

In short, they are choosing majors because of the career outcomes of those majors, not because of any inherent desire to learn those subjects. The problem is that these decisions are often made at age 18 or 19, without any career advice at all or with career advice of the very worst sort. For illustration purposes, let's examine some of the hidden biases in the above choices. For example, it is true that chemical engineering consistently draws top salary offers, but that would be irrelevant if you didn't like chemical engineering or couldn't succeed at it. It is not true that choosing a pre-med major makes you more likely to get into medical school; as long as you do well in the prerequisite courses you can major in anything. It is not true that there are always plenty of jobs for engineers, either. It is true that majoring in nursing or accounting prepares you for careers in nursing or accounting, but it is equally true that majoring in nursing or accounting can lead to many *other* careers.

Let's explore the alternative issue of students who avoid certain majors because they think they have unpromising career outcomes. They may avoid philosophy as a major because they think that businesses wouldn't be interested in philosophy majors. Or they may avoid majoring in music, a subject they really enjoy, because they believe that would be a singularly poor choice for someone who had

a passionate interest in computers. Or they may think that studying English literature is a waste of time, career-wise.

It turns out that each of these propositions is false. According to two major
studies on the topic, liberal arts majors get promoted faster and tend to rise
higher on the organizational charts than engineering and business majors hired
at the same organization at the same time. This is not to say that your major has
no impact on your earnings, but other studies show that hours worked, gender,
attainment of advanced degrees, being taller than average in high school if a male,
and being relatively more attractive than average—but not drop-dead gorgeous—
are influences on earnings. But no one is suggesting that you change your gender
or become taller in high school if that is not your nature.

For example, all types of companies hire liberal arts majors. In fact, even in
high tech companies, one quarter of the people employed do not have technical
degrees. And as it turns out, music is a common major among computer pro-
grammers. Einstein studied music passionately, in addition to physics. Writing
well, which is something one learns to do in an English lit program, is in such
demand in all types of organizations that it is considered a key to management
advancement. According to research monitored by Dr. Howard Figler, a consultant to university career centers, between 40%-60% of all CEOs majored in the
liberal arts as undergraduates. These data may be influenced by issues related to
class as well as choice of major, yet the inference can be made that business is not
the first choice major of many CEOs.

There is an old saying that "Your major may help you get a job in the first place,
but it is your *education* that helps you get promoted." I will go further and say
that an undergraduate curriculum can best provide an education, while graduate
school can best provide specialization. Continuing your education past the bacca-
laureate level is actually a much bigger influence on earnings than your choice of
major. More than half the workers in America have been to college, so it's just not
that powerful a ticket all by itself.

I think students should seek high-paying jobs, but that's a separate issue
from choosing an undergraduate major. If you are only interested in money,
skip college and become a longshoreman. They earn an average of $107,000 per
year in West Coast ports. Although it is true that all art majors earn less than all
engineering majors, it is not true that you as an art major would earn less than
you as an engineering major. Here is a truism for you: individuation will always
exceed group norms. One of the most successful business people I know was an
art major, and his company sells products you can buy in any hardware store in
the country.

Further, when students pick majors based on career outcomes, they sometimes pick majors they don't really enjoy. Sometimes this is true even if they
would have enjoyed the career associated with the major. As just one example, a
lot of pre-med majors would make excellent doctors, but get turned off by years
of laboratory sciences that have little relevance to the curriculum or clinical training provided in medical school. Or they blow their GPAs studying subjects that

aren't really required for success in medical school and then can't get in because of a tarnished record.

Here is the biggest secret in career development: *You can get any job with any major*. I don't mean that all majors prepare you for all jobs equally well, but I do mean that at the juncture of college graduation, no job is inherently sealed off to you simply and solely because of your major. For example, I don't mean to imply that it is easy to get a job in accounting if you've never taken a class in accounting, but it is not at all out of the question. I knew a college student who was a marketing major, who got a temp job with an accounting firm the summer after his junior year. He helped out with some accounting and found out he liked it. He didn't change his major, but he did stay in contact with the firm during his senior year. Upon graduation they hired him, and after a few night classes, he's an accountant today.

Let me be doubly clear in my purpose of discussing the relationship between majors and possible careers: I don't want you to abandon your major or doubt the wisdom of your choice. *I want you to abandon the limitations you have put on yourself.* You cannot do real career development while you are accepting a pre-ordained conclusion. Most people receive tons of career advice and influence from family, friends, neighbors, faculty, and the media that simply don't hold up under scrutiny. Chance, inclination, and extra hard work are far more important in the long run than your major—or even your GPA or whether you were a tall male in high school.

Let's consider what employers themselves say they want in their new hires. According to a survey of corporate recruiters by the National Association of Colleges and Employers, here are the top 10 characteristics of new hires in order of importance:

· Communication skills
· Honesty/integrity
· Teamwork skills
· Interpersonal skills
· Motivation/initiative
· Strong work ethic
· Analytical skills
· Flexibility/adaptability
· Computer skills
· Self-confidence

You will notice that any student with any major could easily possess all ten of these attributes. You will also notice that the only technical item, computer skills, is ranked ninth.

Some majors are obviously preparatory for a particular type of career, for example, elementary education. You can predict that a student pursing this major plans to start her career as an elementary school teacher. In practice, however, careers change and evolve from the initial post-college job in ways that are simply not that predictable, even for those students who have a clear starting point.

By investigating real people with real careers, you will see how this works:

Michael Jordan, legendary basketball player, was a geography major.
Young MC, music mogul, was an economics major.
Lisa Kudrow, actress and star of "Friends," was a biology major.
David Duchovny, actor and star of "The X Files," was an English major.
Carly Fiorina, CEO of Hewlett-Packard, was a philosophy major.
Arnold Schwarzenegger, former Mr. Universe, film star, and governor of economically troubled California, was an economics major.
Jay Leno, king of late night television, was another successful philosophy major.
Barack Obama, president of the United States, was a political science major.

In any case, I think you must by now agree that your major doesn't determine the first job you should seek after college.

The real purpose of a college education is this: To find out what makes you happy. College should also give you the skills you will need to be capable of pursing what makes you happy, once you discover what it is. If you have skills without that knowledge, then you're all dressed up but unsure of where to go; you're armed and dangerous but unsure of your target; you're a power for good but unsure of what good really is.

From HOW TO GET ANY JOB WITH ANY MAJOR by Donald Asher, copyright © 2004 by Donald Asher. Used by permission of Ten Speed Press, an imprint of the Crown Publishing Group, a division of Random House, Inc.

Discussion Questions

1. Do you agree or disagree with Asher when he says that too many students pick their major because of its possible career outcomes and that this is a poor reason for selecting it?
2. Do you agree with Asher that you can get a job with any major? Give reasons for your answer.
3. What does the author mean when he states: "I don't want you to abandon your major or doubt the wisdom of your choice. *I want you to abandon the limitations you have put on yourself*"?
4. Are you surprised at the list of what employers want? Why or why not?
5. Asher says the real purpose of a college education is "to find out what makes you happy." Do you agree? Explain.

Suggestions for Your Journal

How did you select your major? What reasons (including career outcomes) did you have for choosing it? Are the reasons still valid? Why? Have you ever changed (or considered changing) your major? If so, what thoughts and feelings did you have about changing? What was the outcome?

Job Search: Chance or Plan?

Mark Ballard

A former director of career services for the Arts and Sciences at The Ohio State University and retail executive with Victoria's Secret, Gap, and Ann Taylor, Mark Ballard is currently Co-Founder and CEO of Sugardaddy's Sumptuous Sweeties® and Sugardaddys.com®. Ballard offers some excellent advice for initiating the job-search process as freshmen and delineates specific career-planning tasks for each year of student life. Based on extensive experience with college students, he believes his advice, if followed, will generate solid job prospects upon graduation.

I'd like to tell you about Terry—the alumnus who "chanced" his career. His story can provide important insights for your career planning.

Terry was a popular student in high school, was involved in many activities, and graduated in the top 20 percent of his class. Terry could hardly wait to leave his hometown to become a college student. His academic performance was quite respectable. He couldn't believe how quickly the years passed. They passed so quickly that he didn't get involved in any structured *co-curricular* activities because he was "too busy" with school, sports, and friends. For spending money, Terry worked; but his employment experience, for the most part, consisted of stocking shelves at his parent's hardware business during the summers and being a salesperson at an electronics store on weekends.

The quarter before Terry was slated to graduate, he heard about the campus career services office. Terry eagerly signed up for several on-campus interviews with companies that came to campus to interview students. Terry bought a suit, had someone prepare a resume for him, and interviewed with several company representatives. He was confident that he could present himself well in the interviews and would mostly assuredly get an offer from one of the employers with whom he'd interviewed. After all, he'd never had difficulty finding (part-time) jobs. How could a prospective employer turn Terry down with a soon-to-be diploma in hand?

Graduation came and went for Terry. Summer came, and Terry began to worry. Mid-summer, Terry returned to the career services office because the anticipated job offers did not materialize from his interviews. Terry came back looking for additional companies who were coming to campus to interview students and alumni. But there were none during the summer because companies generally complete their hiring visits in April. Terry was unaware of this fact since he didn't attend the on-campus interviewing orientation session: He was "too busy" with college life. Terry left the office dejected, failing to take advantage of the many other employment resources. He vowed to return, but he never got around to it.

In the follow-up questionnaire mailed to alumni six months after graduation, Terry's alma mater received a note from him. Good news: Terry had landed a job!

Well, maybe not good news. The job, which he stumbled on by "accident," was not the kind of job Terry thought he would land with a college degree. Sadly, his college education would not be fully leveraged, nor was his salary comparable to similar graduates.

Here's the moral of Terry's tale: Finding meaningful employment *commensurate* with one's education is not an event that occurs at the end of college. It is a process that begins early in one's collegiate career. Making the transition from academics to the work world doesn't begin with writing a resume, buying a new suit, or getting a job interview. It begins with early research, planning, and action.

To secure meaningful employment upon graduation, begin with the process of self-assessment. As a part of this process, you'll need to be able to answer such questions as, "What do I want to do for work?" and "Where do I want to do it?" "What are my talents, strengths, abilities, and assets?" "What do I enjoy doing?" "What am I curious about, motivated by, and get pleasure from?"

"What are my values—those needs that I want satisfied by work?" (e.g., recognition, independence, money, prestige, social status, responsibility, uncovering knowledge, innovation).

"What are the job tasks or activities of the careers that I am considering, the types of organizations that employ individuals in these occupations, the job outlook/forecast, salary ranges, entrance requirements, and lifestyle issues associated with the jobs and careers I am considering?"

"What are the steps necessary to undertake the decision-making process related to my career? Do I know where to go find out how to write an effective resume and cover letter, interview for job offers, and to learn strategies to find jobs?"

If you can answer the above questions fully, you'll increase your prospects for success in making the transition from college to career.

As an entering student, you're likely saying "It's too early now." "I don't have time." "I'm just a freshman; I have too much on my plate." "I'll deal with job-related issues during my senior year, or when I'm ready to graduate." "I'll figure the job thing out. After all, I figured out how to apply and get accepted to college didn't I?"

It's important that you don't confuse starting the career-planning process with implementing your career decision. While you don't necessarily need to choose a career as a freshman, do begin to think about and get actively involved in the self-assessment process during your early years of college. Your senior year is the time for you to focus attention on *transitional* issues that will take you from academics to the work world, or on to graduate or professional school.

Career planning is a developmental, systematic process of:

1. Learning about yourself (e.g., your interests, abilities, and values),
2. Identifying occupations that correspond to your self-assessment,
3. Exploring the occupational fields that you are considering,
4. Selecting an occupational area to pursue,
5. Readying yourself for the job search process (i.e., resume and application letter writing, job interview skills development, job finding techniques and strategy knowledge), and
6. Securing satisfying employment.

I am sure that it seems the process of career planning could be simplified by proceeding directly to step six—finding a job upon graduation. Remember Terry, however. That's exactly what he did. He jumped into the job search without establishing the foundation of the first five stages. While he landed a job, it was a job in the ranks of the underemployed which can have *ramifications* for a lifetime.

Your career process will be easier if you also fully use the career planning and placement services provided at your university. There, staff members can help you answer the all too familiar question, "What can I do with a major in . . .?" and assist you in finding purposeful, gratifying employment.

As a career services professional, I had the pleasure of working with thousands of students, employers, and alumni. As a business professional, I've interviewed hundreds of college graduates, and I've hired and worked with hundreds of college graduates fresh on-the-job. I can distill what I know about getting that first great job into five recommendations—yes, recommendations for students entering college.

1. Choose to major in a subject that interests you—one that really gets you excited. Don't rely on your parents, peers, or counselors to make the choice for you regarding your academic major or the occupation to pursue. Make the decision yourself. As a related note, given the difficulty of predicting which skills will be in demand even five years from now, not to mention in a lifetime, your best career preparation is one that emphasizes broad knowledge and skills—from the liberal arts to technical and mathematical to scientific; intellectual curiosity; and knowledge of how to learn.

2. Strive for a rigorous academic program and high grades. Yes, grades are important to employers. Job candidates are often rejected from interviews due to low GPA's. GPA's tell employers a great deal about your commitment to achieving excellence—not just getting by.

3. Develop your leadership, writing, oral communication, teamwork, and time management skills by taking active roles of responsibility in student organizations and activities. This involvement will provide you with an opportunity to put knowledge from the classroom into practice.

4. Get career-related experience prior to graduation (that is, through part-time positions, *cooperative education*, internships, and volunteer work). The benefits of such experiences go well beyond making money. You'll have a chance to sample a variety of jobs and work settings, make results-based contributions, identify valuable contacts with professionals for future networking, develop self-confidence, and gain insight when choosing elective courses in your academic program.

5. Use the career planning and placement services on campus early in your academic experience to help you with your career decision making and your job search. By doing so, you can get a head start on your employment future.

You can take the above recommendations a step further by following a year-by-year plan for your job search success. Use this plan as a general strategy to increase the likelihood of your landing the job of your dreams upon graduation.

As a Freshman . . .   The goal of your freshman year should be to learn as much as you can about yourself and the relationship this information has to careers. Consider the following:

In your academic course work, use the required general education courses and other college courses to help you explore your potential. You might wish to take courses and explore subjects that have always been of interest to you but that you've never before had an opportunity to take.

Visit your campus career services office online and in person on your campus to get acquainted with the services and resources of that office.

Explore your interest, abilities, and values. Identify appropriate career choices by using online career guidance systems and tools, meeting with staff members of the career services office for career counseling, attending career awareness workshops offered on campus, and sharing your career goals with your academic advisor.

Learn about *cooperative education* and internship opportunities.

Analyze online job descriptions from a variety of job and company websites, and ask yourself how these positions fit with your identity profile.

Begin investigating and getting involved in at least one of the student organizations and activities on campus to develop leadership, communication, team work, and time management skills.

Find a summer job that will provide you with an opportunity to learn or refine skills that will be attractive to a prospective employer—based on your research.

As a Sophomore . . .   During your sophomore year, your goal should be to concentrate on identifying careers that appeal to you and to begin testing them out.

Use the Internet to research career options, companies, and specific jobs.

Begin the process of informational interviewing—contacting and talking with people employed in the fields you are considering. For example, if you are interested in chemistry, dietetics, or nutrition as a major, consider conducting an informational interview with a nutritionist or nutritional researcher at an area business or hospital. Career services staff members and online networking and professional association sites can help you identify professionals working in occupations that are of interest to you.

Take active roles of responsibility in clubs, organizations, and activities. Cultivate relationships with faculty, advisors, counselors, and others who can help in answering questions that relate to careers and the relationship of course work to careers.

Take time to attend "career days" held on campus and in the community as well as online career fairs. These events provide you with the opportunity to meet representatives from a variety of businesses and organizations. Be sure to ask about cooperative education and internship opportunities. Get ahead of others by getting your name in front of company representatives.

Find out about summer internships and cooperative education opportunities through the career services office and through online internship sites.

Begin developing an electronic resume as well as job interviewing skills. Workshops on these topics are conducted regularly through many career services offices, by a number of community organizations and businesses. There are numerous free online tools to help.

As a Junior . . .   During your junior year, your goal should be to obtain career-related experience.

Prepare for the job search by attending workshops and individual counseling sessions—online and offline—on resumes, application letters, personal webpage/website development, portfolio development, job search strategies, and interviewing skills.

Develop a network of contacts in the field of your choice through continued informational interviewing, involvement in professional associations, online networking groups, and cooperative education or internships.

Continue to attend "career days" held on campus and in the community. Continue to inquire with targeted company representatives about internships and cooperative education opportunities.

Research job leads and make initial contacts in fall for sources of possible employment that have some relationship to your tentative career choice. Gather and electronically file letters of recommendation written on your behalf from past employers, current employers, professors, teaching associates—professionals who can vouch for your skills and abilities.

As a Senior . . .   Your senior year is the culmination of your college education and the launching pad for your future. Your goal is to secure satisfying employment or to get accepted to graduate or professional school should your career interest indicate the need for an advanced degree.

Learn the online and in person procedures for interviewing with organizations that come to campus to interview graduating students.

Research the organizations with which you wish to interview by accessing online company information and tools.

Attend "career day" events held on campus and in the community. Actively participate in career days by distributing resumes, in person and via email, to company representatives. Tell them who you are, what you can do, and the type of position you are seeking.

Interview for jobs during the year with employers who come to campus through the career services office. Note: they are not likely to be there during the summer. (Remember Terry's disappointment?)

Continue gathering electronic letters of recommendation written on your behalf by people who can attest to your skills and abilities. Keep these letters in backup files, too.

Explore, in consultation with career services personnel, other strategies to find employment for your field of interest, such as using the many online listings proprietary to career services offices, making use of online job search sites, enrolling in national employment databases, and learning the process of networking (getting involved with professionals in the field you wish to enter and learning where the hidden job marker is). **The best job search strategy is to use a variety of job**

search strategies simultaneously; don't rely solely on one strategy to find employment.

Choosing a career and finding a professional job takes a tremendous amount of time, effort, and lots of strategic emails. Your time and effort will get noticed by prospective employers.

You need to find out as much as you can about what interests you, what you can do well, and what you want out of life. Even after you've decided on your career direction, you'll find a wide range of job options available to you. There may be occupations that you have never even heard of that would match your education, interests, values, and abilities perfectly. It's important to find out about them as early as possible. By waiting too long to begin proper planning and preparation for a successful career, you run the risk of embarking on the job search scene unaware of what field to pursue, getting frustrated, giving in, giving up, and taking any job you are offered.

Make a commitment to creating your career of choice rather than leaving your career to chance. Use the above outlined plan, and visit your career services office today. You owe it to yourself.

Mark Ballard, "Job Search: Chance or Plan?". Reprinted by permission of the author.

 ## Vocabulary

As you think about this essay, these definitions may be helpful to you:
1. **co-curricular**   being outside of but complementary to the regular curriculum
2. **commensurate**   equal in measure or extent
3. **transitional**   in the process of passing from one state, stage, or place to another
4. **ramifications**   consequences or outgrowths
5. **cooperative education**   a program that combines academic studies with actual work experience

 ## Discussion Questions

1. What is the first important step in the job-search process, according to Ballard?
2. What would you tell an employer about yourself in 30 minutes during a job interview?
3. What are the six steps that Ballard outlines to systematically begin the career-planning process?
4. What type of work experiences can students engage in prior to graduation?
5. What are some strategies students can use during their first year to enhance the career-planning process? As sophomores? Juniors? Seniors?

Suggestions for Your Journal

Describe your dream job. Where would it be? What tasks would you be involved with all day? How would it fulfill your work values? How would it affect your family? How could it affect your lifestyle? Paint a picture of what a typical day would be like.

Which of the tasks or activities on Ballard's list for the first-year college student have you accomplished? What specific steps can you take to complete them by the end of the year?

An Internship—Your First Big Career Break

Dave Horne

Dave Horne brings over 30 years of real experience to the world of career success. As a career counselor and writer he has helped young people avoid painful mistakes during the transition from college to their first job.

Winning your first job in your chosen vocation is a significant success. More than likely, however, it will also be the most difficult undertaking in your career. Outsourcing, immigration, economic conditions, and the growing trend of older workers postponing retirement means that it may be more difficult for you to land your first job in your chosen field than it was for me. That is, it will be if you do what I did and wait until you graduate to start thinking about how you are going to find your first job. If you take that route and walk into a prospective employer's office looking for a full time job without any relevant experience, you are likely to be turned down immediately.

Internships are attractive for a variety of reasons. First, you never have to fire an intern. Internships run for a fixed period of time, often as little as 8 weeks and when it's over, the intern just disappears. Second, intern programs are usually justified as a goodwill gesture to the community and local colleges, not critical resource decisions. Senior executives consider the hiring managers who take on internships as performing a company service rather than consuming additional personnel. Third, interns cost next to nothing, or perhaps even nothing. Most internships pay the prevailing minimum wage, or in the case of a coveted employer, they may not pay at all.

You should be thinking about creating a portfolio of internships during your college years because it will give you four or five experience highlights on your resume rather than just one. You'll have more potential post-graduate job opportunities, more references, and undoubtedly learn more with each new assignment. Most importantly, if you pick assignments with different types of jobs in different size organizations, you will learn more about the kind of environment you will flourish in.

I had never heard of internships when I was going to school, although the idea did occur to me. In order to improve my odds at landing the position I dreamed of, I persuaded a friend of mine to hire me for the summer as his designer. He owned a log cabin company and was having a tough time documenting exactly what it was that his customers were actually buying. While I did design a few homes, it did nothing to help me get a real job after college. That's when I first learned all

216

internships are not the same. When considering an internship, you want to look for the following characteristics:

1. A place that is likely to offer you a job after graduation.
2. A location where you'd like to live.
3. A high quality company with a good reputation.
4. A decent supervisor who will let you do real work.
5. An assignment that complements, not duplicates, other internships.

If you are like most young people, there is probably nothing on your resume yet that will help you win your first real job, or even get you an interview. Your internship portfolio is the only chance you have to create this. You will need project-type assignments, ideally with tangible results or at least an impressive report or presentation. If you work four to five internships during college and create two to three projects that you can list on your resume and talk about in an interview, you will have a stronger chance of landing your first real job.

While it is very important to pick the right internships, the terms of your employment are virtually irrelevant. You will find that some internships pay and some don't. If you need to make money, your choices will be limited. Be aware that payment (or non-payment) is probably non-negotiable. Unlike the real job you'll be chasing after graduation, the terms will be "take it or leave it." On the other hand, the days of the week and hours you work are generally flexible. Having a great company listed on your resume (with one or two meaty accomplishments) is very important, but it is doubtful that anyone will ever ask you how many hours a week you worked. Establish yourself immediately. If you are not given anything meaningful to do, force your boss to take you seriously. Complete everything they assign as fast as possible. Not only will they take notice, but they will quickly realize that they can't invent enough busy work to keep you quiet for the next few months; they will have to actually let you help them do their job. It's important for you to strike quickly, ideally your first day on the job.

When the end of your internship is near, you need to focus on building references for your future. Don't be afraid to ask co-workers and supervisors if you can use them for a reference—they're expecting it. If they say yes, make sure you get private information (home and cell phone numbers, private e-mail addresses, etc.) and ask them for a letter of reference. Offer to draft the letter, welcome their edits, and then get them to sign it. This will eliminate the risk that you lose track of your references in years to come.

Internships are easy to secure and painless to complete. The only big mistake you can make is to fail to go after them. Complete several before the end of your senior year and you probably will have an easier time landing your first real job.

Vocabulary

As you think about this essay, these definitions may be helpful to you:
1. **outsourcing**   to procure goods and services from an outside employer
2. **coveted**   to wish for earnestly
3. **portfolio**   a selection of work compiled over a period of time

 Discussion Questions

1. What reasons does Horne give for why employers hire interns?
2. Why might a "portfolio of internships" help you get a job after graduation? What would be contained in such a portfolio?
3. When considering an internship placement, what characteristics does Horne recommend you look for? What can you add to this list?
4. What does Horne suggest you do if your employer is not giving you real work? What other tactics could you employ?

 Suggestions for Your Journal

Imagine the ideal "portfolio of internships" that you might want to include on your resume by the end of your senior year. What sort of work would you be looking for? What kind of work tasks would you like to do? What type of work experiences do you currently have on your resume? How do they fit into your ideal portfolio? How would you describe them? Where on your campus will you find people to talk to about obtaining internships?

Adjust to Change

Arthur D. Rosenberg

Arthur D. Rosenberg specializes in business analysis, project management, documentation, corporate communications and training. He gives career-related seminars to professional and minority groups.

> *...For the times they are a - changin'.*
>
> —BOB DYLAN

This timeless line chanted by a rock-and-roll poet captured the imagination of an entire generation. No surprise that many of those who attended Dylan's concerts are now scratching their heads in bemusement over the preferences and ideas of the next generation. The patterns of change are enticingly familiar, even in our reluctance to accept them.

Individuals, groups, and species keep pace with change or dwindle into history. Change happens, and if you fail to meet the demands imposed by this change, you will go the way of the dinosaurs. The lesson here is that the skills and talents that get you where you are won't necessarily take you any further.

Change filters down from official decisions, hidden policies, and complex conditions, often as an unexpected side effect. New guidelines and requirements replace the old, and you need to adjust to assimilate these differences. Avoid the tendency toward familiar habit patterns and comfort zones, clinging to what you know and shying away from the uncertain. Don't let holding onto what you have acquired buffer you from recognizing and accepting changes when they occur. For the inevitable cannot be long postponed, much less avoided.

The times are always changing.

Understand that change is not a series of events that differ from one another, but an ebb and flow of all that was and is. Time, motion, and entropy are elements as much as agents of change. The world is altered as it spins, and you must adjust accordingly. Your attitude toward change is reflected in the way you accept it, adjust to it, and use it. Make it work for you.

Keeping up with change means adjusting to the technology, pace, and demands of your environment. The velocity of change accelerates with each fleeting microchip. From Instant Messenger to fax and telephone to wireless, you need to keep up with the latest developments and use them to your advantage.

Technology accelerates the pace of change. Available information and the speed with which it is delivered far exceed the agility of our brains to digest it all, so we use computers to collect, distill, and apply it for us. As soon as the patterns of change become familiar, they too change.

According to the U.S. Department of Labor, the average worker in the United States changes jobs as many as ten times between the ages of eighteen and thirty-eight. They estimate three to seven career changes will occur throughout an average worker's lifetime. A more useful measure of change is the rapid evolution of the marketplace and the need to respond effectively to new and different challenges. Baseball is a microcosm of the pace of business in the 21st century. Batters have to instantly adjust to the location and velocity of the pitch, pitchers alter their approach between right- and left-handed batters, and team owners and coaches revise their plans to compensate for changing personnel from one season to the next.

The most practical way to keep pace with change is to recognize it, react to it, and initiate it in a timely fashion. Anticipating change enables you to prepare for new conditions with purpose and control, and to initiate creative new directions. Passively waiting for things to happen can leave you victimized by change, groping to survive, and uncertain of your future.

Change forces you to consider different ways of solving problems and to reconsider older methods. Opportunities open and abruptly close like windows. The most serious challenge to adjusting to new conditions is force of habit. Learning to react promptly and wisely to change is far more productive. Your career success is likely to depend on how well you can adapt to change, and how quickly you react to the opportunities it can offer.

In the workplace, necessity continues to dictate change. Over time, your career will hinge on your ability to adjust to evolving realities and needs. When major changes are in the air, create an inner dialogue to talk yourself into a positive frame of mind. If you know you've got to do something, an upbeat attitude is guaranteed to work on your behalf.

Vocabulary

As you think about this essay, these definitions may be helpful to you:
1. **bemusement**   puzzlement
2. **entropy**   disorganization or randomness

? Discussion Questions

1. What causes change, according to Rosenberg? Why can't it be avoided?
2. The author says your attitude toward accepting change is very important. What do you think he means by this?
3. What part does technology play in accelerating change? Give a few examples of when technology forced you to change the way you were thinking about or doing things.

4. What are the advantages of anticipating and adjusting to change? What are the dangers of "passively waiting for things to happen"?
5. How can change affect careers? What does Rosenberg suggest you can do to adjust to change in this area?

 ## Suggestions for Your Journal

How flexible are you at handling change? Give an example of when you were confronted with a changing situation and how you reacted to it. What was the outcome? Do you adjust to some kinds of change better than others (for example, daily plans, technical changes, life-changing events)? How? As you plan your career, give some examples of how you can better prepare to recognize, accept, and use change.

Unit Summary

The readings in this unit provide a wide variety of opinions about work and workers. Reflect on your own ideas about your place in the work world and how these writers have added to your understanding of its complexities and challenges.

■ Summary Questions

1. Responding to a recent poll, younger workers indicated that they care more about job satisfaction than job security. How do you think that knowing this might influence what employers offer new workers?
2. Describe how you have searched for a job in the past and the differences having a college degree might make in the way you will search for a job in the future.
3. How do you think the American workplace has changed in the last 5 years? How will your work life be different from that of your parents? How will these differences, if any, affect your life in a way different from theirs?

■ Suggested Writing Assignments

1. The readings in this unit explore several beliefs, attitudes, and perspectives about work. Select one and write a brief essay on why the ideas in this reading agree or disagree with your own ideas about work.
2. Write a brief essay on what you want in your future career (e.g., independence, creativity, security, high salary) and why these work values are essential to you.
3. Write a brief essay about how you are currently approaching the choice of academic major and career field and what you still need to do in order to make an initial decision or confirm one you have already made.

■ Suggested Readings

Arruda, William and Dixson, Kirsten. *Career Distinction*. John Wiley and Sons, NJ: HoboKen, 2007.
Gordon, Virginia, and Susan Sears. *Selecting a College Major: Exploration and Decision Making*. (6th ed.) Upper Saddle River, NJ: Prentice Hall, 2010.
Michelozzi, Betty N. *Coming Alive from Nine to Five*. Mountain View, CA: Mayfield, 2000.
Paprochi, Sherry and Ray Paprochi. *Complete Idiots Guide to Branding Yourself*. NY: Alpha, 2009.
Terkel, Studs. *Working*. New York: Pantheon, 1974.

Unit 9

Setting Future Goals: Now Is the Time to Start

Climb high

Climb far

Your goal the sky

Your aim the star.

—INSCRIPTION ON JOHNS HOPKINS HOSPITAL

MEMORIAL STEPS

Imagine the day you will be wearing a cap and gown and receiving the diploma that attests to your status as a college graduate. What does the future hold for you? Several readings in previous units offered visions of the future from different perspectives. These can stimulate your thinking about what you might hope to accomplish during your college years so that your college education can prepare you for both the workplace and your life in general.

In Unit 1, several authors described the value of a college education and emphasized the importance of taking advantage of the opportunities offered through the experience of higher education. You were asked to examine your reasons for being in college and how these might affect your initial goals for the college experience itself. The beginning of your college life is a good time to set some tentative goals to reach by the day you are ordained a college graduate. Through your college career, you will want to broaden those goals to include specific actions to prepare for the future lifestyle you desire. Some of your ideas might change very much.

You will also want to set goals related to the type of work you want to do and the type of worker you want to become. These should take into account both the type of job and quality of work life you hope to obtain after college. Thoughtful planning now can also improve your effectiveness as a worker later in life.

During the college years many foundational skills and personal competencies can be acquired and practiced, usually in a nonthreatening environment. The quality of your life after college will depend on how well you take advantage of the opportunities presented to you during your college years.

The essay by Mel Levine discusses the transition from school to being a "startup adult." He lists some issues individuals might face *after* graduation. The reading by Neil Howe and William Strauss speculates about how the Millennial Generation will influence history and "achieve greatness" in their own time. Lev Grossman identifies a new group of young people who he calls the "Twixters." He describes a new phase in the life cycle that reflects cultural changes. Christopher Reeve urges college students to maintain their integrity "in a culture that has devalued it" and describes how his injury helped him live a more "conscious" life. The final essay in this unit is by First Lady Michelle Obama who challenges the graduates in this commencement address to use their education as a "building block to a brighter future."

In addition to discussing these issues in class and writing about them in your journal, you might want to talk to family, friends, and others to whom you look for guidance. Examining what is important to you now and in the future is a first step in setting thoughtful, realistic goals for your life after college. Don't wait until the day you march down the graduation aisle to consider who you are and where you want to be when that day arrives.

Here Life Comes

Mel Levine

Mel Levine, M.D., is professor of pediatrics at the University of North Carolina Medical School and director of its Clinical Center for the Study of Development and Learning. He is the founder and co-chair of All Kinds of Minds, a nonprofit institute for the understanding of differences in learning.

Lives flow with heavy undercurrents, much like the open sea; they *undulate* through well-timed waves, such as the preschool period, adolescence, and the so-called golden years of late life. Each arriving era brings its special challenges and opportunities, along with its unique stresses and pressures. A person may or may not be equipped to ride the next wave, to manage the requirements—obvious and hidden—of his or her latest time of life.

A particularly challenging period is the opening stages of a life at work, the school-to-career years, a time that, although rarely thought of as distinct, may be one of the roughest to traverse. These are the startup years, a pivotal time that claims more than its share of unsuspecting victims. In fact, most people are better prepared for their retirement than they are for the startup of their working lives! For some the startup years commence at age sixteen or seventeen, upon their dropping out of high school. For others the startup years may not begin until age twenty-nine, following a residency in plastic surgery.

Many individuals in and around their twenties come to feel abandoned and anguished. They start to question their self-worth, and they are prone to some awful mistakes in their choice of career or in the ways they perform as novices on the job. They suffer from an affliction I call work-life unreadiness, which may have its onset right after high school, in college, during the job search, or during the early phases of a job or a career.

The length of the startup period varies from just a few years to a decade or more of uncertainty and justified anguish. Some emerging adults take longer to start up a stable work life than do others. Some never stop starting; they can't move ahead toward a career because of repeated false starts or because they keep changing course. They start up and stall out! Others feel *stymied* in their work choices, while some of their friends effortlessly and expediently move into job roles that fit them as snugly as their favorite athletic socks.

Clearly, work life is not one's only life! Family life, perhaps spiritual life, sex life, social life, along with assorted other slices of life, operate in concert and sometimes in conflict with work life. To a large extent people are what they do. But we must remember that life at work is influenced by and influences numerous facets of day-to-day existence.

The culture of the modern world affords multiple ways to get lost or ambushed along the work-life trail. More than ever before, young adults are apt to confront job descriptions that are strikingly different from those familiar to elder members of their families. Role models within a family are an endangered species. Even if a young person breaks into the identical occupation as his mother or father, the chances are that its current routines and requirements look nothing like those his parents faced. Practicing medicine or law or tending to the family farm is a whole different ball game these days. Meanwhile, new adults have to face an economic world as *unfathomable* as it is unpredictable.

In their book *Quarterlife Crisis,* Alexandra Robbins and Abby Wilner make the observation, "The whirlwind of new responsibilities, new liberties, and new choices can be entirely overwhelming for someone who has just emerged from the shelter of twenty years of schooling." Startup adults may be totally unprepared for some of the bracing realities of early work life. Some matters they need to consider:

- They are accumulating experience at school and work—no matter what kind of work they're doing. That means it's better to work than be unemployed and have to contend with the costly stigma of being "inexperienced," a common reason for being turned down for a good job.
- Parents are often good sounding boards, if they can be asked not to preach or dispense too much glib, oversimplified advice.
- People should never feel they can't backtrack. Poor decisions are always reversible. Life is full of trials and errors; no one should let an error put the brakes on their forward motion. A startup adult can learn from taking a wrong road.
- Startup adults should never give up on their passions. They should keep finding ways to get where they want to be, namely, getting paid to do things that they love.
- Startup adults have to realize that there is no work entitlement. Their boss doesn't owe them anything, and he is not losing sleep worrying about their self-esteem. But they are being watched, and they need to perform as if they are being scored on their performances. Being impressive actually can be fun.
- Early in a career, it is a good idea to explore diverse roles within a field. That means that a person who wants to become a screenwriter and is having trouble selling her scripts should consider a job as an associate producer or assistant casting director—a job that might eventually lead right back to screenplay writing or branch out into something else worthwhile within the movie world. Early insistence upon a particular role can be counterproductive.
- It is important for startup adults to keep sniffing out the connections between what they are doing and what ultimately they hope to be doing. A person might say, "Eventually I'd like to manage a restaurant; working in this coffeehouse is teaching me a lot about customer service, and I'm observing closely how my superior operates; she's terrific." By the way, such connections are very effectively mentioned during a job interview.

· Everyone should have some well-thought-out alternative plans and then be ready to change course when an excellent opportunity presents itself that fits with someone's overall career aspirations. It is hazardous to wait around for such golden chances and foolhardy to get so stuck on a plan that potential windfalls are missed.

The French philosopher Jean-Paul Sartre once wrote, "Il faut choisir, vivre ou raconter"—in English, "One must choose whether to live one's life or tell it." That advice suggests another *formidable* challenge faced by startup adults. People have to live a life that's right for them, not an existence that *sounds* right. The world is replete with posers, folks of all ages, who are telling their lives rather than living them. A startup adult needs to be especially careful to avoid making important choices solely because a choice would embellish a "cool" story. Although it can be tempting to try to emerge as a *charismatic* character in one's own biography, there has to be more to life than that. The best success stories are about people who have refused to be anyone but themselves.

 Vocabulary

As you think about this essay, these definitions may be helpful to you:
1. **undulate**   to move in a wavy or flowing manner
2. **stymied**   presenting an obstacle
3. **unfathomable**   impossible to comprehend
4. **formidable**   having qualities that discourage approach
5. **charismatic**   a magnetic charm or appeal

 Discussion Questions

1. Why, according to Levine, can the "school-to-work" life stage be one of the most difficult to traverse? Do you agree with him?
2. Why might some "startup" adults be unprepared for the realities of early work life? What can they do to be better prepared?
3. What does Levine say about work entitlement? Do you agree with his stance? If not, why?
4. Why should we explore diverse opportunities within an occupational field early in our careers? Give some examples of alternatives in the general career field you would like to pursue.
5. How does Levine describe the difference between an existence that *sounds* right and living a life that *is* right? Discuss the implications of each of these existences as they influence a "startup" adult.

Suggestions for Your Journal

What advice that Levine gives in this essay makes the most sense for you? Have you ever experienced the feelings of a "startup" adult that Levine describes? When and how? Are you "living" your life or "telling" it? If you are "telling" it, how can you change?

The Next Great Collegiate Generation

Neil Howe and William Strauss

Neil Howe and William Strauss, the authors of *Millennials Rising, Millennials and the Pop Culture* and *The Fourth Turning*, write and lecture frequently on generational issues. They founded LifeCourse Associates, a strategic-planning consulting firm where they host active discussions about generations with readers at www.fourthturning.com.

Every generation has its own strengths and weaknesses, its own potential for triumph and tragedy. The course of human history affords to each generation an opportunity to apply its unique gifts for the benefit of others. Some generations steer their world toward outer-world rationality, others toward inner-world passion. Some focus on graceful refinement, others on the hardscrabble bottom line. The German historian Leopold von Ranke, who weighed many Old World generations on the scales of history, observed that "before God all the generations of humanity appear equally justified." In "any generation," he concluded, "real moral greatness is the same as in any other."

What will Millennials provide for those who come after? It is this future contribution, not what they have done in youth, that will be their test of greatness.

The collective Millennial lifespan—and its influence on history—will stretch far into the Twenty-First Century. In 2004 the first *cohorts* graduated from college. In 2006 they began graduating from business and professional schools, in 2007 they graduated from law schools, and in 2008–2009 they began graduating from medical schools and Ph.D. programs. Over the next two decades, this generation will fill the ranks of young-adult celebrities in the Olympics, pro sports, and entertainment—and the ranks of the military in any wars the nation may wage. In 2007, the first Millennial women reached the median age of first marriage and of giving birth to a first child. The first Millennial men reached that age in 2009. The first Millennial college graduates, women and men, reached those median ages about two years later than their generation as a whole—in 2009 and 2011, respectively. From now through 2020, they will make a major mark on the youth pop culture. A new youth activism had a real impact on national politics in the elections of 2008 and will again in 2012.

Through the 2010's, Millennials will be giving birth in large numbers, returning to college for their fifth-year and tenth-year reunions—and swarming into business and professions, no longer as apprentices. Some will enter state houses and the U.S. Congress. Around 2020 they will elect their first U.S. Senator—around 2030, their first U.S. President. In the 2020's their first children will apply to college. In 2029 and 2039, they will attend their first twenty-fifth and thirty-fifth college reunions. They will occupy the White House into the 2050's, during which period they will

229

also provide majorities in Congress and Senate, win Nobel prizes, rule corporate board rooms, and fill the ranks of collegiate parent bodies. Thereafter, into the 2070's they will occupy the Supreme Court and be America's new elders. And along the way, they will make lasting contributions to literature, science, technology, and many other fields. Their children will dominate American life in the latter half of the Twenty-First Century—and their grandchildren will lead us into the Twenty-Second. Their influence on the American story, and the memory of their deeds and collective *persona*, will reach far beyond the year 2100.

As is true for any generation, history will intrude on the Millennials' collective life story, posing distinct challenges and opportunities. How they respond will alter the way others see them and the way they see themselves. What would one have said about the future of the G.I. Generation of youth back in 1928, before World War II redefined who they were and how they lived their lives? What would one have said about the future of young *Boomers* back in 1962, before the *Consciousness Revolution*? And what of *Generation X* in 1979, before the digital age?

Towards the close of his re-nomination address in 1936, President Roosevelt said:

> *There is a mysterious cycle in human events.*
> *To some generations much is given.*
> *Of other generations much is expected.*
> *This generation of Americans has a rendezvous with destiny.*

Perhaps because we know them better than those two other World War II-era generations, we especially revere today's very old G.I. war veterans and their widows. As young people, the G.I. s understood how much older generations had given them. They wanted to give back, and they did—especially in World War II. Another way they gave back was to nurture a new postwar generation of idealistic Boomers. Those Boomers have given birth to the first Millennials, and the story continues.

The Millennials' greatness as a generation has yet to reveal itself. When the strengths of this generation do appear, it is unlikely they will resemble those of their Boomer parents. Instead, these virtues are more likely to call to mind the confidence, optimism, and civic spirit of the high-achieving G.I.s.

What will happen over the course of their lives is, of course, unknowable. It is possible Millennials will dominate the story of the Twenty-First Century to much the same degree as the G.I. Generation dominated the story of the Twentieth. If Millennials face their own *"rendezvous* with destiny" as they come of age, much will be expected of them by older generations. Will future writers have reason to call them, on their record of achievement, another "great generation"? Time will tell.

Whatever history's challenge—whether economic, political, military, social, or environmental—Millennials may provide just what those times will require. Perhaps they will mobilize to meet it with the upbeat attitude, can-do confidence, and civic spirit that will enhance the prospects for a successful outcome. Whatever the crisis, Millennials will realize that the bulk of their lives will lie in the years beyond it—while those who teach them will realize that the bulk of their lives has already transpired in the years before.

The greater the national peril, the more the nation will focus on this generation. What they need will become a national priority, what they suffer a source of national anguish, and what they achieve a source of national pride. Thus will the decades ahead be a time of historic opportunity for colleges and universities, as they help today's young people achieve greatness in their own time and generation.

Reprinted by permission.

 ## Vocabulary

As you think about this essay, these definitions may be helpful to you:
1. **cohorts**   groups of individuals who are in the same age group
2. **persona**   the image that a person projects in public
3. **Boomers**   individuals born during the baby boom following World War II
4. **Generation X**   the generation following the Boomers
5. **Consciousness Revolution**   the expansion of consciousness followed by a radical shift in priorities (in recent history the ideas that permeated the 1960's and 1970's)
6. **rendezvous**   an appointed time or place

 ## Discussion Questions

1. Have you ever thought of yourself as a member of a certain generation? Do you think your generation will steer toward "outer-world rationality," "inner-world passion," "graceful refinement," "hardscrabble bottom line," or something else?
2. Every generation, according to the authors, has formed distinct values that influence its attitudes and behaviors. What do you think are the defining characteristics of your generation?
3. Do you think your generation has a "rendezvous with destiny"? What current events do you think your generation will be still confronting in the future and how will you respond?

 ## Suggestions for Your Journal

To which generation do you belong (i.e., Boomers, Xers, Millennials)? How is your generation different from past generations? Talk to a family member or a friend from a generation different from yours. Discuss how you see the world differently and what values you have in common. Write about how you agree or disagree with the authors that your generation will meet history's challenge like the G.I. generation.

Grow Up? Not So Fast

Lev Grossman

Lev Grossman is *Time Magazine*'s book critic and one of its lead technology writers. He also blogs about nerd culture for *Time*. He published his novel, *WARP*, in 1997, and his novel, *The Magicians*, was published in 2009.

Michele, Ellen, Nathan, Corinne, Marcus and Jennie are friends. All of them live in Chicago. They go out three nights a week, sometimes more. Each of them has had several jobs since college; Ellen is on her 17th, counting internships. They don't own homes. They change apartments frequently. None of them are married, none have children. All of them are from 24 to 28 years old.

Thirty years ago, people like Michele, Ellen, Nathan, Corinne, Marcus and Jennie didn't exist statistically speaking. Back then, the median age for an American woman to get married was 21. She had her first child at 22. Now it all takes longer. It's 25 for the wedding and 25 for baby. It appears to take young people longer to graduate from college, settle into careers and buy their first homes. What are they waiting for? Who are these permanent adolescents, these twentysomething Peter Pans? And why can't they grow up?

Everybody knows a few of them—full grown men and women who still live with their parents, who dress and talk and party as they did in their teens, hopping from job to job and date to date, having fun but seemingly going nowhere. Ten years ago, we might have called them Generation X, or slackers, but those labels don't quite fit anymore. This isn't just a trend, a temporary fad or a generational hiccup. This is a much larger phenomenon, of a different kind and a different order.

Social scientists are starting to realize that a permanent shift has taken place in the way we live our lives. In the past, people moved from childhood to adolescence and from adolescence to adulthood, but today there is a new intermediate phase along the way. The years from 18 until 25 and even beyond have become a distinct and separate life stage, a strange, transitional never-never land between adolescence and adulthood in which people stall for a few extra years, putting off the iron cage of adult responsibility that constantly threatens to crash down on them. They're betwixt and between. You could call them twixters.

Where did the twixters come from? And what's taking them so long to get where they're going? Some of the sociologists, psychologists and demographers who study this new life state see it as a good thing. The twixters aren't lazy, the argument goes, they're reaping the fruit of decades of American affluence and social liberation. This new period is a chance for young people to savor the pleasures of irresponsibility, search their souls and choose their life paths. But more histori-cally and economically minded scholars see it differently. They are worried that twixters aren't growing up because they can't. Those researchers fear that what-ever cultural machinery used to turn kids into grownups has broken down, that society no long provides young people with the moral backbone and the financial wherewithal to take their rightful places in the adult world. Could growing up be harder than it used to be?

The sociologists, psychologists, economists and others who study this age group have many names for this new phase of life—"youthhood," "adultescence"—and they call people in their 20s "kidults" and "boomerang kids," none of which have quite stuck. Terri Apter, a psychologist at the University of Cambridge in England and the author of *The Myth of Maturity,* calls them "thresholders."

Apter became interested in the phenomenon in 1994, when she noticed her students struggling and *flailing* more than usual after college. Parents were baffled when their expensively educated, otherwise well-adjusted 23-year-old children wound up sobbing in their old bedrooms, paralyzed by indecision. "Legally, they're adults, but they're on the threshold, the doorway to adulthood, and they're not going through it," Apter says. The percentage of 26-year-olds living with their par-ents has nearly doubled since 1970, from 11% to 20%, according to Bob Schoeni, a professor of economics and public policy at the University of Michigan.

Jeffrey Arnett, a developmental psychologist at the University of Maryland, favors "emerging adulthood" to describe this new demographic group, and the term is the title of his book on the subject. His theme is that twixters are misunderstood. It's too easy to write them off as overgrown children, he argues. Rather, he sug-gests, they're doing important work to get themselves ready for adulthood. "This is the one time of their lives when they're not responsible for anyone else or to any-one else," Arnett says. "So they have this wonderful freedom to really focus on their own lives and work on becoming the kind of person they want to be." In his view, what looks like incessant, *hedonistic* play is the twixters' way of trying on jobs and partners and personalities and making sure that when they do settle down, they do it the right way. It's not that they don't take adulthood seriously; they take it so seriously, they're spending years carefully choosing the right path into it.

College is the institution most of us entrust to watch over the transition to adulthood, but somewhere along the line that transition has slowed to a crawl. In a *Time* poll of people ages 18 to 29, only 32% of those who attended college left school by age 21. In fact, the average college student takes five years to finish. The era of the four-year college degree is all but over.

Twixters expect to jump laterally from job to job and place to place until they find what they're looking for. The stable, quasi-parental bond between employer and employee is a thing of the past, and neither feels much obligation to make the relationship permanent. "They're well aware of the fact that they will not work for the same company for the rest of their life," says Bill Frey, a demographer with Brookings Institution, a think tank based in Washington. "They don't think long-term about health care or Social Security. They're concerned about their careers and immediate gratification."

Twixters expect a lot more from a job than a paycheck. Maybe it's a reaction to the greed-is-good 1980s or to the whatever-is apathy of the early 1990s. More likely, it's the way they were raised, by parents who came of age in the 1960s as the first generation determined to follow its bliss, who want their children to change the world the way they did. Maybe it has to do with advances in medicine. Twixters can reasonably expect to live into their 80s and beyond, so their working lives will be extended accordingly and when they choose a career, they know they'll be there for a while. But whatever the cause, twixters are looking for a sense of purpose and importance in their work, something that will add meaning to their lives, and many don't want to rest until they find it. "They're not just looking for a job," Arnett says. "They want something that's more like a calling, that's going to be an expression of their identity." Hedonistic *nomads*, the twixters may seem, but there's a serious core of idealism in them.

Maybe the twixters are in denial about growing up, but the rest of society is equally in denial about the twixters. Nobody wants to admit they're here to stay, but that's where all the evidence points. Tom Smith, director of the General Social Survey, a large sociological data-gathering project run by the National Opinion Research Center, found that most people believe that the transition to adulthood should be completed by the age of 26, on average, and he thinks that number is only going up. In another 10 or 20 years, we're not going to be talking about this as a delay. We're going to be talking about this as a normal trajectory," Smith says. "And we're going to think about those people getting married at 18 and forming families at 19 or 20 as an odd historical pattern."

There may even be a biological basis to all this. The human brain continues to grow and change into the early 20s, according to Abigail Baird, who runs the Laboratory for Adolescent Studies at Dartmouth. "We as a society deem an individual at the age of 18 ready for adult responsibility," Baird points out. "Yet recent evidence suggests that our *neuropsychological* development is many years from being complete. There's no reason to think 18 is a magic number." How can the twixters be expected to settle down when their gray matter hasn't?

Most of the problems that twixters face are hard to see, and that makes it harder to help them. Twixters may look as if they have been overindulged, but they could use some *judicious* support. Apter's research at Cambridge suggests that the more parents sympathize with their twixter children, the more parents take time to discuss their twixters' life goals, the more aid and shelter they offer them, the easier the transition becomes. "Young people know that their material life will not be better than their parents'," Apter says. "They don't expect a safer life than their parents had. They don't expect more secure employment or finances. They have to put in a lot of work just to remain O.K." Tough love may look like the answer, but it's not what twixters need.

If twixters are ever going to grow up, they need the means to do it—and they will have to want to. There are joys and satisfactions that come with assuming adult responsibility, though you won't see them on *The Real World*. To go to the movies or turn on the TV is to see a world where life ends at 30. There are few road maps in the popular culture—and to most twixters, this is the only culture—to get twixters where they need to go. If those who are 30 and older want the rest of the world to grow up, they'll have to show the twixters that it's worth their while. "I went to a Poster Children concert, and there were 40-year olds still rocking," says a 26-year-old twixter. "It gave me hope."

Vocabulary

As you think about this essay, these definitions may be helpful to you:
1. **flailing**   moving or swinging about
2. **hedonistic**   a way of life where the sole purpose is pleasure and happiness
3. **nomads**   people who have no fixed residence but move from place to place
4. **neuropsychological**   a science concerned with the psychology of behavior and the mind as they relate to the brain and nervous system
5. **judicious**   using sound judgment

Discussion Questions

1. Do you know any young people who fit the role of "twixters"? How does the author's description fit them? How are they different?
2. How and why do you think the twixter phenomenon has appeared in today's culture?
3. What role do you think the rapidly changing workplace has played in creating the "twixters"?
4. Do you agree that society is "in denial" about the twixters' existence? Why or why not?
5. What do you think of the author's suggestion that there might be a "biological basis" to this new twixter phenomenon?

Suggestions for Your Journal

Write about how you envision your life after graduation. Do you think you could become a twixter during that period of time? Do you want to be? What are or should you be doing now to prepare for your life after graduation?

If you are an older student, what is your opinion of the author's depiction of this new life stage? Were you ever a twixter or do you know any? How do they (you) compare to Grossman's description?

To the Graduates

Christopher Reeve

Christopher Reeve gave this commencement address to the graduates of a large mid-western university in June 2003. Reeve was an actor with many movie credits, but perhaps he is best known as "Superman." He was paralyzed after a riding accident in 1995 and spoke to that change in his life in this address. Christopher Reeve died in 2004.

I am extremely honored to address so many of you who are graduating today. I wanted to be here to pay tribute to the long-standing ideals of this university: compassion for our fellow human beings, the aspiration to be champions in all arenas of life, and the desire to make a difference.

At this university, students and faculty understand the importance of public service on both a local and global scale. Some focus on the environment, others on community outreach, education, social programs, health research, and many other programs. I salute these points of pride to congratulate you for your outstanding achievements. But I also want to sound a note of caution as you leave this sanctuary of learning, self-discovery, and ethical conduct to make your way in the outside world.

You have been taught to work hard, not to cheat, and balance your own advancement with service to others. But when you look beyond this campus, you witness seemingly endless examples of questionable conduct in government, religion, business, the media, and even sports. Our intelligence agencies are being challenged to explain their recommendation for the invasion of Iraq. The Catholic Church is embroiled in a crisis of misconduct and cover-ups. CEOs of major corporations are facing fines and imprisonment for their greed at the expense of the employees who helped create their success. The reputation of one of the most respected newspapers in the country has been severely damaged by a reporter who could not resist plagiarizing in his zeal to succeed. Even the achievements of one of our favorite baseball players will probably be eclipsed by controversy over his use of an illegal bat.

The challenge before you will be to maintain your integrity in a culture that has devalued it. You will have to bring your own personal and professional ethics with you on the journey when you leave here today, because you may not find anyone to guide you. Living a moral life in an indifferent world is likely to be more difficult than you can imagine. How will you succeed?

The answer may be found in a few simple words written by Abe Lincoln: "When I do good I feel good. When I do bad I feel bad. And that is my religion." All of us have a voice inside that will speak to us if we let it. Sometimes it is easy to hear; sometimes we have to turn down the volume of distracting noise around us so we can listen. That voice tells us if we are on the right track. It lets us know if we give as much as we take, if we welcome the opinions of others, and at least accept diversity even if we are not able to embrace it.

As you go forward, hopefully that inner voice will remind you of some of the points of pride that bring such distinction to your university. You will discover that you can go far by being conscientious, but you will go farther and find true satisfaction by being conscious. If you have already achieved self-aware-ness and set specific goals for yourself, that is fine. If you don't know who you are or what to do next, don't worry about it. Your life should not run on a schedule, and you may go down some dead end streets until you find the right road. Don't be afraid to question assumptions you may have lived with since childhood. Take your time and seek true independence as you search for mean-ing and fulfillment.

Perhaps the greatest reward for living a conscious life is that it prepares you to cope with adversity. If you are open to change and new experiences, if you are accustomed to self-discipline, if you respect others and nurture your relation-ships, then you will have built a solid platform that will support you and help you deal with anything that comes your way. I'm not saying all of that is easy. But sitting here today I can honestly tell you that you don't need to break your neck to learn the value of living consciously. I was lucky to grow up unthreatened by change and eager for new experiences. Thirty years as an actor before my injury taught me self-discipline and helped me cope with rejection and failure. My mar-riage and my relationships with friends and family were alive and well before the accident. Since then they have grown even stronger and given me the ability to recover and go forward.

That catastrophic event also changed my perspective about other things in life. Outside of my circle of family and friends, I didn't appreciate others nearly as much as I do now. Once I trained with actual paraplegics to portray one in a film. Every evening as I drove away from the rehab center I quickly pushed those suffer-ing patients out of my mind, relieved that I was not one of them. Less than a year later I became paralyzed myself. Did I need to learn something about compassion and humility? No doubt about it.

It was not until I was immersed in my own rehabilitation that I realized an apparent tragedy had created a unique opportunity. Spinal cord patients like the ones I once dismissed were now in the next room, traveling down the same hall-ways, and struggling right beside me in physical therapy. I came to know people of all ages and from all walks of life that I would otherwise never even have met. For all our differences, what we had in common was our disability and the desire to find a reason to hope. I was inspired by so many and gradually discovered that I had been given a job that would create urgency and a new direction in my life: I could do something to help.

Thanks to the education you have received and the ideals that guide this distinguished university, you have already learned some of the most important principles you will ever need to know: compassion for our fellow human beings, the aspiration to be champions in all arenas of life, and the desire to make a difference. To all of you leaving today I can only say, on behalf of all those who will look to you for guidance and leadership, take those principles with you and hold them close.

Congratulations on all your achievements. I wish you the best of luck.

 Discussion Questions

1. How does Christopher Reeve define a "moral life"?
2. How does he suggest you can achieve it?
3. What is the difference between being "conscientious" and being "conscious"?
4. In what ways did Reeve's disability change his life?
5. What did he advise these graduates to consider as they enter a culture that makes it difficult to maintain integrity?

 Suggestions for Your Journal

What emotions did you feel as you read Christopher Reeve's address? How would your life change if you had to face the kind of catastrophe that he suffered? Do you live a "moral life"? If so, how? If not, do you even aspire to one? Explain.

The First Lady's Challenge to the Graduates

Michelle Obama

Michelle Obama gave this commencement address to the graduates at the University of California-Merced. She speaks of the value of an education as well as community service and the transformative effects they can have on our communities and nation.

Thank you. Thank you so much, Class of 2009. All I can say is wow, and good afternoon, everyone. I am so proud of these graduates. We have to just give them one big round of applause before I start. This is just an amazing day...

To the graduates and their families and the entire community of Merced, I am so pleased, so thrilled, so honored to be here with all of you today.

Now, I know we've got a lot of national press out there, and a few people may be wondering why did I choose the University of California-Merced to deliver my first commencement speech as First Lady. Well, let me tell you something, the answer is simple: You inspired me, you touched me. You know, there are few things that are more rewarding than to watch young people recognize that they have the power to make their dreams come true. And you did just that. Your perseverance and creativity were on full display in your efforts to bring me here to Merced for this wonderful occasion.

So let me tell you what you did. If you don't know, parents, because some of you were involved, my office received thousands of letters and, of course, Valentines cards from students; each and every one of them so filled with hope and enthusiasm. It moved not just me but my entire staff. They came up to me and said, "Michelle, you have to do this." "You have to go here!" ... I received letters from everyone connected to this university—not just students, but they came from parents, and grandparents, and cousins, and aunts, and uncles, and neighbors, and friends, all of them telling me about how hard you all have worked and how important this day is for you and for the entire Merced community ... Well, let me tell you, it worked, because I'm here! ... I am honored by your efforts and happy to be with you to celebrate this important milestone...

Merced's make-up may have changed over the years, but its values and character have not—long, hot days filled with hard work by generations of men and women of all races who wanted an opportunity to build a better life for their children and their grandchildren; hardworking folks who believed that access to a good education would be their building blocks to a brighter future.

You know, I grew up in one of those communities with similar values. Like Merced, the South Side of Chicago is a community where people struggled financially, but worked hard, looked out for each other and rallied around their children. My father was a blue-collar worker, as you all know. My mother stayed at home to raise me and my brother. We were the first to graduate from college in our immediate family.

I know that many of you out here are also the first in your families to achieve that distinction, as well. And as you know, being the first is often a big responsibility, particularly in a community that, like many others around our country at the moment, is struggling to cope with record high unemployment and foreclosure rates; a community where families are a single paycheck or an emergency room visit away from homelessness.

And with jobs scarce, many of you may be considering leaving town with your diploma in hand. And it wouldn't be unreasonable. For those of you who come from communities facing similar economic hardships, you may also be wondering how you'll build decent lives for yourselves if you choose to return to those communities.

But I would encourage you to call upon the same hope and hard work that brought you to this day. Call upon that optimism and tenacity that built the University of California at Merced to invest in the future of Merced in your own home towns all across this country. By using what you have learned here, you can shorten the path perhaps for kids who may not see a path at all.

And I was once one of those kids. Most of you were once one of those kids. I grew up just a few miles from the University of Chicago in my hometown. The university, like most institutions, was a major cultural, economic institution in my neighborhood. My mother even worked as a secretary there for several years.

Yet that university never played a meaningful role in my academic development. The institution made no effort to reach out to me—a bright and promising student in their midst—and I had no reason to believe there was a place for me there. Therefore, when it came time for me to apply to college, I never for one second considered the university in my own backyard as a viable option.

And as fate would have it, I ultimately went on and accepted a position in student affairs at the University of Chicago more than a decade later. What I found was that working within the institution gave me the opportunity to express my concerns about how little role the university plays in the life of its neighbors. I wanted desperately to be involved in helping to break down the barriers that existed between the campus and the community.

And in less than a year, through that position, I worked with others to build the university's first Office of Community Service. And today, the office continues to provide students with opportunities to help reshape relationships between the university and its surrounding community. Students there today are volunteering in local elementary schools, serving as mentors at high schools, organizing neighborhood watches, and worshiping in local churches.

But you know a little something about working with your community here, don't you, Merced? UC Merced, its faculty and its students seem to already have a handle on this need and it speaks once again to the character of this community. As I learned more about what you have done, I am so impressed with how the students, faculty and the community are collaborating to ensure that every child in this community understands there is a place for them at this big beautiful university if they study hard and stay out of trouble…

So the faculty, the students, local leaders, Merced alumni, everyone here is doing their part to help the children of Merced realize that access to a quality education is available to them as long as they work hard, study hard and apply themselves.

It is this kind of commitment that we're going to need in this nation to put this country back on a path where every child expects to succeed and where every child has the tools that they need to achieve their dreams. That's what we're aiming for. And we're going to need all of you, graduates, this generation, we need you to lead the way.

Now, let me tell you, careers focused on lifting up our communities—whether it's helping transform troubled schools or creating after-school programs or training workers for green jobs—these careers are not always obvious, but today they are necessary. Solutions to our nation's most challenging social problems are not going to come from Washington alone. Real innovation often starts with individuals who apply themselves to solve a problem right in their own community. That's where the best ideas come from.

And some pretty incredible social innovations have been launched by young people all across this world.

Teach for America in this country is a great example. It was created by Wendy Kopp as a part of her undergraduate senior thesis in 1989. And now, as a result of her work then, more than 6,200 corps members are teaching in our country's neediest communities, reaching approximately 400,000 students.

And then there's Van Jones, who recently joined the Obama administration, a special adviser to the President on green jobs. Van started out as a grassroots organizer and became an advocate and a creator of "green collar" jobs—jobs that are not only good for the environment, but also provide good wages and career advancement for both skilled and unskilled workers; jobs similar to the ones being created right here at UC Merced as this green campus continues to grow.

And then one of my heroes, Geoffrey Canada, grew up in the South Bronx. After graduating from Bowdoin and getting his masters at Harvard, he returned to New York City and used his education to ensure that the next generation would have a chance at the same opportunity. Geoffrey's Harlem Children's Zone is a nationally recognized program that covers 100 blocks and reaches nearly 10,000 children with a variety of social services to ensure that all kids are prepared to get a good education.

And in an effort to invest in and encourage the future Wendy Kopps, Van Joneses and Geoffrey Canadas, the Obama administration recently launched the Office of Social Innovation at the White House. The President has asked Congress to provide $50 million in seed capital to fund great ideas like the ones I just described. The Office is going to identify the most promising, results-oriented non-profit programs and expand their reach throughout the country.

And this university is blessed with some of the leading researchers and academics who are focusing already their attention on solving some of our nation's most critical issues, like the energy crisis, global warming, climate change, and air pollution.

And you, the students, the graduates and faculty on this campus, you're capable of changing the world, that's for sure. Where you are right now is no different from where Wendy and Van and Geoffrey were when they graduated, remember that. You too can have this same transformative effect on the community of Merced and our entire nation. We need your ideas, graduates. We need your resourcefulness. We need your inventiveness.

And as the students who helped build this school, I ask you, make your legacy a lasting one. Dream big, think broadly about your life, and please make giving back to your community a part of that vision. Take the same hope and optimism, the hard work and tenacity that brought you to this point, and carry that with you for the rest of your life in whatever you choose to do. Each and every single day, some young person is out there changing the ways—the world in ways both big and small.

But let me tell you something, as you step out into that big, open world, and you start building your lives, the truth is that you will face tough times, you will certainly have doubts, let me tell you, because I know I did when I was your age. There will be days when you will worry about whether you're really up for the challenge. Maybe some of you already feel a little of that right now. Maybe you're wondering: Am I smart enough? Do I really belong? Can I live up to all those expectations that everyone has of me?

And you will definitely have your share of setbacks. Count on it. Your best laid plans will be consumed by obstacles. Your excellent ideas will be peppered with flaws. You will be confronted with financial strains as your loans become due and salaries fall short of both expectations and expenses. You will make mistakes that will shatter your confidence. You will make compromises that will test your convictions. You will find that there is rarely a clear and direct path to any of your visions. And you will find that you'll have to readjust again and again and again. And there may be times when you wonder whether it's all worth it. And there may be moments when you just want to quit.

But in those moments, those inevitable moments, I urge you to think about this day. Look around you. Look around you. There are thousands and thousands of hardworking people who have helped you get to this point, people who are celebrating with you today, who are praying for you every single day, and others who couldn't be here, for whatever reason. I want you to think of the people who sacrificed for you—you know that—family members who worked a third job to get you through, who took on the extra shifts to get you through, who put off doing something important for themselves to get you to this day.

And think about the friends who never got the chance to go to college but were still invested in your success—friends who talked you out of dropping out, friends who kept you out of trouble so that you could graduate on time, friends who forced you to study when you wanted to procrastinate.

Most importantly, though, think of the millions of kids living all over this world who will never come close to having the chance to stand in your shoes—kids in New Orleans whose schools are still recovering from the ravages of Katrina; kids who will never go to school at all because they're forced to work in a sweat shop somewhere; kids in your very own communities who just can't get a break, who don't have anyone in their lives telling them that they're good enough and smart enough to do whatever they can imagine; kids who have lost the ability to dream. These kids are desperate to find someone or something to cling to. They are looking to you for some sign of hope.

So, whenever you get ready to give up, think about all of these people and remember that you are blessed. Remember that you are blessed. Remember that in exchange for those blessings, you must give something back. You must reach back and pull someone up. You must bend down and let someone else stand on your shoulders so that they can see a brighter future.

As advocate and activist Marian Wright Edelman says, "Service is the rent we pay for living … it is the true measure, the only measure of our success." So, graduates, when times get tough and fear sets in, think of those people who paved the way for you and those who are counting on you to pave the way for them. Never let setbacks or fear dictate the course of your life. Hold on to the possibility and push beyond the fear. Hold on to the hope that brought you here today, the hope of laborers and immigrants, settlers and slaves, whose blood and sweat built this community and made it possible for you to sit in these seats.

There are a lot of people in your lives who know a little something about the power of hope. Don't we, parents and grandparents? Look, I know a little something about the power of hope. My husband knows a little something about the power of hope.

You are the hope of Merced and of this nation. And be the realization of our dreams and the hope for the next generation. We believe in you. Thank you so much, and good luck. God bless you all.

Remarks by the First Lady at the University of California-Merced Commencement, May 16, 2009. www.whitehouse.gov.

Discussion Questions

1. Why did the First Lady choose this particular university to deliver her first commencement speech? Under what circumstances could you use this technique to bring about a desired outcome?
2. As a young, promising student she was never contacted or recruited by the "university in her back yard." How did she change this when she later worked at the same university?
3. How does she suggest these graduates "pay back" those who have supported them throughout their education? How can they give back to their communities?
4. Michelle Obama talks about how community service can have a transformative effect on our nation. What examples does she give to illustrate this concept?

 Suggestions for Your Journal

Michelle Obama emphasizes the importance of community service in her address. What type of community service have you performed? How has it affected you personally and educationally? What type of service learning opportunities does your campus offer? If you have never performed community service, why not? Do you believe it can transform people and communities in the way the First Lady describes?

Unit Summary

In Unit 9 you have read several authors' perceptions of how life after college might be different, along with some of their suggestions about goal setting. The following questions and writing assignments may help you clarify your aspirations for what you want in the future and how you might begin to prepare for it now.

■ Summary Questions

1. As you look forward to your years in college, have the authors of the readings in this unit given you any new insights into how you should prepare for the future? If so, what are they? What steps can you take now to prepare for your life after college (e.g., improve your communication skills, develop technological competencies, and manage money)?
2. How important is having a degree to you? What are the reasons for its importance to you?
3. In Unit 8, Rosenberg writes about the importance of keeping pace with change. As you set long-term goals, how will you accommodate change in your plans?

■ Suggested Writing Assignments

1. If you wrote an essay in Unit 1 about your reasons for being in college, reexamine these reasons. Are they still the same? Have they changed? Have you added any? What has influenced your thinking the most?
2. How has the prospect of finding a job after college influenced your initial choice of major? Have your experiences so far confirmed that decision? In what way? If you are considering a change, discuss some possible alternatives and why you are considering them.
3. Discuss how you intend to prepare yourself to become an effective worker in tomorrow's workplace. Describe specific ways, such as work and volunteer opportunities, campus involvement, and academic and other experiences, that will help you acquire the general competencies and skills necessary to be effective.

■ Suggested Readings

Brockman, John. *The Next Fifty Years-Science in the First Half of the Twenty-First Century*. New York: Vintage Books, 2002.

Luscher, Keith. *Don't Wait Until You Graduate*. Far Hills, NJ: New Horizon Press, 2003.

Strauss, William and Howe, Neil. *Millennials and the Pop Culture*. Great Falls, VA: LifeCourse Associates, 2006.

Author Index

Subject Index